Research *for the* Psychotherapist

Pelham, William

U g Vermont

March 28 - cheryl
April 18 - Alexandra
51 BIRCH STREET

Research *for the* Psychotherapist

From Science to Practice

Jay Lebow

Routledge
Taylor & Francis Group
New York   London

Routledge is an imprint of the
Taylor & Francis Group, an informa business

Published in 2006 by
Routledge
Taylor & Francis Group
270 Madison Avenue
New York, NY 10016

Published in Great Britain by
Routledge
Taylor & Francis Group
2 Park Square
Milton Park, Abingdon
Oxon OX14 4RN

Printed in the United States of America on acid-free paper
10 9 8 7 6 5 4 3 2 1

International Standard Book Number-10: 0-415-95226-3 (Softcover)
International Standard Book Number-13: 978-0-415-95226-2 (Softcover)
Library of Congress Card Number 2005033951

Library of Congress Cataloging-in-Publication Data

Lebow, Jay.
   Research for the psychotherapist : from science to practice / Jay Lebow.
      p. cm.
   Includes bibliographical references and index.
   ISBN 0-415-95226-3 (pb : alk. paper)
   1. Psychotherapy--Research. 2. Psychotherapy. I. Title.

RC337.L44 2006
616.89'14072--dc22   2005033951

Taylor & Francis Group
is the Academic Division of Informa plc.

Visit the Taylor & Francis Web site at
http://www.taylorandfrancis.com

and the Routledge Web site at
http://www.routledge-ny.com

DEDICATION

To my parents, William and Ellen Lebow,
who instilled in me the spirit of both psychotherapist and researcher

CONTENTS

Part III

Research Focused on or Relevant to Couple and Family Therapy

PREFACE

It is often said that science and the clinical practice of psychotherapy inevitably inhabit different worlds, and thus research has little relevance for the practice of psychotherapy. At times, the acrimonious exchanges between ivory tower researchers and science-phobic therapists appear to confirm this belief. Symmetrically escalating exchanges with little or no acknowledgment of the unique contribution of each viewpoint produce little dialogue or progress. And surveys of psychotherapists typically reveal research to number among the less important influences on their practice compared with supervision, coursework, and even the impact of their own personal therapy.

And yet, such disconnection and dissonance limits the possibilities for both research and practice. For researchers, a disconnect from the world of clinical practice leaves them insulated, limited in their understanding of the pragmatic importance of various questions, and without a major core group to whom they can disseminate their (frequently useful and relevant) findings. For clinicians, a disconnect from the world of science leaves their enterprise in a prescientific state. They thereby remain practitioners of a craft that resembles art more closely than it does science, lacking the vital empirical data that can test the accuracy of their beliefs or the impact of their services.

The lack of collaboration between researchers and practitioners also remains substantially out of touch with the developments in both arenas over the last quarter century. We now are heir to many years of research both directly assessing psychotherapy and the various phenomena in focus in clinical practice (e.g., human personality, systems, psychopathology). That research provides many extraordinary insights into various human conditions and into what is likely to prove most helpful in treatment. It also has developed many useful ways of assessing progress in ongoing clinical practice. And we also are heir to the 100 years of the history of psychotherapy, which has led to a point where most clinicians focus less on which theory is the best descriptor of the human condition, and more toward how to best help the individual clients they are seeing. Questions such as what is most effective in treating various difficulties and how best to achieve such proximate goals as building the client–therapist relationship are ever present for most therapists; these are precisely the sorts of questions most readily informed by research.

In today's mental health care, the ethical practice of psychotherapy must be informed by the best research available. *Informed* is the relevant word here and elsewhere in this volume, because clinical practice is far too complex an endeavor with far too many variables and decisions to ever be fully dictated by specific research findings. Skillful practice involves finding the right way to bring research to bear on the clinical questions in focus in psychotherapy.

But, if there is, increasingly, general agreement that research should have a role in informing clinical practice, how to present research in a way that engages and helps inform practice? This book is the culmination of my efforts over the last decade to wrestle with this problem. I am both a psychotherapist and a researcher on psychotherapy. I have worked in community mental health, private practice, university, hospital, and institute settings. In each setting, I have tried to grasp how psychotherapists used research, what enabled the incorporation of research into practice, and what constraints mitigated that incorporation.

I have presented research, research findings, and reviews of the pertinent literature, and looked at the impact of those efforts. And although those efforts had value, I noticed that only the most research-oriented attended those workshops and presentations, and that the reviews, though published in prominent prestigious journals, were actually poorly disseminated. And I noticed that, although I went to research meetings filled with findings of great relevance to the practice of psychotherapy, few clinicians knew about that research. In fact, psychotherapists, impressed with research, were sometimes as likely to quote the results of poor research, used as part of the public relations effort of a presenter, as that better grounded research that I had found so useful.

My good fortune was that, as I was grappling with these issues, Richard Simon, editor of the *Psychotherapy Networker,* approached me about writing an article aimed at psychotherapists about the research assessing family therapy. That resulted in much positive feedback about the value of that article and an offer from Rich to write a column for the *Psychotherapy Networker* titled "From Science to Practice" focused on bringing information and issues from science to the practicing psychotherapist. What I became aware of in writing that column was the absence of other similar vehicles. Researchers talk to researchers. Clinicians talk to clinicians. Developers of approaches present research in support of their approaches as part of their presentations. But almost no one makes an effort to translate research in a balanced way to psychotherapists and students of psychotherapy.

Ten years later, we had accrued two dozen of those columns. George Zimmar, publishing director at Routledge, approached me about building a book around the columns, a compendium of a range of descriptions of diverse research activities and controversies in research aimed at psychotherapists. This book is the product of that invitation. All of the columns from the *Networker* have been updated and revised for this volume, and six additional chapters, aimed at topics that seemed vital to address in a volume of this kind, have been written and added.

The goal of this volume is to have the clinician or clinician-in-training reader engage with research and participate in a process of digesting it. Hopefully, this will not merely be about accepting findings as static "truths" applicable to practice, but raising questions about the research and findings, engaging in debate about the issues, and becoming an informed consumer of this information. Although it is certainly an intention of this volume to communicate the state of research about several key issues relevant to psychotherapy (e.g., Does psychotherapy work? What can we say about the impact of controversial treatments such as Eye Movement Desensitization and Reprocessing (EMDR)? How important is the therapist's contribution to psychotherapy?), the more important meta-level goal is to help clinician readers become skilled consumers of research. This is not a comprehensive volume aimed at summarizing all the research that is relevant to psychotherapy, but one aimed to provide a view of some of the most interesting and clinically significant research and research controversies. I hope this volume can help its readers develop an open and informed view toward research, so that they can best learn from the findings available and those yet to come.

This book begins with an introductory section, *Psychotherapy and Psychotherapy Research,* that orients the reader to the relationship between research and clinical practice and provides some guidelines for how to look at research. That's followed by sections describing research focused on psychotherapy, research focused on or relevant to couple and family therapy, incorporating research methods into one's own practice, and research in psychology that informs the practice of psychotherapy. Each of the chapters assumes a specific focus, looking to inform about some issue relevant to clinical practice. Most of the chapters center on describing relevant findings from psychotherapy research, though there also are chapters focused on the discussion of controversies in the world of research that have relevance for psychotherapy, and other chapters that discuss clinically relevant findings from basic research on social and psychological processes. The topics covered are intended to be representative of the most significant research findings about psychotherapy and controversies in today's psychotherapy research, though, again, this volume does not intend to speak comprehensively to all such relevant findings or controversies. Each chapter ends with a References section, as well as a section entitled Resources, which point to key sources for the article that can be used for follow-up by the reader. Ultimately, my hope is that you, the reader, will consider each essay in the context of your own experience and engage with the growing body of research that can help inform practice.

ACKNOWLEDGMENTS

I would like to thank George Zimmar, publishing director at Routledge, for suggesting the idea for this volume and supporting its publication, and Dana Bliss at Routledge for his help with the process of publication. I'd also like to especially thank Rich Simon of the *Psychotherapy Networker* for helping cocreate the idea of developing a series of short essays designed to speak to psychotherapists and focused on topical discussions of relevant issues in psychotherapy research and how to translate the findings from research into practice. Rich also helped suggest the topics for many of these chapters and has often helped me to recognize drifts into language that stood in the way of communicating. I'd also like to thank the *Psychotherapy Networker* for permitting the reproduction of some of the material in this volume. In addition, I'd like to thank Molly Gasbarrini for her help in editing the chapters in this volume; Danielle Shannon and Maria Muro for helping with the secretarial tasks; the administration of the Family Institute including William Pinsof, Cheryl Rampage, Jennifer Nastasi, and Angie Heisler for providing support for this effort; and my family for tolerating the many hours at the computer that this kind of project entails. And to you, the reader, who might find a way someday to have some of what is described in this volume inform how you think about psychotherapy and how you practice. Throughout the examples and case studies in this volume, the names of individuals have been changed to protect their identities.

ABOUT THE AUTHOR

Jay Lebow is a clinical psychologist and research consultant at The Family Institute at Northwestern, and clinical professor of Psychology at Northwestern University. He is board certified in family psychology. He is a clinical member and approved supervisor of the American Association for Marriage and Family Therapy, a fellow of the American Psychological Association and its Divisions of Clinical and Family Psychology, a fellow of the Academy of Family Psychology, and a former member of the board of the Illinois Association of Marriage and Family Therapists. Dr. Lebow has served as treasurer and a member of the board of directors of the American Family Therapy Academy, president of the American Psychological Association's Division of Family Psychology, and a member of the board of directors of the American Board of Family Psychology.

His publications include three edited volumes: *Family Psychology: The Art of the Science* (with William Pinsof), *The Clinical Handbook of Family Therapy*, and the *Integrative/Eclectic Volume of the Comprehensive Handbook of Psychotherapy*. He is also the author of 100 book chapters and articles, including an end-of-decade review of couple therapy; the practice update concerned with couple therapy for the American Association for Marriage and Family Therapy; a chapter reviewing the research literature in family therapy for the *Annual Review of Psychology*; chapters overviewing couple and family therapy in *Comprehensive Clinical Psychology*, the *Psycholosgist's Desk Reference*, and the *Comprehensive Textbook of Psychiatry*; as well as numerous articles and chapters dealing with integrative therapy, research in couple and family therapy, and assessment and treatment in divorce when there is conflict over child custody and visitation. He is a contributing editor and writes a regular column on the relation of research to practice for the *Psychotherapy Networker* and is on the editorial boards of the *Journal of Marital and Family Therapy, Family Process,* and *In Session.*

Dr. Lebow lectures in the Master of Science in Marital and Family Therapy Program and leads a practicum group from the doctoral clinical psychology program at Northwestern University. He also is involved in The Family Institute's ongoing treatment research concerned with assessing progress in psychotherapy and the development of the Systemic Therapy Inventory of Change. Dr. Lebow received undergraduate and graduate degrees from Northwestern University and is also a graduate of The Family Institute's post-graduate training program.

Part I

Psychotherapy and Psychotherapy Research

1

MERGING SCIENCE AND PRACTICE
IN PSYCHOTHERAPY

Researchers in the mental health field and psychotherapists are sometimes pictured as having little in common, and arguments between researchers and practitioners sometimes demonstrate all the qualities of poor communication manifested in couples. Yet, ultimately, good practice and good research in the mental health field must inform one another. This chapter examines the relationship between science and practice in psychotherapy.

Somehow, we have entered the 21st century with research and practice often operating in separate spheres, at times competing rather than complementing one another. We need to refocus our vision to be able to see psychotherapy as a coherent whole, to draw from each of its constituent parts, and transcend the older conceptualization of practice and science as two disparate activities conducted by different groups aimed toward different ends. The science and practice subsystems within psychotherapy are each best served when they provide feedback to, inform, and influence each other.

THE DIVIDE BETWEEN SCIENCE AND PRACTICE

Historically, science and practice have unfortunately largely occupied different worlds within the mental health fields. There have been many sources for the divide between those doing research and those in clinical practice.

- Those who do research and those who engage in practice typically live their professional lives in different communities. Most communicate with others who are, like themselves, using languages that are quite distinct, allowing for little in the way of mutual influence.
- Scientists and practitioners interface with different constituencies and focus their attention in divergent directions. Scientists must respond to grant review committees, which are focused on the scientific rigor of research and emphasize carefully building new research in a logical sequence based on the foundation of the methods and findings of previous research. These review committees also emphasize the importance of structuring proposed research in relation to *Diagnostic and Statistical Manual of Mental Disorders* (*DSM*) disorders or concerns about public health issues. In contrast, clinicians relate primarily to clients, who look for help with the complex problems they experience in their lives (problems which only occasionally center on *DSM* diagnoses), and who need that help now rather than some time down the road after all of the important research illuminating a problem area or treatment is completed.
- Some prominent researchers and clinicians ignore and, at times, even disparage the work of the other group in their writings and presentations (thus modeling disengagement).
- Many of the scientists who study treatment are rooted in cognitive-behavioral models, whereas the majority of therapists are rooted in other traditions.
- The styles of publications and presentations that focus on science and those that focus on practice are so vastly different, and there is a relative paucity of efforts to translate between these domains so that clinicians and researchers might better understand and be able to use each other's work.

These differences can easily lead to a field divided, with a gap the size of the Grand Canyon. Our field has seen polemics against scientists (seen as too positivist and locked in the ivory tower) and clinicians (seen as "unscientific" and arbitrary in their choices). Surveys of therapists show little use of research findings (Goldfried, Greenberg, & Marmar, 1990). Even some of my colleagues who are both clinicians and researchers admit to using research sparsely in their clinical practice. Similarly, one often encounters research that has failed to take into account typical methods of clinical practice or how the information collected might prove useful.

THE NEED FOR COMMON GROUND

Does it make any sense to engage in practice without reference to relevant research or to engage in research that fails to be informed by the work of clinicians and bears no relation to practice? My reading of the history of psychotherapy is that when either activity occurs insulated from the other, bad things happen. On the practice side, we have seen the promulgation of strategies of intervention that are less effective than they might be because they fail to incorporate what the research evidence shows about clients and about psychotherapy. One classic example is the prominent set of methods, centered on creating highly emotionally arousing confrontation and enactments, to treat families with schizophrenic members (Whitaker, 1958). These therapies clearly increased "expressed emotion" in these families, a quality that research has demonstrated to be highly toxic within these families, most especially for their schizophrenic members. Therapies informed by the research about expressed emotion, such those developed by Carol Anderson (Hogarty et al., 1991), Ian Falloon (1988), and William McFarlane (McFarlane, Link, Dushay, Marchal, & Crilly, 1995), have moved in a very different direction, creating therapies that number among the most effective methods for intervening with these problems. Another example from family psychology of a therapy remaining limited in its effectiveness because of its failing to incorporate a relevant body of research can be found in the early Palo Alto model for family therapy (Watzlawick et al., 1990; Watzlawick, Weakland, & Fisch, 1974). That model, for all of its insightful theoretical formulations, completely ignored any attention to the building of a therapeutic alliance (even showing a degree of disdain for the building of alliances with clients), despite the fact that the importance of alliance in the change process numbers among the most firmly established findings in psychotherapy research. And despite numerous studies that have shown the efficacy of special strategies of intervention, we continue to see treatment of such difficult-to-treat problems as obsessive-compulsive disorder and panic disorder with methods that fail to draw on the principles that have demonstrated effectiveness.

In a similarly short-sighted manner, scientists have invested in the refinement and testing of some treatments that were so limited in their scope that the findings would have almost no utility for those in real-world practice, whereas little attention has been focused on several of the mostly widely practiced psychotherapies such as the humanistic- and solution-oriented therapies. We've also seen scientists create "new" treatments built from the ground up without regard to longstanding, finely honed similar methods already widely disseminated in clinical practice. And we've frequently encountered a total dismissal by researchers of treatments that have not been empirically tested, failing to discriminate between treatments that have shown to be ineffective from approaches that have merely not been tested.

And yet, I believe it is a time in which we are beginning to see progress in the rapprochement between science and practice. We are beginning to see more research that begins with questions that have relevance for clinical practice, therapies that are shaped in relation to research findings, a body of useful findings from research from which clinicians can draw in their practice, more research done by clinician/researchers, and more effective dissemination of research findings.

In part, the rapprochement of science and practice represents a developmental step in the evolution of the field. The early history of psychotherapy is an account of brilliant men and women bringing their observation skills to the process of uncovering how the human mind operates and how change may be stimulated. The efforts of such seminal figures as Freud, Jung, Rogers, and Sullivan number among the most valuable contributions to human progress, yet all were limited due to their being involved in the earliest phases of exploration. Like Columbus, these pioneers explored uncharted territory, but also like Columbus, they had to create their own maps as they moved forward and remained subject to the idiosyncrasies they encountered. Busy with this work of establishing the acceptance of psychotherapy, few of those who developed treatments in real-world treatment settings had the time or focus to begin the process of bringing researchers into the study of their methods. Aaron Beck (1995) and Carl Rogers (1992) stand out as the outstanding exceptions to this trend.

In an analogous process, scientists whose input might have relevance to psychotherapy (both psychotherapy researchers and those focused on explicating basic human processes) had to begin their work in a way that produced little in the way of clinically useful findings. These researchers first needed to establish a place for themselves and their type of research in the academic world by beginning the slow process of building a knowledge base about human psychology through asking simple questions that typically did not have great clinical relevance. Following the process of science, before they could ask the kinds of questions most relevant to clinical practice (such as how best to deliver a particular intervention), they first needed to explore more basic questions, such as identifying the key aspects of dysfunctional processes.

In the first 70 years of the practice of psychotherapy, with few research findings to build on, the development of therapies remained only marginally influenced by research. And practice had even less influence on the advance of the science. Each group needed to cultivate its own territory, and the first steps for each almost inevitably were disconnected from the other. However, after 100 years of the development of the science of human psychology and the practice of psychotherapy, the time is clearly propitious for better integration of science and practice.

EXAMPLES OF HOW RESEARCH AND PRACTICE CAN INFORM ONE ANOTHER FROM FAMILY PSYCHOLOGY AND FAMILY THERAPY

Consider some key examples from the domains of family psychology and family therapy.

There is an overwhelming body of evidence now available for the powerful ways that families affect individuals and individuals affect one another in families. Specific research has demonstrated beyond question that the quality of family life affects enormously and is affected by such "individual" problems as depression and physical health (Beach, 2001). In demonstrating these linkages, family scientists have provided the empirical evidence for the systemic viewpoint, perhaps the most crucial core understanding of couple and family therapists. Families do matter and are potent forces in the process of change.

The wide range of more specific findings that has emerged from the science of family psychology also offers many understandings that offer the potential to help improve practice. Such diverse research as that explicating the profiles of domestic batterers, the expected challenges in divorce and physical illness, and the impact of parental depression on children have great bearing on our work as clinicians.

A greater clarity is also emerging about the kinds of information from research about families and about therapy that truly would be of interest and clinically useful to practitioners. And we are beginning to see a greater openness on the part of clinicians to incorporating research findings into what is done in psychotherapy.

To cite one such example from family psychology, John Gottman's research on the predictors of success in marriage has become a core building block for numerous approaches to couple therapy (Gottman, 1998). Most couple therapists, drawing from Gottman's research, now know that when they see the "four horsemen" of criticism, defensiveness, contempt, and stonewalling in a couple, extraordinary measures are required. And couple therapists regularly draw on such Gottman findings as his documentation of the importance of the ratio of positive to negative behaviors in couples, the importance of positive sentiment override, and the difficulties associated with accelerated "startup" and "emotional flooding."

Another example from family psychology of the influence of science on practice lies in the large number of those who work with families with acting out adolescents and use or draw from one of the five evidence-based treatments for adolescent substance abuse or delinquency: Jim Alexander and Tom Sexton's Functional Family Therapy, Scott Henggeler's Multi-Systemic Therapy, Howard Liddle's Multi-Dimensional Family Therapy, Patricia Chamberlain's Treatment Foster Care model, and Jose Szapocznik's Brief Strategic Therapy. Notably, each of these approaches began with a mix of understandings and techniques developed in clinical work with these families coupled with understandings from research about these families, followed by the refinement of the clinical approach through feedback from empirical testing. That is, each of these approaches was built on an amalgamation of the best that science and practice have to offer.

It also should be emphasized that the teams that developed each of these therapies (along with John Gottman and others like him) have found ways to present the science of their work in ways that speak to and influence practitioners. Transcending the science/practice rift depends not only on doing good work but finding effective means of communicating across the divide. A similar landscape has begun to develop in the context of many of other therapies, including virtually all cognitive-behavior therapy (Nathan & Gorman, 2003), interpersonal therapy (Klerman, Weissman, Rounsaville, & Chevron, 1995), Les Greenberg's version of experiential therapy (called emotion-focused therapy) (Greenberg & Elliott, 2002), group therapies (Burlingame, Fuhriman, & Johnson, 2004), some psychoanalytic therapy (Clarkin & Levy, 2003), Miller and Duncan's version of solution focused therapy (Miller, Duncan, & Hubble, 2002), and most integrative therapies (Lebow, 1997; Norcross & Goldfried, 2005).

CLOSING THE GAP

These are positive signs. Yet, what I am describing is progress in the relationship between science and practice, not a full paradigm shift to a comfortable, connected mutual influence. Some of the old complaints remain, and sometimes exchanges between researchers and clinicians still look like those families that struggle to have any useful communication. The divide can be great, as it was in the recent debates about empirically supported psychotherapies (Chambless & Hollon, 1998; Levant, 2004). To enable us to narrow the gap, there need to be more structures that bring scientists and clinicians together. Communication between scientists and practitioners is essential. And this dialogue can't be expected to be perfectly smooth, nor should it be. As we know from couple therapy, the right kind of spirited argument also can be useful. It is also essential to maintain realistic expectations for the product of this dialogue. We can always expect there to be differing viewpoints on issues; some will disagree and some will pay little attention. The key question is not whether there is full agreement or disagreement, but whether conversation between the scientists and practitioners moves forward, and whether that discourse promotes mutual understanding and a helpful exchange of ideas.

Ultimately, research must inform our practice, not dictate it (Lebow, 2000). There are simply too many complexities in clinical practice for every intervention to be driven by a research. But clinical decision making needs to be informed by research. To ignore the findings from the sciences of psychology, sociology, psychiatry, and psychotherapy research is to remain working in the context of the 19th century, not the 21st. And a similar frame holds true for scientists, who need to focus more on questions that matter to clinicians, the clinical ramifications of their findings, and the clinical implications that flow from the way they frame the questions in their research.

I have come to use a great deal of research in my clinical practice. The vast array of findings now existent often helps me shape a specific intervention. I even believe that in the wake of some data, we may be on ethically unjustifiable grounds when we fail to offer a particular intervention with a particular problem (e.g., sex therapy for sexual difficulties). I also see each case as a further test of my own therapeutic method, which I believe is in an endless recursive process of refinement as I learn more about what works in my own hands. The well-documented findings about the importance of therapeutic alliance and the therapist in psychotherapy have always meant a good deal to me. One of the limiting factors in all psychotherapy research is that it cannot tell you how a method will work for you, only for the generic therapist. We still need to see how methods work for us, determine our strengths, and develop our best method of working.

The clinical phenomenon is so complex that it never will be fully driven by research, only informed by it. Important judgments about efficacy and ethics in the context of specific cases, must always remain in the hands of the therapist. In the 21st century, we can expect to have therapy be more informed and more interventions supported and shaped by research findings. Yet, the process of treatment will never be amenable to a simple formula.

I expect that over the next decade we will see a greater and greater confluence between research and practice. I have spent a significant part of my career attempting to bridge the gap between research and practice. After two decades of grappling with the problem of how to integrate these two endeavors, I have emerged with an equivocal conclusion: research and practice are neither the natural antagonists that some might suggest nor the easy partners that others might. Each of us can have a role in improving that relationship and bridging the gap. For clinicians, this principally lies in keeping abreast of the developments in research and applying them in practice; for researchers, in focusing their research in ways that are germane to practice. And for both researchers and clinicians, in remaining respectful and interested in the work of the other (Beutler, Williams, Wakefield, & Entwistle, 1995; Kazdin, 2001; Orlinsky, 1994; Robbins, Bachrach, & Szapocznik, 2002).

RESOURCES

Beutler, L. E., Williams, R. E., Wakefield, P. J., & Entwistle, S. R. (1995). Bridging scientist and practitioner perspectives in clinical psychology. *American Psychologist, 50*(12), 984–994.

Orlinsky, D. E. (1994). Research-based knowledge as the emergent foundation for clinical practice in psychotherapy. In P. Talley & H. H. Strupp (Eds.), *Psychotherapy research and practice: Bridging the gap* (pp. 99–123). New York: Basic Books.

REFERENCES

Beach, S. R. H. (Ed.). (2001). *Marital and family processes in depression: A scientific foundation for clinical practice.* Washington, DC: American Psychological Association.

Beck, A. T. (1995). Cognitive therapy: Past, present, and future. In M. J. Mahoney (Ed.), *Cognitive and constructive psychotherapies: Theory, research, and practice* (pp. 29–40). New York: Springer Publishing.

Beutler, L. E., Williams, R. E., Wakefield, P. J., & Entwistle, S. R. (1995). Bridging scientist and practitioner perspectives in clinical psychology. *American Psychologist, 50*(12): 984–994.

Burlingame, G. M., Fuhriman, A. J., & Johnson, J. (Eds.). (2004). Current status and future directions of group therapy research. In J. L. DeLucia-Waack, D. A. Gerrity, C. R. Kalodner, & M. T. Riva (Eds.), *Handbook of group counseling and psychotherapy* (pp. 651–660). Thousand Oaks, CA: Sage Publications.

Chambless, D. L., & Hollon, S. D. (1998). Defining empirically supported therapies. *Journal of Consulting & Clinical Psychology, 66*(1): 7–18.

Clarkin, J. F., & Levy, K. N. (2003). A psychodynamic treatment for severe personality disorders: Issues in treatment development. *Psychoanalytic Inquiry, 23*(2): 248–267.

Falloon, I. R. (1988). Behavioral family management in coping with functional psychosis: Principles, practice, and recent developments. *International Journal of Mental Health, 17*(1): 35–47.

Goldfried, M. R., Greenberg, L. S., & Marmar, C. (1990). Individual psychotherapy: Process and outcome. *Annual Review of Psychology, 41*: 659–688.

Gottman, J. M. (1998). Psychology and the study of the marital processes. *Annual Review of Psychology, 49*: 169–197.

Greenberg, L. S., & Elliott, R. (2002). Emotion-focused therapy. [References]. In F. W. Kaslow (Ed.), *Comprehensive handbook of psychotherapy: Integrative/eclectic* (pp. 213–240). New York: John Wiley & Sons.

Hogarty, G. E., Anderson, C. M., Reiss, D. J., Kornblith, S. J., Greenwald, D. P., Ulrich, R. F., et al. (1991). Family psychoeducation, social skills training, and maintenance chemotherapy in the aftercare treatment of schizophrenia: Vol. II. Two-year effects of a controlled study on relapse and adjustment. *Archives of General Psychiatry, 48*(4): 340–347.

Kazdin, A. E. (2001). Bridging the enormous gaps of theory with therapy research and practice. *Journal of Clinical Child Psychology, 30*(1): 59–66.

Klerman, G. L., Weissman, M. M., Rounsaville, B., & Chevron, E. S. (1995). Interpersonal psychotherapy for depression. *Journal of Psychotherapy Practice & Research, 4*(4): 342–351.

Lebow, J. (1997). The integrative revolution in couple and family therapy. *Family Process, 36*(1): 1–17.

Lebow, J. (2000). What does the research tell us about couple and family therapies? *Journal of Clinical Psychology, 56*(8): 1083–1094.

Levant, R. F. (2004). The empirically validated treatments movement: A practitioner/educator perspective. *Clinical Psychology: Science & Practice, 11*(2): 219–224.

McFarlane, W. R., Link, B., Dushay, R., Marchal, J., & Crilly, J. (1995). Psychoeducational multiple family groups: Four-year relapse outcome in schizophrenia. *Family Process, 34*(2): 127–144.

Miller, S. D., Duncan, B. L., & Hubble, M. A. (2002). Client-directed, outcome-informed clinical work. [References]. In F. W. Kaslow (Ed.), *Comprehensive handbook of psychotherapy: Integrative/eclectic* (pp. 185–212). New York: John Wiley & Sons.

Nathan, P. E., & Gorman, J. M. (2003). A guide to treatments that work. *Psychotherapy Research, 13*(1): 128–130.

Norcross, J. C., & Goldfried, M. R. (Eds.). (2005). *Handbook of psychotherapy integration* (2nd ed.). London: Oxford University Press.

Orlinsky, D. E. (1994). Research-based knowledge as the emergent foundation for clinical practice in psychotherapy. In P. Talley & H. H. Strupp (Eds.), *Psychotherapy research and practice: Bridging the gap* (pp. 99–123). New York: Basic Books.

Robbins, M. S., Bachrach, K., & Szapocznik, J. (2002). Bridging the research-practice gap in adolescent substance abuse treatment: The case of brief strategic family therapy. *Journal of Substance Abuse Treatment, 23*(2) 123–132.

Rogers, C. R. (1992). The processes of therapy. *Journal of Consulting and Clinical Psychology, 60*(2): 163–164.

Watzlawick, P., Fisch, R., Andolfi, M., de Shazer, S., Lipchik, E., Reamy-Stephenson, M., et al. (1990). Strategic and structural approaches. J. K. Zeig & W. M. Munion (Eds.), *What is psychotherapy? Contemporary perspectives.* New York: Norton.

Watzlawick, P., Weakland, J. H., & Fisch, R. (1974). *Change: Principles of problem formation and problem resolution.* Oxford, UK: W. W. Norton.

Whitaker, C. A. (1958). *Psychotherapy of chronic schizophrenic patients.* Oxford, UK: Little, Brown.

2

A CLINICIAN'S PRIMER FOR EVALUATING RESEARCH ABOUT PSYCHOTHERAPY

It is essential for psychotherapy to be informed by relevant research, but how is a practicing therapist to assess whether findings presented are solidly grounded and widely applicable? This chapter provides some guideposts for reading research and summaries of research.

Most psychotherapists want to have what they do in practice be consistent with the latest research. But how does one stay current with relevant findings? There is no central clearinghouse that evaluates clinically relevant research, disseminates key findings, and places research in context. Each clinician needs to become a good consumer of research.

The first task lies in knowing where to look for research relevant to practice. The good news is that such research is reported in many accessible sources. Newspapers and magazines often report the results of research, particularly when the research involves a controversial topic, such as the impact of selective serotonin reuptake inhibitors (SSRIs), or efforts to change gays into heterosexuals. The quality of these reports vary from very thorough, balanced summaries in places such as the science pages of the *New York Times,* to what essentially are writeups of press releases by those with a vested interest in the findings of a piece of research. Practitioner-friendly professional magazines such as the *APA Monitor,* published by the American Psychological Association (APA); *Psychotherapy Networker; In Session;* and *Family Therapy Magazine,* published by the American Association of Marriage and Family Therapy, provide generally reliable summaries. And, of course, there are the research journals themselves which publish most of the original research and the reviews of that research. That literature is typically more arcane and difficult to decipher without a strong background and interest in research methodology, though there are publications, such as *Clinical Psychology: Research and Practice* that are easier to follow. And, of course, there are the ubiquitous online sources that can vary from comprehensive, knowledgeable, and balanced to outright ridiculous.

Whether encountering a newspaper article, book, research article, or web site, a report of one study or a review of studies, the criteria for evaluating research remains more or less the same. Here are a few of the most salient factors.

WHO DID THE RESEARCH?

Good research mostly emanates from those who regularly are involved in research. And the most questionable reports often come out of politically related think tanks with an axe to grind. Of course, a researcher with a wonderful reputation can produce a poorly executed study, but looking at the source often can provide a quick clue to the quality of the effort.

WHERE HAS THE STUDY BEEN PUBLISHED?

Almost every piece of research can get published somewhere. The research that is most reliable and valid appears in the best research journals. So learn to discriminate between journals. Among the most highly regarded for research relevant to psychotherapy are the *Journal of Consulting and Clinical Psychology, Journal of Abnormal Psychology,* and *Archives of General Psychiatry.* Raise more questions about articles in small journals that are not in the collections of most libraries.

HAS THE CONCLUSION BEEN REPLICATED IN NUMEROUS STUDIES?

A frequently encountered phenomenon in research is one where findings that come to be widely reported are not replicated in further research. When encountering the result of a single study, no matter how well conducted, we must determine whether that result is found again in further research. Therefore, reports that summarize the findings from more than one study are innately superior to the findings of single studies.

HOW WELL WAS THE RESEARCH CONDUCTED IN TERMS OF METHODOLOGY?

Methods are less intrinsically interesting than findings and often are skipped over in lay summaries of research. But research is only as good as its methodology. Each study can be evaluated in terms of level of potential threats to what is called internal validity, the possibility that the study found what it did because of an error or failing to account for some key influence. Threats to validity include such concerns as people knowing what the study was about and responding to that, using instruments that don't tap what the instruments are supposed to measure, and sloppily following the procedures in the study. It's difficult to determine if a comparison between two treatments means anything if one of the treatments is carried out poorly. Cook and Campbell have written the definitive book on threats to methodology (Cook, Campbell, & Peracchio, 1990; Shadish, Cook, & Campbell, 2002).

DOES THE EXPLANATION OFFERED BY THE AUTHORS FIT WITH WHAT IS FOUND? ARE THERE ALTERNATIVE EXPLANATIONS FOR THE FINDINGS REPORTED?

Sometimes, a study is conducted reasonably well, but the conclusions drawn extend well beyond the data. A classic example lies in studies assessing correlation (how two things covary) leading to conclusions about causation (what causes what?) that are not warranted. For example, David Blankenhorn (Blankenhorn, 1996) has argued that living together before marriage causes higher levels of marital dissolution, based on data that showed that those who live together before marriage divorce more than those who do not live together first (40% vs. 31% at 10 years). However, that there is a covariation does not mean that one variable caused the change in the other even if one variable came first (here, living together or not doing so). The error in Blankenhorn's widely disseminated logic stems from the fact that those who live together before marriage and those who don't do so also vary in a number of other important ways (religiosity, social conservative behavior) and that it is almost certainly these ways rather than something about the process of living together itself that result in the group who cohabitate to have a slightly higher rate of divorce.

IS THE STUDY APPLICABLE TO MOST PEOPLE?

This question, labeled the "generalizability" of the study, is a crucial one in psychotherapy research (Cook et al., 1990; Shadish et al., 2002). Many findings are based on only a narrow population, especially one limited in diversity (Sue, 1995). When that is the case, it limits the applicability of the findings to others until research is completed on a broader range of people.

HOW CLINICALLY SIGNIFICANT ARE THE FINDINGS?

Most research is ultimately about a comparison between groups of subjects or between subjects before and after treatment, and these comparisons are reported in statistical tests. In typical published research, a statistically significant effect is reported (if there were no such effect, the study is unlikely to be published), but it still remains essential to understand how clinically meaningful the effect is. For example, those receiving a treatment for obsessive-compulsive disorder may improve in statistical terms, but the far more important question is do they improve enough for that change to be clinically meaningful (in, for example, truly being able to have their lives be less disrupted by the obsessive-compulsive disorder). Neil Jacobson (Jacobson & Revenstorf, 1988) proposed several criteria for judging clinical significance: for example, assessing the extent to which those receiving a treatment come to be able to function as do others who never had the particular problem that is the focus of the treatment.

CONCLUSION

These are some criteria for judging research. And there's a great deal of useful research to learn from. Try to read or listen to the claims with an open but cautious attitude. How solid is the evidence for what is being claimed? And talk to others, particularly your more research-oriented colleagues, about the research you read or hear about. Such conversations can help put research in perspective. As a community of researchers and clinicians, we have much to learn from one another.

RESOURCES

Shadish, W. R., Cook, T. D., & Campbell, D. T. (2002). *Experimental and quasi-experimental designs for generalized causal inference*. Boston, MA: Houghton Mifflin.

REFERENCES

Blankenhorn, D. (1996). *Fatherless America: Confronting our most urgent social problem*. New York: Harper Perennial.

Cook, T. D., Campbell, D. T., & Peracchio, L. (1990). Quasi experimentation. In M. D. Dunnette & L. M. Hough (Eds.), *Handbook of industrial and organizational psychology* (vol. 1, 2nd ed., pp. 491–576). Palo Alto, CA: Consulting Psychologists Press.

Jacobson, N. S., & Revenstorf, D. (1988). Statistics for assessing the clinical significance of psychotherapy techniques: Issues, problems, and new developments. *Behavioral Assessment, 10*(2):, 133–145.

Shadish, W. R., Cook, T. D., & Campbell, D. T. (2002). *Experimental and quasi-experimental designs for generalized causal inference*. Boston, MA: Houghton Mifflin.

Sue, S. (1995). The implications of diversity for scientific standards of practice. In S. C. Hayes & V. M. Follette (Eds.), *Scientific standards of psychological practice: Issues and recommendations* (pp. 265–279). Reno, NV: Context Press.

Part II
Research Focused on Psychotherapy

3

THERAPY BY THE NUMBERS: CRITICS CLAIM EMPIRICALLY SUPPORTED TREATMENTS (ESTs) UNDERMINE CLINICAL CREATIVITY

This chapter provides a view of the controversy about the generation of lists of empirically supported treatments. Few issues have divided the worlds of science and practice as the generation of such lists. Although listings of empirically supported treatments are becoming more commonplace (Chambless & Ollendick, 2001; Nathan & Gorman, 2003; Ollendick & Davis, 2004), the level of controversy today remains as great as when the first such lists were issued.

The uncertain relationship between the art and science of psychotherapy has for decades been at the heart of many clinical researchers' misgivings about their therapist colleagues (Barlow et al., 1993; Beutler et al., 1995). According to these critics, too many therapists practice without the slightest attention to the research literature and the decades of findings regarding which therapeutic methods have proven effective for which kinds of problems (Lilienfeld, 2002). Rather than following the model of medicine, in which what is considered acceptable practice is shaped and refined by rigorous research procedures, the therapy field, its critics contend, has been shaped far more by persuasive innovators and intellectual fashions than by anything resembling scientific inquiry. As a result, important distinctions between untested methods and empirically proven approaches have been obscured.

In 1995, a task force acting under the auspices of the Division of Clinical Psychology of the APA, a group that included many of the most prominent therapy researchers in the country, decided it was finally time to establish the scientific foundations of clinical practice. Under the direction of Diane Chambless, then of the University of North Carolina, it set out to establish clear, objective criteria to distinguish those treatment procedures that had been scientifically proven to be effective with specific psychological conditions from those that had not (Chambless, 1999; Chambless & Ollendick, 2000). This task force became responsible for issuing a list of empirically supported treatments (ESTs), a kind of Good Housekeeping Seal of Approval for psychotherapies.

To join the elite ranks of "well-established" therapies, Chambless and colleagues laid out the following standards:

- To make sure that approval of a treatment is not determined by the enthusiasm of a single investigator, two different and independent studies, each undertaken by a different researcher, must show the treatment to be more effective than no treatment, a placebo, or an alternative treatment.
- To avoid any ambiguity about the therapeutic factors accounting for an approach's effectiveness, the method itself must be guided by a treatment manual that makes explicit the exact procedures and interventions to be used with each client.
- To establish with which specific treatment group a particular approach is effective, all the clients being studied must be shown to be suffering from the same psychological disorder (e.g., depression, anxiety, schizophrenia, chemical dependence).

These criteria created by Chambless and her colleagues have become the standard for assessing treatments as empirically supported in a wide array of efforts (Nathan & Gorman, 2003; Ollendick & Davis, 2004)

Cognitive Therapy for Depression (Beck, 1976), developed by Aaron Beck and colleagues of the University of Pennsylvania, offers a clear example of the typical stages of development involved in becoming recognized as an EST:

A specific disorder was identified as the focus of treatment. Beck aimed the therapy at a distinct diagnostic category—depression and its specific symptoms. He also created a number of valid and reliable measures (most prominently, the Beck Depression Inventory [Beck & Beamesderfer, 1974]) to quantify and assess the impact of his interventions.

A step-by-step treatment strategy was developed. Beck and his colleagues identified a number of typical ways depressed people think, centered on their amplifying negative thoughts while minimizing their sense of competence. They then created a clear and replicable treatment aimed at altering these thought patterns by teaching clients to logically examine their thoughts, develop more balanced self-talk, track their depressed feelings and behaviors, and increase their activity.

A treatment manual was created to explicitly direct clinicians' interventions and decision making. Beck and colleagues developed a treatment manual that purported to describe what interventions to deliver and when during the various phases of therapy.

Treatment effectiveness was clearly demonstrated. Beck and colleagues first showed that clients treated with Cognitive Therapy for Depression had fewer symptoms of depression than those who received no treatment. They subsequently have proved it to be at least as effective as medication in several studies.

Yet, despite the fact that more than 20 therapies have met the task force's standard for well-established treatments and more than 50 have qualified as "probably efficacious" treatments pending further studies, the effect of ESTs on clinical practice has been limited so far. Although such ESTs as Beck's depression treatment (Rush & Beck, 1988), David Barlow's therapy for anxiety disorders (Barlow, 1994), and Sue Johnson's and Les Greenburg's Emotionally Focused Couples Therapy (Johnson, 1998; Greenberg, 2002) have all grown in popularity in recent years, most ESTs have yet to become part of the practice of most practitioners.

So, why have therapists and the public not responded more enthusiastically to the evidence that certain therapeutic procedures seem to yield consistently good results? Why haven't ESTs revolutionized clinical practice? There appear to be several reasons why the movement to codify psychotherapy's ESTs has so far generated limited enthusiasm among both therapists and the general public. In fact, such is the controversy surrounding the whole concept of ESTs that the task force's report and listing have still not received the official imprimatur of the American Psychological Association. Among the criticisms are the following:

>**ESTs ignore the importance of the therapist.** Some therapists charge that ESTs place too much emphasis on the technical aspects of treatment. Psychologists Mark Hubble, Barry Duncan, and Scott Miller (1999), along with others, have tried to highlight the evidence that the most important factors in treatment outcome have far more to do with the strength of the therapeutic relationship and the hope and expectation of success than with any specific therapeutic technique, no matter how clearly delineated and manualized. They point to meta-analyses that suggest that technique may account for no more than 15% of the improvement clients make in therapy (Lambert & Barley, 2001; Wampold, 2001).

>**ESTs limit the focus of therapy and hamstring creativity.** Stan Messer of Rutgers University suggests that the use of treatment manuals and the focus on diagnostic groupings ignores the inherent complexities of therapy (Messer, 2004). Messer describes a hypothetical client—married but involved with another woman—in the throes of a life crisis and manifesting numerous symptoms of depression. Should the therapist use an EST for the depressive symptoms or should he lead the client to a wider ranging self-examination? Messer asks what it would mean to offer an EST for depression to such a client. He contends that the preoccupation with merely alleviating symptoms and treating *Diagnostic and Statistical Manual of Mental Disorders (DSM)-IV* syndromes only represent a small part of what most skilled therapists are concerned with.

>**ESTs favor therapies that are easily researched rather than those most deserving research.** Cognitive-behavioral approaches now comprise more than 80% of approved therapies on the APA task force's list. Many therapists argue that these approaches are no more effective than other therapies, but merely lend themselves to manualized treatment and the other quantifiable procedures necessary to establish therapies as empirically supported. Meanwhile, critics point out that there has been virtually no testing

of such major approaches to psychotherapy as Gestalt therapy, object relations therapy, or Bowen therapy (Hubble et al., 1999).

ESTs potentially narrow the field of reimbursable treatments and represent a threat to therapists' freedom of choice. The loudest opposition to ESTs arises out of the fear that at some point in the future they will become the only therapies eligible for third-party reimbursement. It was probably for this reason that the APA refused to officially endorse its task force's listing of ESTs. Recognizing that managed care already makes decisions about reimbursement based on *DSM* diagnoses, critics contend it's not a big leap to imagine reimbursements in the future being limited to a select group of highly routinized treatments on a managed care "approved" list.

Meanwhile even those skeptical about ESTs recognize that they can offer benefits to therapists who know how to incorporate them into their current treatment approaches. For those willing to pick and choose, ESTs offer an abundance of tested treatment ideas and intervention packages that may be applied with a range of problems. In the context of his multimodal therapy, for example, noted psychotherapist Arnold Lazarus moves in and out of ESTs, applying techniques he believes are helpful while maintaining an independent theoretical framework (Lazarus & Beutler, 1993). And certainly when a clinician has to contend with an uncooperative case manager, ESTs bolster the argument for therapy instead of medication.

At the moment, it is unclear whether ESTs will move beyond being a collection of tested tools and become reductive clinical procedures that are unsuited to the complexity of therapeutic problems and hamstring the creativity of clinicians. But although their impact on therapists' future freedom of choice in selecting their practice methods remains to be seen, ESTs do provide research-minded therapists a link between scientifically evaluated interventions and their day-to-day work.

RESOURCES

Chambless, D. L., Baker, M. J., Baucom, D. H., Beutler, L. E., Calhoun, K. S., Crits-Chistoph, P., et al. (1998). Update on empirically validated therapies II. *The Clinical Psychologist, 51*: 3–16.

Messer, S. B., (2001). Empirically supported treatments: What's a non-behaviorist to do? In B. D. Slife, R. N. Williams, & S. H. Barlow (Eds.), *Critical Issues in Psychotherapy: Translating New Ideas Into Practice*. Thousand Oaks, CA: Sage Publications.

Nathan, P. E., & J. M. Gorman. (2003). A guide to treatments that work. *Psychotherapy Research 13*(1): 128–130

The website of the Society for a Science of Clinical Psychology includes papers about the selection of ESTs: http://www.wpic.pitt.edu/research/sscp/empirically_supported_treatments.htm

REFERENCES

Barlow, D. H. (1994). Effectiveness of behavior treatment for panic disorder with and without agoraphobia. In B. E. Wolfe & J. D. Maser (Eds.), *Treatment of panic disorder: A consensus development conference* (pp. 105–120). Washington, DC: American Psychiatric Association.

Barlow, D. H., Morrow-Bradley C., et al. (1993). Relationship between the scientist and the practitioner. In J. A. Mindell (Ed.), *Issues in clinical psychology* (pp. 11–35). Madison, WI: Brown & Benchmark/Wm. C. Brown Publishers.

Beck, A. T. (1976). *Cognitive therapy and the emotional disorders.* Oxford, UK: International Universities Press.

Beck, A. T., & Beamesderfer, A. (1974). Assessment of depression: The depression inventory. In P. Pichot & R. Olivier-Martin (Eds.), *Psychological measurements in psychopharmacology.* Oxford, UK: S Karger.

Beutler, L. E., Williams, R. E., Wakefield, P. J., & Entwistle, S. R. (1995). Bridging scientist and practitioner perspectives in clinical psychology. *American Psychologist, 50*(12): 984–994.

Chambless, D. L. (1999). Empirically validated treatments—What now? *Applied & Preventive Psychology, 8*(4): 281–284.

Chambless, D. L., & Ollendick, T. H. (2000). Empirically supported psychological interventions: Controversies and evidence. *Annual Review of Psychology, 52*: 685–716.

Chambless, D. L., & Ollendick, T. H. (2001). Empirically supported psychological interventions: Controversies and evidence. *Annual Review of Psychology, 52*: 685–716.

Greenberg, L. S. (2002). *Emotion-focused therapy: Coaching clients to work through their feelings.* Washington, DC: American Psychological Association.

Hubble, M. A., Duncan, B. L., & Miller, S. D. (Eds.). (1999). *The heart and soul of change: What works in therapy.* Washington, DC: American Psychological Association.

Johnson, S. (1998). Emotionally focused couple therapy. In F. M. Dattilio (Ed.), *Case studies in couple and family therapy: Systemic and cognitive perspectives. The Guilford family therapy series* (pp. 450–472). New York: Guilford Press.

Lambert, M. J., & Barley, D. E. (2001). Research summary on the therapeutic relationship and psychotherapy outcome. *Psychotherapy: Theory, Research, Practice, Training, 38*(4): 357–361.

Lazarus, A. A., & Beutler, L. E. (1993). On technical eclecticism. *Journal of Counseling & Development, 71*(4): 381–385.

Lilienfeld, S. O. (2002). The scientific review of mental health practice: Our raison d'etre. *Scientific Review of Mental Health Practice, 1*(1): 5–10.

Messer, S. B. (2004). Evidence-based practice: Beyond empirically supported treatments. *Professional Psychology: Research & Practice, 35*(6): 580–588.

Nathan, P. E., & Gorman, J. M. (2003). A guide to treatments that work. *Psychotherapy Research, 13*(1): 128–130.

Ollendick, T. H., & Davis, T. E. III. (2004). Empirically supported treatments for children and adolescents: Where to from here? *Clinical Psychology: Science & Practice, 11*(3): 289–294.

Rush, A., & Beck, A. T. (1988). Cognitive therapy of depression and suicide. In S. Lesse (Ed.), *What we know about suicidal behavior and how to treat it* (pp. 283–306). Northvale, NJ: Jason Aronson.

Wampold, B. E. (2001). *The great psychotherapy debate: Models, methods, and findings.* Mahwah, NJ: Lawrence Erlbaum Associates.

4

THE PUSH FOR EVIDENCE: DEFINING THE ROLE FOR EVIDENCE-BASED PRACTICE

The role of evidence-based practice has emerged as one of the major controversies in psychotherapy. This chapter looks at the debate about evidence-based practice in the context of a recent effort within the American Psychological Association (APA) to delineate what is meant by evidence-based practice and how it should inform practice.

In 2004–2005, a longstanding controversy in the world of psychotherapy researchers about how treatment research should be conducted and influence practice boiled over into a heated public argument in forums such as the science section of the *New York Times*. This national attention to what previously had been seen by most outsiders as an esoteric disagreement between researchers, if they knew about it at all, stemmed from the appointment of a task force aimed at addressing what constitutes evidence-based practice by the president of the APA, Ron Levant of Nova Southeastern University. In forming this task force, Levant sought to expand the purview of what is considered evidence beyond the clinical trial research that typifies drug studies in medicine and which have become the predominant method in federally funded research assessing psychotherapy and which has been used as the criterion for therapies being evaluated as empirically supported treatments (ESTs).

Ironically, given the level of acrimony that ensued around the creation of this task force, Levant's intension in organizing this group was to help bridge the gap between researchers and practitioners (Levant, 2004). He hoped to use this platform to build a consensus across researchers engaged in various types of treatment research and between researchers and clinicians about how practice might best be informed by research. Such a consensus has inevitably become mired in quicksand when that dialogue has centered exclusively on the extent to which therapists should practice ESTs. Yet, in looking to move beyond the narrow frame of the results of tightly controlled efficacy studies to include such factors in what is regarded as evidence-based as the consensus of skilled clinicians and less well-controlled forms of research in real-world clinical settings, Levant invoked the ire of those identified with more tightly controlled research methods.

It didn't help that Levant was quoted in the *New York Times* as saying, "This entire approach to develop manuals and require practicing psychologists to use them is fundamentally insane," (Carey, 2004, p. 43) questioning the use of treatment manuals, one of the foundations of the EST movement. Although Levant subsequently identified that he was misquoted, this statement was taken by those most invested in the kind of research (which always use treatment manuals) as creating a caricature of their ideas. In a letter to the *New York Times* responding to this comment and other critiques of the EST movement in the earlier story, a group of prominent researchers, including John Weisz of the University of California Los Angeles and Philip Kendell of Temple University, whose research focuses on evaluating child treatments, stated, "Efforts to identify effective treatments would seem to be our professional and ethical obligation to those who seek our help" (Weisz, Abidin, et al., 2004). And there were further rejoinders from those researchers identified with other traditions of investigation, whose challenge to the EST movement had already been reinvigorated over the last few years with the publication of several critiques of the studies that examined psychotherapy in the classic drug study design.

Most therapists and the public might wonder about how such a difference of opinion about what might seem to be an arcane topic, the comparative value of different methodologies for studying psychotherapy, could have importance beyond the province of academic discourse.

Yet, this debate has vast importance for the practice of psychotherapy over the next few decades. In a world increasingly conscious of the importance of accountability, showing that therapy "works" and which therapies "work" has become vitally important to third-party payers and the public. And deciding what is meant by *works* is in part determined by how the question is framed; a product of the kind of evidence regarded as relevant to answering the question. Anchored in the foundation of the kind of evidence crucial for those in the EST movement, some third-party payers have already begun to mandate the practice of one of the ESTs given the presence of particular disorders such as dysthymic disorder. And considerable government resources have already begun to be invested in the dissemination of these treatments.

Researchers divide into two very different positions in the debate about the kind of research most relevant for the practice of psychotherapy. The first group, most of whom are researchers and who most frequently are cognitive-behavior therapists, are those who believe in the superiority of what are called "randomized clinical trials" for assessing psychotherapy (Kazdin, 2003; Lilienfeld, 2002). This group believes that therapies are analogous to medications and need to be assessed in tightly controlled research that establishes specific variants of therapy as safe and effective for the treatment of particular disorders; essentially drug research without the drugs. Their worldview focuses on the universe of disorders identified in the Diagnostic and Statistical Manuel (*DSM*) of the APA and establishing which are the most effective treatments for these disorders. The mechanism they believe will best test these treatments is the comparison of the outcomes of those receiving these treatments with the outcomes of those who have the same disorder and do not receive treatment. This is the essence of the randomized clinical trial; the standard method by which drugs are evaluated for their efficacy and safety across a diverse array of problems from diabetes to heart disease to schizophrenia. This kind of research makes up the preponderance of research on mental health treatment funded over the last 20 years by the National Institute of Health.

From the vantage point of those who share this viewpoint, the best relationship between research and practice lies in carefully controlled research establishing those treatments that impact on specific disorders followed by dissemination of these therapies to practicing therapists through the publication of treatment manuals describing these approaches and training in those methods. And therapists who practice methods that are not established as effective in this way when there are such methods available are viewed as behaving irresponsibly. Diane Chambless, Professor of Psychology at the University of

Pennsylvania, said, "In meeting my commitment to be ethical in my practice, if I do an evaluation with a client and find that the client has a problem that can be treated by an EST in which I have no competence, whereas my own approach has unknown efficacy, I should try to refer the client to someone who does have that competence, unless the fully informed client prefers to take his or her chances with an approach of unknown efficacy" (Diane Chambless, personal communication, 2004). Dr. Chambless also suggests that ESTs should at least be the first treatment alternatives tried in a case, and the lists of ESTs suggest the most useful directions for continuing education for practicing therapists. Dr. Chambless headed the first major effort to construct a list of ESTs as the head of a task force devoted to this task of the Society of Clinical Psychology of the APA.

The second group of researchers in this controversy has a quite different vantage point, believing the value of clinical trial research has been grossly exaggerated by its supporters and that different types of research offer greater promise for positively impacting on psychotherapy. Bruce Wampold of the University of Wisconsin persuasively argued such a position in the best-selling book *The Great Psychotherapy Debate* (2001), suggesting that that therapist differences are much more important than differences that flow from technique. Wampold says,

> Clinical trials, by their very nature, focus on treatment differences and ignore other important sources of variability. Despite this maniacal focus on treatments, very little evidence has ever been presented that one treatment is superior to another, generally or for specific disorders. Much of the variability that can be identified is due to the therapists—some therapists consistently produce better outcomes than others. These results are consistent with our inclinations as clinicians when we are asked to make a referral—we think of the best therapist we know, rather than think of a particular approach to treatment. If it was my cousin who needed treatment, for instance, I would refer him or her to the best provider in his or her town. (Bruce Wampold, personal communication, 2004).

In a similar vein, Drew Westen, professor of psychology at Emory University, along with his colleagues Catherine Novotny and Heather Thompson-Brenner, in what has quickly become the definitive critique of the clinical trial in research on psychotherapies in the prestigious *Psychological Bulletin*, enumerated the deficits of the clinical trial research that constitutes the foundation for ETSs (Westen, Novotny,

& Thompson-Brenner, 2004). They convincingly point to several factors that make the present version of clinical trial research funded by National Institute of Mental Health a poor method for finding out about what works in psychotherapy. These include:

1. The foundation of this research in the *DSM* diagnostic system. They point out that a very small percentage of those who seek therapy do so because they have a particular *DSM* diagnosis such as obsessive-compulsive disorder. Instead, people mostly seek psychotherapy for problems in living. And they point to ways the *DSM* system itself is less than ideal such as when it suggests the existence of two highly co-morbid separate disorders, generalized anxiety disorder and dysthymic disorder, rather than a more generic problem in dealing with negative affect. Westen and colleagues suggest that in examples such as this one, the focus on symptoms moves away from what would be a more useful focus on the core problem.

2. That most clients don't have one clear primary problem for which they seek treatment as do the clients in the clinical trial research focused around single problems where clients with multiple problems are excluded from studies. This leaves those in that research highly unrepresentative of the people seen in clinical practice.

3. That clinical trial research focused on disorders ignores the central importance that differences in individual personality have in treatment, and fails to factor in the adaptations in approach that are needed in response to personality differences.

4. That the treatment manuals used to direct the course of treatment in clinical trial research impose significant limitations. Manuals can easily prove rigid or unable to speak to the range of treatment decisions. And in a remarkable and very telling description of the problematic way manuals have come to strangely interface with the various broad schools of treatment, Westen and colleagues record how a method designed to represent commonplace brief psychoanalytic practice transformed into the manualized treatment called Interpersonal Psychotherapy. This lead to Interpersonal Psychotherapy becoming established as an effective psychotherapy for depression, whereas psychoanalytic psychotherapy (which it was supposed to represent) could not qualify for the list (because it was studied as Interpersonal Psychotherapy).

5. That although findings from mental health services indicate that longer therapies typically are more successful, such lengthy

treatments are rarely studied in randomized clinical trials. They note that the almost complete focus of clinical trial research on brief therapies seems more likely to be the product of the effort of researchers to mimic drug studies and on costs of research rather than on the ecological fit with therapy. In a survey of 242 clinicians in more typical practice, done by Westen and colleagues, successful therapies for specific *DSM* conditions, such as panic disorder or dysthymic disorder, typically ranged from 52 to 75 sessions. And Westen and colleagues highlight that brief therapies seldom are effective in leading to the kind of change that prevents recurrence of problems.

Westen says,

> The problem is when researchers overgeneralize both the findings and the power of clinical trials to answer many of the questions clinicians face in everyday practice, often using samples that do not resemble those in practice, studying disorders that do not exist in pure form in clinical practice, studying treatments that deal with only a small piece of what most patients present with, and concluding that success rates that usually hover around 30–40% represent the treatment of choice, when they have never compared their treatments to what good clinicians in the community do. Perhaps these success rates are better than what most clinicians obtain in everyday practice, but I doubt it. (Drew Westen, personal communication, 2004).

Such criticisms have led this group of researchers to seek other methods to learn about psychotherapy. These methods include surveys of clients and therapists, like the Consumers Reports survey of its readers' experiences with psychotherapy (Seligman, 1995) or the one reported by Westen previously; studies of the impact of general processes in treatment that transcend orientation, such as the establishment of a therapeutic alliance and how these factors impact on treatment outcome; effectiveness research that examines the impact of typical treatments on specific client populations with specific kinds of difficulties in real-world settings; and progress research, in which client gains are regularly tracked during treatment by the therapist, without regard to the kind of intervention. These methods provide information about psychotherapy not available from clinical trials.

And a number of organizations have begun to look into alternative ways of looking at how various kinds of research can best impact practice. The Division of Psychotherapy of the APA has published a volume edited by John Norcross (Norcross, 2002), titled *Psychotherapy Relationships That Work,* which accentuates research-based conclusions that center on broad general factors in treatment, such as creating and maintaining a string therapeutic alliance. Larry Beutler and Louis Castonguay have led a task force of APA's Division of Clinical Psychology focused on Principles of Change mixing treatment, participant, and relationship factors. And the Division of Counseling Psychology of APA has suggested an approach in which a number of therapy levels are evaluated: (1) whether therapy in general works, (2) whether kinds of therapy work, (3) whether specific treatments for specific conditions work, and (4) specific treatments for specific difficulties in specific populations (that is, paying attention to culture). The Counseling Psychology task force (Wampold, Lichtenberg, & Waehler, 2002) emphasizes that diagnosis, the center of the EST movement, should not be privileged as the way of assessing psychotherapies. And they hold that the choice of treatment is ultimately a local decision made by the practitioner on the basis of the best information available. Moreover, they emphasize the need to track outcomes in any environment.

The proponents of clinical trials argue that the critics of the clinical trial method exaggerate their claims and create a caricature of the method. Chambless says,

> It's simply not true that those of us who advocate learning about ESTs think that the therapeutic relationship isn't important; that we claim ESTs cure most clients in a brief period; that we advocate clinicians slavishly following manuals; that we exclude clients with comorbidity from our research protocols; and that ESTs only help clients in research settings and so forth. It's a puzzle to me that so many of these myths continue to be repeated despite our efforts to correct them. (Diane Chambless, personal communication, 2004).

And it certainly is true that those who promote clinical trial research increasingly have produced manuals that include considerable flexibility for clinical decision making, and are also trying to study longer treatments and treatments in more natural community treatment settings. Additionally, they are attending more to diversity in the samples on which treatments are tested. Nonetheless, the core value of the clinical trial method lies in its narrow focus, which provides a laboratory for intensely studying treatment processes, and each of the criticisms stated by Westen and colleagues still applies to most of the existent clinical trial research.

So what are we to make of the kinds of controversies described here when they catch our eye in the newspaper? Do the arguments in the cross fire have importance for what we do as clinicians or are they just headline-grabbing bravado? A couple of overarching conclusions emerge. Research is becoming and must become even more a crucial input into practice, but that fact should not be confused with the need to simply accept the notion that practice is better when directed by lists of best treatments for specific disorders. There is a position that combines the best of research-informed decision making and clinical wisdom that is evident in the best work in psychotherapy research and the best clinical practice. Research has grown as an input in practice. Some of this growth has been the product of clinical trial research, a rarefied environment in which aspects of treatment can be carefully studied. Sometimes treatments emerge that are so especially effective for those with particular difficulties (psycho-educational family treatments for schizophrenia and cognitivey-behavioral therapies for panic disorder being two examples) that there are clear treatments of choice transcending all other factors. However, this has been the case only in relation to a few very specific clinical problems. For most problems, a range of approaches seems to be effective, and other factors (such as the skill of the therapist or the strength of the alliance) appear far more important than the treatment chosen.

As Levant suggests, the polarization is clearly greatest at the ends of the continuum, between those few researchers who believe the only ethical treatment is that demonstrated to be efficacious and a clinical trial, and those clinicians with no use for any form of research. On one side are those who would like to return to the days of letting it all hang out and working fully from the gut. Guts are helpful (as long as they don't stick out too much) but easily become confused. On the other are those who look to transform psychotherapy into behavioral psychopharmacology without the drugs. For all the reasons that Westen suggests, this is a pathway that is equally fraught with difficulty as ignoring research entirely.

Yet there is a considerable consensus emerging about some aspects of this debate. There seems to be agreement that research must be an input in practice, but only can inform practice, not dictate what is done in psychotherapy. Chambless says, "I don't think clinical practice can ever be entirely driven by data because we will never have empirical findings on which to base every decision" (Diane Chambless, personal communication, 2004); a comment with which the critics of

ESTs would surely agree. And there is agreement that there must be a partnership between researchers and clinicians. Weisz and his colleagues (2004) in their letter state, "We see clinical scientists and clinical practitioners as essential partners." These words are echoed by Ron Levant.

Building on such common ground, the Levant APA task force ultimately produced a report and set of recommendations that supported the importance of evaluation and treatment being solidly grounded in evidence, but which also suggested that research evidence constitutes only one of several vital factors which must be considered in making decisions about treatment. The report concluded that clinician expertise and client values are coequal inputs that, together with research evidence, provide the foundation for evidence based practice. This report and its recommendations were subsequently approved by the governance of the APA.

Hopefully, the work of this task force betokens broader movement toward a consensus that can assimilate the best of what the clinical trial evidence, other sources of evidence, and clinical traditions of practice have to offer us. As Levant has suggested, this would logically lead to a vision of the psychotherapist as what George Stricker has termed a "local clinical scientist" (Stricker & Trierweiler, 1995), who draws from the results of research studies but also uses clinical expertise in hypothesis testing in practice to process the effects of the ways he or she is working with a client in treatment. Levant and his task force envision an appropriate place for a range of kinds of evidence, including clinical trial research, other psychotherapy research, and the evidence immediately available in the clinical process. Hopefully, Ron Levant's APA task force has helped move the field away from becoming bogged down in the rhetoric of debate about the role of evidence toward identifying ways for helping psychology and psychotherapy become more anchored in the best traditions of research, while allowing for the room for improvisation that is essential to most successful treatment.

RESOURCES

Chambless, D. L., Baker, M. J., Baucom, D. H., Beutler, L. E., Calhoun, K. S., Crits-Christoph, P., et al. (1998). Update on empirically validated therapies II. *The Clinical Psychologist, 51*: 3–16.

Wampold, B. E. (2001). *The great psychotherapy debate: Models, methods, and findings*. Mahwah, NJ: Lawrence Erlbaum Associates.

Westen, D., Novotny, C. M., & Thompson-Brenner, H. (2004). The empirical status of empirically supported psychotherapies: Assumptions, findings, and reporting in controlled clinical trials. *Psychological Bulletin, 130*: 631–663.

REFERENCES

Carey, B. (2004, August 10). For psychotherapy's claims, skeptics demand proof. *New York Times*, p. 43.

Chambless, D. L., Baker, M. J., Baucom, D. H., Beutler, L. E., Calhoun, K. S., Crits-Christoph, P., et al. (1998). Update on empirically validated therapies II. *The Clinical Psychologist, 51*: 3–16.

Kazdin, A. E. (Ed.). (2003). *Methodological issues & strategies in clinical research* (3rd ed.). Washington, DC: American Psychological Association.

Levant, R. F. (2004). The empirically validated treatments movement: A practitioner/educator perspective. *Clinical Psychology: Science & Practice, 11*(2): 219–224.

Lilienfeld, S. O. (2002). The scientific review of mental health practice: Our raison d'etre. *Scientific Review of Mental Health Practice, 1*(1): 5–10.

Norcross, J. C. (Ed.). (2002). *Psychotherapy relationships that work: Therapist contributions and responsiveness to patients*. London: Oxford University Press.

Seligman, M. E. P. (1995). The effectiveness of psychotherapy: The *Consumer Reports* study. *American Psychologist, 50*(12): 965–974.

Stricker, G., & Trierweiler, S. J. (1995). The local clinical scientist: A bridge between science and practice. *American Psychologist, 50*(12): 995–1002.

Wampold, B. E. (2001). *The great psychotherapy debate: Models, methods, and findings*. Mahwah, NJ: Lawrence Erlbaum Associates.

Wampold, B. E., Lichtenberg, J. W., & Waehler, C. A. (2002). Principles of empirically supported interventions in counseling psychology. *Counseling Psychologist, 30*(2): 197–217.

Weisz, J., Abidin, R., et al. (2004) Letter. *Newsletter of the Society of Clincal and Adolescent Psychology, 19*(3), 22.

Westen, D., Novotny, C. M., & Thompson-Brenner, H. (2004). The empirical status of empirically supported psychotherapies: Assumptions, findings, and reporting in controlled clinical trials. *Psychological Bulletin, 130*(4): 631–663.

5

WHAT CAN WE SAY ABOUT THE
EFFECTIVENESS OF PSYCHOTHERAPY?

There has been considerable debate about the effectiveness of psychotherapy. This chapter examines that debate and available findings about outcomes in psychotherapy.

In 1953, Hans Eysenck (Lambert & Bergin, 1994) issued a major challenge to the practice of psychotherapy by suggesting that the data available indicated that psychotherapy was ineffective. Eysenck compared the impact of a diverse array of psychotherapies aimed at a wide range of undifferentiated difficulties by comparing the change in clients who received treatment with a set of norms he developed for the change in individuals who did not receive psychotherapy. Eysenck's comparisons found little difference between those who received therapy and those who did not, an effect partially attributable to the considerable improvement of those who did not receive treatment.

Eysenck's challenge raised a question about whether psychotherapy, long shielded behind closed doors, could withstand examination into its effectiveness in helping individuals with their problems. And although this represented somewhat of a public relations disaster for psychotherapy in the mid-1950s, it also spurred the growth of psychotherapy research. Eysenck's challenge was met by several thoughtful rejoinders illuminating his errors in evaluating contemporary research of that time, especially in grossly overestimating the level of change that typically occurs without treatment (Garfield et al., 1990). Fortunately, the debate spurred much more methodologically rigorous psychotherapy research.

Today, we are heirs to the 50 succeeding years of psychotherapy research. What ultimately does this research tell us?

1. Psychotherapy works! The great majority of clients who receive psychotherapy improve. Typically, three clients of four decrease their dysfunctional symptoms and increase their positive functioning in psychotherapy. Meta-analyses point to an effect size for psychotherapy of about 0.8, suggesting that statistical effects in studies that compare psychotherapy with no therapy are what is termed "large" (compared with, for example, the effect of smoking on health, which is statistically a small effect) (Smith & Glass, 1977). Not only is this a considerable level of success but also compares quite favorably with the approximately 25–30% who improve without psychotherapy (Lambert & Bergin, 1994; Smith & Glass). And these changes remain substantial when comparisons are to placebo control groups who receive something that looks like psychotherapy (that is, clients and therapists talking), but without a method of intervention.

2. Psychotherapy significantly ameliorates such commonly encountered problems as depression, anxiety, substance abuse, adolescent delinquency, and childhood conduct disorder (Lambert & Bergin, 1994; Lambert & Hill, 1994). Psychotherapies have been found to impact a wide array of client difficulties, and to be particularly effective when the treatment is specifically shaped in relation to the client difficulty. Psychotherapies appear to be roughly equally effective in treating adults, children, and families (Lambert & Bergin, 1994; Lebow & Gurman, 1995; Weisz, Huey, & Weersing, 1998). These rates of success are typically at least as good as, and often superior to, the effects of medication.

3. Psychotherapy in combination with medication offers the most effective treatment for such pervasive disorders as schizophrenia, bipolar disorder, and childhood autism (Dixon et al., 2001). Again, treatments work best when specifically structured in response to these disorders.

These conclusions provide considerable support for the impact of psychotherapy. Yet research on psychotherapy also points to the limitations of psychotherapy, including the following considerations.

1. Not all clients are helped by psychotherapy. Whatever the difficulty, there remain 20%–40% of clients who do not achieve the level of functioning of those who never had the particularly presenting problem. There are always some who don't change and even a small percentage (approximately 5%) who deteriorate over the time of treatment (Lambert & Bergin, 1994).

2. Change is often temporary. Long-term follow-ups at 2–10 years after the end of treatment typically find large percentages of clients who return to having difficulties without further treatment (Lambert & Bergin, 1994). The maintenance of change seems to present a particular challenge in problems such as substance abuse and depression (Moos, 2003).

3. Many clients abandon psychotherapy prematurely, before it is able to have an effect. Although there are many cases in which change occurs quickly through some brief, focused intervention or through simply generating greater hope (psychologist Ken Howard [Kopta, Howard, Lowry, & Beutler, 1994] pointed that 5%–10% of clients improve before the first session), most clients who leave treatment early benefit insufficiently (Lambert & Bergin, 1994).

4. Psychotherapies have been principally tested on middle- to upper-class populations around the world. Indications are that at least some methods of psychotherapy do less well with the economically disadvantaged. A major issue within these populations is a demonstrated lower level of client engagement (Sue, Chun, & Gee, 1995).

5. There is much less evidence about the impact of psychotherapy in real-world settings than in special settings created for the purposes of conducting treatment research. There's both good news and bad news here. The good news is that large-scale research surveying outcomes in typical practice settings finds outcomes as good or better than in those obtained in academic research settings. The bad news is that when the treatments that are established as effective in academic research settings are disseminated to real-world settings, the outcomes are almost always less positive than in the more rarefied settings (though the outcomes remain positive) (Lambert & Bergin, 1994; Lambert & Hill, 1994;

Nathan & Gorman, 2002a; Weisz, Jensen, & McLeod, 2005; Weisz, Weiss, & Donenberg, 1993).

These limitations have led to efforts to (1) create special therapies that target particular problems for which the end states achieved at termination are less than optimal, (2) build stronger alliances that help more clients engage in psychotherapy, and (3) develop ways to help clients maintain change. Specific treatments have been developed that target a myriad of difficulties, including obsessive-compulsive disorder, depression, generalized anxiety disorder, attention deficit disorder, substance use disorders, and bipolar disorder. These treatments are aimed at increasing the levels of impact on individuals with these problems beyond that which can be achieved with broad psychotherapies (Nathan & Gorman, 2002b). The research indicates that these treatments have indeed increased the level of impact, though still there remains a substantial group of nonresponders to treatment for all these problems.

Treatments are also continually being reshaped to increase the likelihood of maintaining change. Although in the early stages of assessment, methods that extend over longer periods and that include booster sessions appear to be promising (Snyder & Ingram, 2000). And how to increase the acceptability of treatment and successfully build therapeutic alliances is increasingly a focus of psychotherapy research (Kazdin & Wilson, 1978; Norcross, 2002). Several innovative methods have been developed, particularly in the context of clients who typically are less interested in treatment (Miller, Meyers, & Tonigan, 1999; Santisteban et al., 1996).

Looking at comparisons of how well various kinds of treatments work compared with one another, the research suggests a mixed set of conclusions. On the whole, meta-analyses show no differences between schools of treatment in their impact (Lambert & Bergin, 1994). However, it is clear that in considering several very difficult-to-treat problems such as obsessive-compulsive disorder and panic disorder, highly specialized treatments are more successful (Nathan & Gorman, 2002b).

Nonetheless, research shows that common factors underlie much of what is effective in psychotherapy regardless of the treatment (Hubble, Duncan, & Miller, 1999; Lambert & Bergin, 1994; Norcross, 2002; Orlinsky, Grawe, & Parks, 1994). A recent volume, the result of a task force within the American Psychological Association, documented the enormous importance that has emerged for such factors as the therapeutic alliance, therapist empathy, and goal consensus involved in the therapy relationship (Norcross, 2002). Other potent common factors, such as the generation of hope and positive expectation, also clearly transcend the particular treatment (Frank, 1963; Lambert & Bergin, 1994; Lambert & Hill, 1994).

In sum, today's psychotherapist can take comfort in the strong support psychotherapy research has had for the field. Yet, we should not fall prey to the myths proffered by the pharmaceutical companies who oversell what drugs can do, assuring us that change is certain and easy. The best practice of psychotherapy is grounded in the full range of research available about psychotherapy. That kind of therapy draws on the research on common factors to maximize these aspects of treatment, yet also seeks to choose the most appropriate intervention strategy for a specific case.

RESOURCES

Lambert, M. J., & Bergin, A. E. (1994). The effectiveness of psychotherapy. In A. E. Bergin & S. L. Garfield (Eds.), *Handbook of psychotherapy and behavior change* (4th ed., pp. 143–189). Oxford, UK: John Wiley & Sons.

Norcross, J. C. (Ed.). (2002). *Psychotherapy relationships that work: Therapist contributions and responsiveness to patients.* London: Oxford University Press.

Orlinsky, D. E., Grawe, K., & Parks, B. K. (1994). Process and outcome in psychotherapy: Noch einmal. In A. E. Bergin & S. L. Garfield (Eds.), *Handbook of psychotherapy and behavior change* (4th ed., pp. 270–376). Oxford, UK: John Wiley & Sons.

REFERENCES

Dixon, L., McFarlane, W. R., Lefley, H., Lucksted, A., Cohen, M., Falloon, I., et al. (2001). Evidence-based practices for services to families of people with psychiatric disabilities. *Psychiatric Services, 52*(7): 903–910.

Frank, J. D. (1963). *Persuasion and healing.* Oxford, UK: Schocken.

Garfield, S. L., Bergin, A. E., Rice, L. N., Greenberg, L. S., Pinsof, W. M., Andreozzi, L. L., et al. (1990). The state of the art and the progression of science in family therapy research. *Journal of Family Psychology, 4*(1): 99–120.

Hubble, M. A., Duncan, B. L., & Miller, S. D. (Eds.). (1999). *The heart and soul of change: What works in therapy.* Washington, DC: American Psychological Association.

Kazdin, A. E., & Wilson, G. (1978). Criteria for evaluating psychotherapy. *Archives of General Psychiatry, 35*(4): 407–416.

Kopta, S. M., Howard, K. I., Lowry, J. L., & Beutler, L. E. (1994). Patterns of symptomatic recovery in psychotherapy. *Journal of Consulting & Clinical Psychology, 62*(5): 1009–1016.

Lambert, M. J., & Bergin, A. E. (1994). The effectiveness of psychotherapy. In A. E. Bergin & S. L. Garfield (Eds.), *Handbook of psychotherapy and behavior change* (4th ed., pp. 143–189). Oxford, UK: John Wiley & Sons.

Lambert, M. J., & Hill, C. E. (1994). Assessing psychotherapy outcomes and processes. In A. E. Bergin & S. L. Garfield (Eds.), *Handbook of psychotherapy and behavior change* (4th ed., pp. 72–113). Oxford, UK: John Wiley & Sons.

Lebow, J. L., & Gurman, A. S. (1995). Research assessing couple and family therapy. *Annual Review of Psychology, 46*: 27–57.

Miller, W. R., Meyers, R. J., & Tonigan, J. (1999). Engaging the unmotivated in treatment for alcohol problems: A comparison of three strategies for intervention through family members. *Journal of Consulting & Clinical Psychology, 67*(5): 688–697.

Moos, R. H. (2003). Addictive disorders in context: Principles and puzzles of effective treatment and recovery. *Psychology of Addictive Behaviors, 17*(1): 3–12.

Nathan, P. E., & Gorman, J. M. (2002a). Efficacy, effectiveness, and the clinical utility of psychotherapy research. [References]. In P. E. Nathan & J. M. Gorman (Eds.), *A guide to treatments that work* (2nd ed., pp. 642–654). London: Oxford University Press.

Nathan, P. E., & Gorman, J. M. (Eds.). (2002b). *A guide to treatments that work* (2nd ed.). London: Oxford University Press.

Norcross, J. C. (Ed.). (2002). *Psychotherapy relationships that work: Therapist contributions and responsiveness to patients.* London: Oxford University Press.

Orlinsky, D. E., Grawe, K., & Parks, B. K. (1994). Process and outcome in psychotherapy: Noch einmal. In A. E. Bergin & S. L. Garfield (Eds.), *Handbook of psychotherapy and behavior change* (4th ed., pp. 270–376). Oxford, UK: John Wiley & Sons.

Santisteban, D. A., Szapocznik, J., Perez-Vidal, A., Kurtines, W. M., Murray, E. J., & LaPerriere, A. (1996). Efficacy of intervention for engaging youth and families into treatment and some variables that may contribute to differential effectiveness. *Journal of Family Psychology, 10*(1): 35–44.

Smith, M. L., & Glass, G. V. (1977). Meta-analysis of psychotherapy outcome studies. *American Psychologist, 32*(9): 752–760.

Snyder, C. R., & Ingram, R. E. (Eds.). (2000). *Handbook of psychological change: Psychotherapy processes & practices for the 21st century.* New York: John Wiley & Sons, Inc.

Sue, S., Chun, C.-A., & Gee, K. (1995). Ethnic minority intervention and treatment research. In J. F. Aponte, & R. Y. Rivers (Eds.), *Psychological interventions and cultural diversity* (pp. 266–282). Needham Heights, MA: Allyn & Bacon.

Weisz, J. R., Huey, S. J., & Weersing, V. R. (1998). Psychotherapy outcome research with children and adolescents: The state of the art. *Advances in Clinical Child Psychology, 20*: 49–91.

Weisz, J. R., Jensen, A. L., & McLeod, B. D. (2005). Development and dissemination of child and adolescent psychotherapies: Milestones, methods, and a new deployment-focused model. [References]. In E. D. Hibbs & P. S. Jensen (Eds.), *Psychosocial treatments for child and adolescent disorders: Empirically based strategies for clinical practice* (2nd ed., pp. 9–39). Washington, DC: American Psychological Association.

Weisz, J. R., Weiss, B., & Donenberg, G. R. (1993). The laboratory and the clinic: Effects of psychotherapy on children and adolescents. *Bollettino di Psicologia Applicata, 208*: 3–16.

6

THE SCIENCE OF CLINICAL ARTISTRY: RESEARCH-BASED PRINCIPLES FOR EFFECTIVE PRACTICE

Some views of the essence of effective treatment accentuate treatment strategies, whereas others have focused on client factors or the client–therapist relationship. This chapter describes the viewpoint developed by Larry Beutler that concentrates on articulating principles of change across all of these dimensions.

Larry Beutler is a researcher who doubles as a perpetual-motion machine. He has served as lead investigator in countless research studies and won numerous awards, including the Distinguished Research Career Award from the International Society for Psychotherapy Research. In his spare time, he has managed to write more than 200 articles and several books, as well as edit two of the most prominent journals in psychology, the *Journal of Consulting and Clinical Psychology* and the *Journal of Clinical Psychology*. But for all of his academic absorption, Beutler, a therapist himself, remains deeply attuned to the real-life, everyday concerns of clinicians.

For some time, he has been grappling with a question that nearly every working therapist asks: How can I get better treatment outcomes? One pathway may be to use only "empirically supported treatments" (ESTs) that have been scientifically demonstrated to work well for specific disorders; this list of mostly cognitive-behavioral approaches has been compiled and endorsed by a task force of the American Psychological Association's (APA) Division of Clinical Psychology (Chambless & Hollon, 1998). A significant limitation of the EST concept, however, is that relatively few therapists have been trained in the highly structured, manualized therapies that have been sanctioned by the APA task force. If a couple seeks your help for intimacy troubles, for example, but you don't happen to be well-versed in the EST approved for couple work—behavioral marital therapy—you're out of luck.

It occurred to Beutler, therefore, that it would be far more useful for therapists to have access to a set of guiding principles that would maximize the chances that clients would improve *regardless* of a clinician's favored theoretical orientation (Beutler, Consoli, & Lane, 2005). So Beutler and colleagues John Clarken and Bruce Bongar plumbed through the research on psychotherapy (Beutler, Clarkin, & Bongar, 2000). First, they looked to see which client and therapist factors have consistently proven to have an effect on treatment outcome in psychotherapy research, examining 2,000 studies assessing a wide range of therapies aimed at treating depression, chemical dependency, and severe mental illness. They looked at these studies, not for the main findings about whether a particular treatment worked, but for how client or therapist characteristics, such as the client's level of functioning and kind of problem, affected treatment outcome. Through these efforts they pared an initial list of 30 key aspects of clients' lives that appeared to affect subsequent treatment decisions to less than a dozen key factors. They then proposed a number of hypotheses about how client, therapist, and pairings of client and therapist factors would affect change. Beutler and his colleagues then tested how well these hypotheses fit the data in 248 of the best studies assessing treatment outcome, arriving at a number of guidelines for treatment. To be sure what they found was broadly applicable, they also assessed how well their hypotheses held up in a large number of studies assessing clients with other diagnoses and problems, and conducted a number of studies themselves testing whether these hypotheses applied in a group of clients treated locally. This extensive state-of-the-art process has led to Beutler and his colleagues offering a number of guidelines for practice that they hold to be widely applicable across therapists, problems, and clients. Beutler believes that these guiding principles support a treatment planning model he calls "Systematic Treatment Selection," which allows therapists to work with maximum flexibility, creativity, and effectiveness within their favored approaches and—with luck—put an end to the clash of "dueling modalities" that has plagued the field for so long.

Some of Beutler's guidelines center on the type of client, some on the type of treatment, some on relationship factors, and some on the interactions between these kinds of factors.

CLIENT PROGNOSIS

Beutler's first set of guidelines focus on client predisposing variables, such as level of distress and coping style. Some of these findings are surprising; for example,

- Less change can be expected when clients show low levels of distress about their problems.

The implication seems clear: When clients appear unruffled about serious difficulties, an effective early strategy may be to ratchet up their distress level, rather than immediately trying to soothe them. For instance, if a client, Mike, comes into mandated therapy after a drunk-driving arrest, yet dismissively claims he "just likes a few brews," his therapist, Susan, might look for ways to heighten Mike's concern about his alcohol consumption. If Mike is a runner who cares about his physical condition and appearance, Susan might give him factual information about the health consequences of alcohol abuse and recommend Alcoholics Anonymous meetings, where the group process would be likely to further raise his level of concern.

Also striking is the extent to which the social support that clients experience in the world is directly linked to their outcomes in psychotherapy. Specifically, Beutler finds that

- Clients experiencing multiple problems or chronic difficulties have better outcomes when their therapists facilitate their gaining social support.

Following this guideline, when Mike presented for therapy after a recent hospitalization, Susan worked with him to build a support network of friends. As Mike encountered difficulties, he was able to draw on these friends to help him avoid rehospitalization.

LEVEL AND INTENSITY OF CARE

Beutler's second set of guidelines are concerned with the level and intensity of care, such as choosing the frequency of sessions or choosing between group, family, and individual therapy. These guidelines include the following:

- Multiperson (group or family) therapies increase the likelihood of improvement in those who have multiple problems or chronic problems.
- More frequent sessions are called for with clients who are more functionally impaired.

Again, the clinical implications are clear: favor group or family therapy in those with chronic or multiproblem difficulties, and see those with great impairment more than once per week. At first blush, the first finding may seem somewhat counterintuitive, because the focused, one-on-one attention provided by individual therapy might seem a more logical choice for an overwhelmed client. On the other hand, the role modeling and range of coping skills offered by multiperson therapy may be particularly valuable for clients who have trouble generating workable solutions of their own. Irrespective of modality, group-based treatment can provide a solid sense of belonging and support that may be especially important for severely troubled clients, who often feel isolated and stigmatized.

THERAPIST SKILLS

Beutler's third set of guidelines focus on the intervention, relationship, and skill factors the therapist brings to the therapy, such as the therapeutic alliance. These guidelines include some widely circulated understandings about psychotherapy:

- Change is greatest when the therapist is skillful and provides trust, acceptance, acknowledgement, collaboration, and respect for the client, and does so in an environment that supports risk and provides maximal safety.
- Therapeutic change is most likely when procedures do not evoke client resistance.

Client change depends substantially on the creation and maintenance of a good therapeutic alliance, and therapists must work to be skillful and maintain a strong sense of acceptance, empathy, and connection. Change also depends on the therapist's being able to deliver interventions in an acceptable manner that does not evoke forces within clients that move against change.

Beutler also suggests that

- Therapeutic change is most likely when clients directly deal with the behavioral and emotional aspects of life they avoid.
- Therapeutic change is most likely if the initial focus of change efforts is to build new skills and alter disruptive patterns.

Both of these guidelines support directly helping clients to engage with their difficulties. Change is enhanced when therapists help clients to directly and safely experience aspects of life they are avoiding, and first build new skills and enable symptom reduction through direct interventions aimed at these targets. Although "let the client set the agenda" sounds like an enlightened policy, it can also be a recipe for stalled therapy. This finding suggests that the effective clinician will not hesitate to be directive—gently but persistently encouraging foot-dragging clients to confront their most disabling problems. For a psychodynamic therapist, this may mean nudging a reluctant client to deal with painful, unresolved feelings about his distant father. For a Bowenian, it might involve coaching the client to pay a visit to his elderly parents to find out more about his father's life. The bottom line: especially with avoidant clients, be prepared to take charge. For example, early in therapy, Jane actively intervened to help Bob, her client, to face his shyness and its consequences, rather than supporting his attempts to defocus from these issues that brought him in to therapy. She helped Bob move through a set of behavioral tasks around social situations aimed to help him lessen his fears, leading to considerable gains in alleviating his symptoms.

MATCHING THE INTERVENTION TO THE CLIENT

Perhaps the most interesting and valuable set of principles Beutler and colleagues articulate focus on matching treatment and clients. The first of these guidelines holds that

- Therapeutic change is greatest when interventions favor skill building and symptom removal for clients who externalize (i.e., who are action oriented, aggressive, extroverted, hedonistic, and stimulation seeking) or insight and relationship-focused procedures among clients who internalize (i.e., who are self-critical, withdrawn, self-reflective, and inhibited).

This finding points to the crucial importance of the personality dimension of the tendency to internalize or externalize for therapist decision making. Beutler concludes that direct interventions that build skills such as cognitive or structural interventions work best with those who externalize, whereas the generation of insight through methods such as psychoanalytic approaches or relating as in experiential methods has more effect for those who internalize. The concept of tailoring your approach to your client's personality is far removed from the one-size-fits-all philosophy of certain schools of therapy—"insight is necessary" (psychodynamic), "you need to better manage your feelings" (cognitive), or "you must get in touch with your emotions" (Gestalt and humanistic). A more appropriate maxim would be "different strokes for different folks." This finding rings with common sense: a client is apt to be more willing to take the kinds of risks that therapy demands if the path toward change is in tune with his or her character.

When faced with a depressed client who internalizes, a therapist might therefore focus therapy toward the process of understanding the antecedents of the client's difficulty in the events in his family of origin. In a client who externalizes, the same therapist would do better to begin with some active mode of intervening directly with the depression, such as questioning the beliefs of the client about depressive ideas, as in cognitive therapy.

The second matching guideline suggests that

- Therapeutic change is greatest when the directiveness of the intervention is lower when resistance is high and higher when resistance is low, or when the intervention meets resistance with paradoxical prescription.

In this way, encountering client cooperation or indifference to the therapy process becomes a marker for a choice of the direction for intervention. Those clients who cooperate and work directly to change are best served with direct means that help them move toward their goals. However, clients who show difficulty with cooperation and compliance are best treated with interventions that do not push them to change, or even suggest the merits of not changing. Following this guideline, when Susan discovered that following her directive interventions focused on stress reduction that Harvey, her client, failed to attend several sessions, she switched to a strategy of suggesting that he did not need to change his behavior if he was not ready to. This, in turn, allowed Harvey to become comfortable again with the therapy process, leading to his eventual improvement.

Beutler's final matching principle is that

- The likelihood of change is greatest when the client's level of emotional stress is moderate.

This guideline suggests that the importance of keeping the client's level of emotional arousal moderate; when the client is flooded with emotion or without emotion change, is likely to occur less. The implication here is that in the most successful therapies, therapists help clients high in emotional stress to reduce their levels of emotion, and those low in emotion to deepen their feeling. Following this guideline, when Sandra presented overwrought about the loss of her job, Lisa first worked with her to help her moderate her level of stress through cognitive-behavioral interventions, and, only then, began to explore the meaning of her job loss.

These matching principles are far removed from some well-known edicts of certain schools of therapy. It is not that "insight is necessary," "you need to better manage your feelings," or "you need to get in touch with your emotions," but "different strokes for different folks." The level of emotion, the directiveness, and the balance of skill building and insight need to be matched to the needs of the client.

These guidelines have been demonstrated to have considerable power in predicting who will change in Beutler's own research samples of clients in therapy (Beutler et al., 2005; Beutler & Harwood, 2000; Norcross, Beutler, & Clarkin, 1998). In one study assessing treatment of alcoholism, three-quarters of the changes occurring could be accounted for by simply looking at the matching of clients' functional impairment and the intensity of treatment, clients' resistance and therapists' directiveness, and therapists' emotional activation and level of client distress. That is, when therapists intervened in ways that fit with the qualities of the client (e.g., provided more direction with less resistant clients), change was far more likely to occur. Similarly, in another study of the treatment of depressed clients, benefit was greatest when the level of client resistance was properly matched with directive or nondirective intervention, and when the level of client distress was properly matched with the level of arousal induced in the therapy to keep the level of distress moderate. In more recent studies, Beutler and his colleagues have also begun to show that when such guidelines guide intervention, better outcomes are achieved than when they do not.

In directing his attention to the way he wishes his findings to be utilized, Beutler surprisingly draws on his hobby, natural horsemanship, once prominently depicted in the movie, *The Horse Whisperer*.

Natural horsemanship does not use the pain and dominance typical in the "breaking" of a horse, but rather a gentle approach in which the trainer is a partner and a guide. He states he can teach anyone to be able to display this form of horsemanship in the right context in 30 minutes, but that the true test of the student's learning comes when asked to teach the horse a complex task in a new environment. Skillfulness involves not following rote programs, but bringing creativity to the new situation. Beutler relates that if the student has become an artist-practitioner, she will know how to break the tasks down and to construct inventive methods for evoking wanted behaviors. If not, the techniques will get in the way. Beutler suggests truly effective psychotherapy requires clinicians to master basic principles of therapeutic influence, then to use them creatively and flexibly within the changing settings created by the endless variety of clients' personalities and needs. Therapy, he believes, is both careful science and inspired art. Beutler's deepest hope is that the research-based principles he articulates will serve as a platform from which genuine clinical artistry can spring.

RESOURCES

Beutler, L. E. (2000). Empirically based decision making in clinical practice. *Prevention and Treatment* 3:1–12.

Beutler, L. E., & Harwood, T. (2000). *Prescriptive psychotherapy: A practical guide to systematic treatment selection*. London: Oxford University Press.

REFERENCES

Beutler, L. E., Clarkin, J. F., & Bongar, B. (2000). *Guidelines for the systematic treatment of the depressed patient*. London: Oxford University Press.

Beutler, L. E., Consoli, A. J., & Lane, G. (2005). Systematic treatment selection and prescriptive psychotherapy. [References]. In J. C. Norcross & M. R. Goldfried (Eds.), *Handbook of psychotherapy integration* (2nd ed., pp. 121–143). London: Oxford University Press.

Beutler, L. E., & Harwood, T. (2000). *Prescriptive psychotherapy: A practical guide to systematic treatment selection*. London: Oxford University Press.

Chambless, D. L., & Hollon, S. D. (1998). Defining empirically supported therapies. *Journal of Consulting & Clinical Psychology, 66*(1): 7–18.

Norcross, J. C., Beutler, L. E., & Clarkin, J. F. (1998). Prescriptive eclectic psychotherapy. In R. A. Dorfman (Ed.), *Paradigms of clinical social work* (vol. 2, pp. 289–314). Philadelphia: Brunner/Mazel.

7

TRANSFORMATION NOW! (OR MAYBE LATER): CLIENT CHANGE IS NOT AN ALL-OR-NOTHING PROPOSITION

Some crucial aspects of psychotherapy transcend the particular clients, therapists, or treatments involved. The research of James Prochaska and his colleagues has illuminated one such crucial dimension: the clients' stage of change. Understanding where clients are in the stages of change can be enormously beneficial to the progress of psychotherapy.

According to conventional wisdom, people enter therapy to actively resolve their problems, reduce their symptoms, and retool their lives. That's a dangerous assumption, say psychologists James Prochaska, Carlo DiClemente, and John Norcross (Prochaska, 2000; Prochaska & DiClemente, 1983; Prochaska, DiClemente, & Norcross, 1995; Prochaska, Johnson, & Lee, 1998; Prochaska & Norcross, 2002). Their large-scale studies suggest that people progress through several predictable, well-defined stages on the way to change, and are apt to take resolute action only toward the tail end of the process. This means that only a small percentage of new therapy clients are ready to actively resolve their difficulties—a reality that clinicians can't afford to ignore, the researchers say. They urge clinicians to assess each client's readiness to change and to tailor therapy accordingly, or risk alienating clients who may conclude that the therapist is clueless about their needs.

Prochaska, professor of psychology at the University of Rhode Island, and DiClemente, professor of psychology at the University of Maryland, have examined the stages of change that people traverse in dealing with such problems as depression, anxiety and panic disorders, marital discord, eating disorders, smoking, alcoholism, and delinquency. In cross-sectional studies involving more than 3,000 individuals, they asked people to identify their major problems, their plans for change, and the specific actions they were taking to bring change about. Most of these subjects came from household samples, while others were in treatment for medical or mental health problems. Regardless of their family and cultural background, the nature of the problem they faced, and whether they had enlisted professional help, Prochaska, DiClemente, and their colleagues (DiClemente, Prochaska, Fairhurst, & Velicer, 1991; Prochaska, 1999; Prochaska, DiClemente, & Norcross, 2003; Prochaska et al., 1994) found that, across studies, people negotiated five discrete stages as they progressed toward change.

PRECONTEMPLATION

In this initial stage, individuals are largely unaware of their problems and have no intention of changing their behavior. People who go into therapy at this stage typically do so in response to pressure from others—a spouse who threatens to leave them, an employer who threatens to fire them, a court that threatens to jail them, or parents who threaten severe consequences. Precontemplators often wish *other* people would change, as in, "How can I get my wife to quit nagging me?"

CONTEMPLATION

Contemplators are aware that they face problems and are seriously thinking about grappling with them within the next six months. But they have not yet made a commitment to take action, usually because they still feel daunted by the effort required to overcome the problem, or because they still feel positively about some aspect of their troublesome behavior. Bad habits die harder than we may realize: when Prochaska and DiClemente followed 200 contemplators who were considering quitting smoking, most of them were still "thinking about it" 2 years later (DiClemente et al., 1991).

PREPARATION

Individuals at this stage intend to take action within the next month. Preparers may have already made some small attempts to modify their behavior—such as trying relaxation exercises when they feel anxious—but these attempts typically have been sporadic and only partially effective. They may be developing strategies for a more committed program of change, such as mapping out an action plan, going public with their intention to behave differently, and getting social support. Most still feel twinges of ambivalence about taking the plunge.

ACTION

In this stage, individuals are taking concrete steps to change their behavior, experiences, or environment in order to overcome their problems. Actors endorse statements such as, "Anyone can talk about changing, but I am actually doing something about it." Because action often brings up feelings of guilt, failure, coercion, and yearning to resume the old behavior, clients typically need a lot of support during this period. A sobering statistic: at any given time, only 10%–15% of people in the process of change are engaged in the action stage (Prochaska, 2000).

MAINTENANCE

During this stage, people work to consolidate their gains and prevent relapse. For some problems, such as alcohol abuse or recurring depression, maintenance might last a lifetime. Remaining free of the problem and behaving in ways incompatible with the problem—such as engaging in positive self-talk or calling a friend when one begins to feel blue—are key signs that a person has reached this stage.

GUIDELINES FOR TREATMENT

Prochaska and DiClemente believe that any clinician, regardless of approach, can offer better-targeted and more effective therapy by observing the following principles:

Don't assume that all clients are at the action stage—or want to be. Therapists often design excellent action-oriented treatments only to discover that the client is not yet ready to embrace change. As a result, clinicians may label the client "resistant" and become quickly frustrated with the case. Remember, only 10%–15% of people are in the action stage.

Assess the client's stage of change. This need not be complicated. You might simply ask, "Do you think that any particular behavior is a problem for you now?" After the client has identified a behavior, follow up with, "When do you intend to change that?"

Go slowly. Rather than rushing straight toward action, help your clients to move only one stage further along the continuum—for example, from precontemplation to contemplation, from feeling it's someone else's problem to thinking about trying to do something about it themselves in the next few months. The researchers found that when people progressed from one stage to the next during the first month of treatment, they doubled their chances of taking action within the next six months.

Anticipate backsliding. Although the term "stages of change" suggests that change marches forward in a step-by-step, linear fashion, it actually occurs in a spiral pattern, which encompasses both forward and backward movement. Some people successfully move into action only to relapse and slide all the way back to the precontemplation stage. Therapists should educate clients about the spiraling nature of change to help counteract shame and discouragement about regressing to earlier stages. To minimize backsliding, relapse prevention should be a key part of any treatment plan.

Do the right thing at the right time. An intervention that is effective at one stage might not work at another. For example, precontemplators typically aren't prepared to take in a lot of information and are best helped by observations and interpretations that gently raise their awareness of their difficulties. By contrast, those in the action stage respond best to specific, behavior-change interventions coupled with steadfast support from the therapist.

Avoid inappropriate interventions. One of the most frequent mistakes therapists make is to deliver insight to an individual who is in the action stage—for example, devoting sessions to the impact of a client's family of origin on his marriage at a time when he is actually ready to change his spousal relationship. The likely result: a bored, frustrated client. Another common mismatch arises when clinicians offer action interventions to precontemplators or contemplators, which can leave them feeling inadequate and even hopeless. In both cases, clients are likely to feel deeply misunderstood—and misunderstood clients are more apt to drop out of therapy.

Honor every stage of change. Because the changes that clients make during the action stage tend to be the most visible and dramatic, clinicians often equate change with action. But Prochaska and DiClemente's research illuminates the fact that each stage is a critical element of the change process, and that negotiating each one requires substantial effort and courage on the part of clients. To help people make enduring change, we must be willing to invest considerable energy and patience in each stage—and to validate our clients as they take each small, significant step toward their goals.

Prochaska, DiClemente, and Norcross offer a view of therapy that can prove extremely valuable to all therapists regardless of their theoretical orientation or the kinds of clients treated in their practice. Ever since I first encountered their research, I have kept track of where each client falls in terms of their stages of change. Although tracking where clients are in their stage of change requires a little effort, few pieces of information have proven as valuable. Clients clearly find psychotherapy more engaging and make more progress when the approach is matched with their stage in the change process.

RESOURCES

Prochaska, J. O., DiClemente, C. C., & Norcross, J. (1998). Stages of change: Prescriptive guidelines for behavioral medicine and psychotherapy. In G. P. Koocher, J. C. Norcross, & S. S. Hill (Eds.), *Psychologist's desk reference* (pp. 230–235). New York: Oxford University Press.

Prochaska, J. O., DiClemente, C. C., & Norcross, J. (1995). *Changing for good.* New York: Avon Books.

REFERENCES

DiClemente, C. C., Prochaska, J. O., Fairhurst, S. K., & Velicer, W. F. (1991). The process of smoking cessation: An analysis of precontemplation, contemplation, and preparation stages of change. *Journal of Consulting & Clinical Psychology, 59*(2): 295 304.

Prochaska, J. O. (1999). How do people change, and how can we change to help many more people? [References]. In M. A. Hubble, B. L. Duncan, & S. D. Miller (Eds.), *The heart and soul of change: What works in therapy* (pp. 227–255). Washington, DC: American Psychological Association.

Prochaska, J. O. (2000). Change at differing stages. In C. R. Snyder & R. E. Ingram (Eds.), *Handbook of psychological change: Psychotherapy processes & practices for the 21st century* (pp. 109–127). Hoboken, NJ: John Wiley & Sons.

Prochaska, J. O., & DiClemente, C. C. (1983). Stages and processes of self-change of smoking: Toward an integrative model of change. *Journal of Consulting & Clinical Psychology, 51*(3): 390–395.

Prochaska, J. O., DiClemente, C. C., & Norcross, J. (1995). *Changing for good.* New York: Avon Books.

Prochaska, J. O., DiClemente, C. C., & Norcross, J. (1998). Stages of change: Prescriptive guidelines for behavioral medicine and psychotherapy. In G. P. Koocher, J. C. Norcross, & S. S. Hill (Eds.), *Psychologist's desk reference* (pp. 230–235). New York: Oxford University Press.

Prochaska, J. O., DiClemente, C. C., & Norcross, J. C. (2003). In search of how people change: Applications to addictive behaviors. [References]. In P. Salovey & A. J. Rothman (Eds.), *Social psychology of health: Key readings in social psychology* (pp. 63–77). New York: Psychology Press.

Prochaska, J. O., Johnson, S., & Lee, P. (1998). The transtheoretical model of behavior change. In S. A. Shumaker, E. B. Schron, & J. K. Ockeane (Eds.), *The handbook of health behavior change* (2nd ed., pp. 59–84). New York: Springer Publishing.

Prochaska, J. O., & Norcross, J. C. (2002). Stages of change. [References]. In J. C. Norcross (Ed.), *Psychotherapy relationships that work: Therapist contributions and responsiveness to patients* (pp. 303–313). London: Oxford University Press.

Prochaska, J. O., Velicier, W. F., Rossi, J. S., Goldstein, M. G., Marcus, B. H., Rakowski, W., et al. (1994). Stages of change and decisional balance for 12 problem behaviors. *Health Psychology, 13*(1): 39–46.

8

BEYOND INTUITION: RESEARCH ON PSYCHOTHERAPEUTIC PROCESS

Psychotherapeutic process research examines how processes in therapy unfold either through direct observation of therapy or through asking clients and therapists to report on their experiences. This chapter looks at the vital role this kind of research can have for clinical practice, primarily focusing on the research of Leslie Greenberg, illuminating processes in experiential therapy.

Most research assessing psychotherapy follows a simple organization focused on treatment outcome. Clients are evaluated before and after receiving treatment, and the differences between how clients are before and after treatment are compared with the changes in others with similar difficulties who do not receive treatment. Therapy "process research" brings a much different lens to research, examining what clients and therapists actually do in treatment and the immediate impact of what is happening. Process research operates on the principle of smaller is better, intensely examining what occurs during important moments in therapy to provide clues to how therapists can be more effective. Process research aims at the creation of a roadmap to help guide therapists: a roadmap that includes markers pointing to where the client and therapist are in the treatment process, how they are experiencing the treatment, what might be most useful to do at various junctures, and how best to deliver specific interventions.

Process research is very clinician friendly. The questions raised by process research coincide with the kind of information most often found to be of greatest value by therapists, for whom the most relevant questions often surround such issues as "What do I do now?" and "How can I best do it?" Instead of pushing therapists to change their fundamental approach to intervention to learn wholly different methods, process research aims toward the much easier-to-digest goal of helping refine how particular methods of therapy can best be delivered and offered in the most timely way.

Over the last two decades, Leslie Greenberg, professor of psychology at York University in Toronto, has been widely identified as the dean of the process research movement (Greenberg, 1986; Greenberg & Pinsof, 1986). Arguing for the rigorous observation of how change in therapy actually takes place, Greenberg says, "We need to observe the process of change to provide us with the kind of explanation that involves a new understanding of what actually occurs, rather than relying on automatic theoretical explanations from our favorite, often too strongly held, theory" (Leslie Greenberg, personal communication, 2001). In particular, Greenberg emphasizes the importance of closely observing those key moments in therapy when something happens that moves clients forward toward the changes they seek. Greenberg's focus has been on pragmatic questions such as, "Under what circumstances are particular interventions most helpful?" and "How are different parts of the treatment process experienced?" and "How can we most effectively deliver interventions?"

Greenberg's work is also quite remarkable in another way. Instead of concentrating his attention on the much-studied cognitive-behavioral therapies, the typical interventions examined in research, Greenberg has focused on experiential and humanistic therapies, treatments often thought of as incompatible with research. Greenberg's studies typically focus on the treatment he has developed, "emotion-focused therapy," and on the Gestalt therapy and experiential techniques that have been major influences on his own approach to treatment. For example, he has conducted studies of such venerable experiential techniques as Fritz Perl's two-chair and empty-chair techniques (Greenberg & Malcolm, 2002). By example, Greenberg shows that a science-based, inquisitive attitude can be brought to any approach. His research illuminates when such methods are most helpful, how they work, and how they can best be delivered.

The outcome research of Greenberg and that of his colleagues Robert Elliott and Sue Johnson on emotion-focused therapy has clearly demonstrated the effectiveness of this approach. Emotion-focused therapy aims toward the identification and processing of client emotion, using the alliance between client and therapist to facilitate the client's experiential processing. The research evaluating this treatment has progressed so far that emotion-focused therapy regularly appears on lists of empirically supported therapies, lists typically dominated by cognitive-behavioral therapies (Greenberg & Elliott, 2002; Johnson & Lebow, 2000). Emotion-focused therapy emerges from the outcome research as a well-established therapy for treating marital distress and depression, and there are a few suggestive studies indicating its effectiveness as an intervention for posttraumatic stress disorder.

METHODOLOGY

Psychotherapy process may be studied in at least two different ways. In the simpler method, clients or therapists complete questionnaires describing what occurs in therapy and how they feel about the process. Alternatively, actual tapes of therapy sessions can be transcribed and coded for their content and emotional climate. The questionnaire method is simple and taps subjective experience, but can be prone to distortions. The coding method is more objective but is expensive and time consuming. The best research often includes both forms of data collection.

In his research, Greenberg uses both approaches, subdividing sessions into a series of therapeutic tasks, in the tradition of what's called "task analysis," identifying the key in-session events that lead up to a client's resolution of specific types of problems (Greenberg, 1992). Within the context of emotion-focused therapy, the key tasks that Greenberg has focused on include dealing with experiential processing difficulty (feeling overwhelmed, stuck, or unclear), problematic reaction points (puzzling overreactions to specific situations), self-evaluative splits (self-criticism, feeling torn), self-interruption splits (blocked feelings), unfinished business (lingering bad feeling regarding a significant other), vulnerability (painful emotion related to self), and relational rupture (disrupted bonds with the therapist).

In this research, sessions are videotaped and the behavior of both clients and therapists are reviewed and coded by raters who score each participant's behavior along a number of dimensions such as the expression of feeling, the amount of empathy, or the degree of blaming.

This direct observation of what clients and therapists do is supplemented by asking clients about their experience of these key moments in treatment, a research technique known as "interpersonal process recall." Clients are asked how they felt at these moments and what they found helpful. Through interpersonal process recall, the client's experience also becomes an essential aspect of the analysis.

Greenberg views a goal of this kind of analysis of the process of treatment as akin to building a periodic table of basic elements of psychotherapeutic process (Greenberg & Elliott, 2002; Greenberg, Rice, & Elliott, 1996). The taxonomy that Greenberg believes we need to build from such study of therapy process would include the naming the different problematic states of mind that occur in therapy (such as being disheartened or feeling disengaged), and suggesting the tasks therapists successfully invoke to help ameliorate those states. Such an organizational device would suggest the therapeutic tasks that can ameliorate particular emotional states. Greenberg's emphasis remains on the short-term effects of particular interventions: the immediate impacts of what therapists do in treatment.

Of course, interventions don't occur in a vacuum; they must be applied in response to the client's experience in session. In Greenberg's research, therapeutic tasks are always thought of in relation to what Greenberg and his colleagues term "markers," clinical road signs pointing to specific intervention strategies. Markers identify the states of mind in which clients respond positively to different interventions.

Consider this example from Greenberg's research on the classic empty-chair technique from Gestalt therapy. In the empty-chair technique, the therapist suggests that the client speak to an imagined person in the empty chair about matters that remain unresolved. Through task-analysis research, Greenberg found that the markers for when the empty-chair technique is most useful are readily identifiable. The indicators include (1) statements describing lingering unresolved feelings, such as resentment, hurt, and grief; (2) mention of a significant other toward whom there are negative feelings; (3) difficulty in fully expressing the feelings; and (4) the client's indication that the experience of not being able to express the feelings is negative. Through a series of studies, Greenberg and his colleagues have been able to delineate the ideal resolution process using the empty chair (Elliott, Watson, Goldman, & Greenberg, 2004; Greenberg & Malcolm, 2002; Paivio & Greenberg, 1995). In this process, the client first expresses blame, complaint, or hurt to someone who has negative meaning for them in the empty chair. The client then differentiates these feelings from one another, often reliving a related memory. Resolution involves the intense expression of a specific emotion, usually anger or sadness, and the mobilization and expression of a previously unmet need. When successful, there is a shift to a more affiliative and less dominant position on the part of the "other" and self-validation in which the "other" is held accountable for their damaging actions.

Greenberg found that when the technique was invoked, intense expression of feeling was found in almost all of those who reached resolution and few of those who did not. And the expression of one's own need was present in almost all of those receiving resolution and few who did not. Resolvers differed from nonresolvers as well in the degree to which they could identify the positive aspects of the other and their amount of self-validation. Interestingly, the presence of blame and hurt did not at all differentiate those who resolved from those who did not reach resolution.

OTHER PROCESS RESEARCH

Other researchers have applied process research to a wide array of interventions. Howard Liddle and his colleagues at the University of Miami Medical School found that the task of building a therapeutic alliance with substance-abusing, inner-city African-American adolescents is helped along when they introduce the theme of the developmental journey required to move from being a boy to being a man (Banks, Hogue, Timberlake, & Liddle, 1996). Jim Alexander and colleagues at the University of Utah found that the gender of the therapist can determine what joining techniques work best (Newberry, Alexander, & Turner, 1991). Clients experienced male therapists positively early in therapy when they employed active, directive interventions, but female therapists employing such interventions early on weakened their clients' sense of alliance. Alexander believes this has to do with the traditional gender expectations of his Utah client population. Patricia Chamberlain and colleagues at the Oregon Social Learning Center found that prompting clients to do homework, a core ingredient of their behavioral family therapy for oppositional disorders in children, increased client resistance (Chamberlain & Baldwin, 1988). After this finding, the group began viewing this noncompliance as a marker for moving toward a less directive stance and framing homework in a more collaborative way.

The goal of process research is to better understand what is actually occurring in therapy, providing information that's pragmatic and immediately applicable. Although outcome studies on therapeutic approaches refer to decision making over the entire course of treatment, findings from process research can guide not only individual sessions, but the timing of particular interventions within the session. This work has great promise for advancing the practice of therapy, regardless of the clinician's school of practice.

CLINICAL APPLICATIONS

Even without the elaborate methodology of trained researchers, clinicians can use modified forms of process-research techniques to better understand what's going on in their own consulting rooms. For example, there are several good, brief, client-reported measures of the therapeutic alliance that can assess this vital aspect of therapy and assist with clinical decision making. The Working Alliance Inventory (Horvath & Greenberg, 1986), developed by Adam Horvath of Simon Fraser University in British Columbia and Leslie Greenberg, is most widely used in individual therapy, and the Therapy Alliance Scales (Pinsof & Catherall, 1986), developed by William Pinsof, is useful in couples and family therapy.

Recently, a couple I was seeing spent so much of their time arguing about their contrasting views about sex and money in sessions that I had little sense of their respective alliances in the therapy. Strikingly, Pinsof's Couple Therapy Alliance Scale indicated that the wife had experienced a strong sense of alliance, whereas the husband had a very tenuous one. Their clear feedback helped focus me on increased efforts to improve my alliance with the husband and his therapy goals.

Inventories that describe the interventions therapists employ are another kind of easy-to-use measure. Often, at the end of sessions, I complete a simple process inventory—the Integrative Therapy Session Report (ITSR), developed by William Pinsof, Bart Mann, and myself—which provides a concise overview of the focus and interventions employed in a session. The value of examining such a snapshot of the therapy can be considerable, especially when looking at the client's overall progress. When Cathy and George, a couple I was seeing, went through a period of increased alienation from each other, I used the ITSRs that I'd completed describing the sessions over that period to examine what I was doing. I noticed how stuck I'd become in exploring family-of-origin issues during this time (work that felt quite positive during the sessions). This work was important, but also meant a decline in the here-and-now focus of our work. Returning attention to communication and mutual problem solving broke the downward spiral.

The anthropological technique of interpersonal process recall (Elliott, 1986) can also be easily adapted to the clinical setting. The method involves simply asking clients to identify the key moments in therapy and explain why they were important. The meanings clients assign to such moments are often different from what therapists imagine. For example, James, a depressed client, identified that the key moment for him in treatment was something quite undramatic—his appreciation of my patience as he, with great difficulty, tried to learn what it meant to focus on his own well-being.

Unfortunately, those funding research on therapy are much less interested in learning from discoveries about therapy process than they are about the identification of broader packages of methods that work and the dissemination of those methods. Thus funding for this body of research remains limited and the advance of process research is much slower than that of the outcome research. It will be some considerable time before Greenberg's periodic table is completely filled in.

Nonetheless, Greenberg and others like him have begun to identify a very useful set of research methods that might ultimately be much more valuable for practice than the larger outcome studies. Several suggestive findings have begun to evolve from this kind of research. Certainly, this work has a great deal of promise for advancing the practice of therapy, as Greenberg has shown, regardless of the therapist's school of practice.

Although funding for research into the process of therapy is limited, it must increase if we are ever to become a more empirically driven enterprise. Meanwhile, by incorporating the perspective of process researchers into our own practices, we can heighten our awareness of what leads up to the "intuitive" leaps that yield helpful interventions, and do what we can to help fill in Greenberg's periodic table from our own caseloads.

RESOURCES

Greenberg, L. S. (1986). Change process research. *Journal of Consulting & Clinical Psychology, 54*(1): 4–9.

Greenberg, L. S., & Pinsof, W. M. (Eds.). (1986). *The psychotherapeutic process: A research handbook*. New York: Guilford Press.

REFERENCES

Banks, R., Hogue, A., Timberlake, T., & Liddle, H. (1996). An Afrocentric approach to group social skills training with inner-city African American adolescents. *Journal of Negro Education, 65*(4): 414–423.

Chamberlain, P., & Baldwin, D. V. (1988). Client resistance to parent training: Its therapeutic management. In T. R. Kratochwill (Ed.), *Advances in school psychology* (vol. 6, pp. 131–171). Hillsdale, NJ: Lawrence Erlbaum Associates.

Elliott, R. (1986). Interpersonal Process Recall (IPR) as a psychotherapy process research method. In L. S. Greenberg & W. M. Pinsof (Eds.), *The psychotherapeutic process: A research handbook* (pp. 503–527). New York: Guilford Press.

Elliott, R., Watson, J. C., Goldman, R. N., & Greenberg, L. S. (2004). Empty chair work for unfinished interpersonal issues. In R. Elliott, J. C. Watson, R. N. Goldman, & L. S. Greenberg (Eds.), *Learning emotion-focused therapy: The process-experiential approach to change* (pp. 243–265). Washington, DC: American Psychological Association.

Greenberg, L. S. (1986). Change process research. *Journal of Consulting & Clinical Psychology, 54*(1): 4–9.

Greenberg, L. S. (1992). Task analysis: Identifying components of intrapersonal conflict resolution. In S. G. Toukmanian & D. L. Rennie (Eds.), *Psychotherapy process research: Paradigmatic and narrative approaches* (Sage Focus ed., vol. 143, pp. 22–50). Thousand Oaks, CA: Sage Publications.

Greenberg, L. S., & Elliott, R. (2002). Emotion-focused therapy. [References]. In F. W. Kaslow (Ed.), *Comprehensive handbook of psychotherapy: Integrative/eclectic* (vol. 4, pp. 213–240). New York: John Wiley & Sons.

Greenberg, L. S., & Malcolm, W. (2002). Resolving unfinished business: Relating process to outcome. *Journal of Consulting & Clinical Psychology, 70*(2): 406–416.

Greenberg, L. S., & Pinsof, W. M. (Eds.). (1986). *The psychotherapeutic process: A research handbook.* New York: Guilford Press.

Greenberg, L. S., Rice, L. N., & Elliott, R. K. (1996). *Facilitating emotional change: The moment-by-moment process.* New York: Guilford Press.

Horvath, A. O., & Greenberg, L. S. (1986). The development of the Working Alliance Inventory. In L. S. Greenberg & W. M. Pinsof (Eds.), *The psychotherapeutic process: A research handbook* (pp. 529–556). New York: Guilford Press.

Johnson, S., & Lebow, J. (2000). The "coming of age" of couple therapy: A decade review. *Journal of Marital & Family Therapy, 26*(1): 23–38.

Newberry, A. M., Alexander, J. F., & Turner, C. W. (1991). Gender as a process variable in family therapy. *Journal of Family Psychology, 5*(2): 158–175.

Paivio, S. C., & Greenberg, L. S. (1995). Resolving "unfinished business": Efficacy of experiential therapy using empty-chair dialogue. *Journal of Consulting & Clinical Psychology, 63*(3): 419–425.

Pinsof, W. M., & Catherall, D. R. (1986). The integrative psychotherapy alliance: Family, couple and individual therapy scales. *Journal of Marital & Family Therapy, 12*(2): 137–151.

9

EVIDENCE-BASED TREATMENTS FOR ANXIETY

*There is a great deal of debate about how much empirically sup-
ported therapies should become the treatments of choice for specific disorders. Nonetheless, with some especially hard-to-treat
disorders such as the various pervasive manifestations of anxiety,
the very impressive levels of impact of these treatments suggest
that these treatments may well be more effective than other treatments for these problems. This chapter describes the evidence-
based treatments for anxiety disorders.*

Most therapists know that the value of empirically supported therapies for real-world therapy is a hotly debated subject these days. Critics
repeatedly point out that, outside of therapy-outcome studies, clients
rarely present themselves with the sort of single, focal, uncomplicated,
pure *Diagnostic and Statistical Manual*-delineated diagnosis around
which most empirically validated treatments are structured and show
such nice success rates (Westen, Novotny, & Thompson-Brenner,
2004). To many therapists, manualized treatments feel rigid, agenda-
driven, and unequal to the messy reality they see in their offices every

day. Even therapists who work on manual-driven projects have been known to report, off the record, that after the first few sessions, their work becomes increasingly variable and idiosyncratic—just like other therapists.

Nonetheless, it cannot be denied that some empirically supported treatments (EST) for certain problems have been proven highly effective (Nathan & Gorman, 2002). Probably the best example of a set of disorders for which ESTs have produced exceptional results is the domain of anxiety treatment. The ESTs developed to treat anxiety have consistently demonstrated *better* results than medications without the side effects and treatment dropout that often accompany medications (Barlow, 2002).

PANIC DISORDER

Panic disorder affects between 3 and 6 million Americans, and is twice as common in women as men. People diagnosed with it have recurrent unexpected panic attacks that include a variety of unpleasant symptoms, including palpitations, pounding heart or accelerated heart rate, sweating, trembling or shaking, sensations of shortness of breath or smothering, choking feelings, chest pain or discomfort, lightheaded or fainting sensations, and fears of losing control. They also typically have pervasive fears of future attacks. Often, the *fear* of the fear is worse than the attacks themselves, so that people with panic disorder are endlessly worried about and preoccupied with the possibility of having an attack. Some of these clients also manifest agoraphobia and as a result have a hard time even leaving home and engaging with the world (Barlow, 2003).

Although traditional talk therapies do not appear to have much impact on panic, there are several variants of cognitive-behavior therapy (CBT) that have been demonstrated to effectively ameliorate this disorder. Most of these treatments share several interventions in common, including increasing clients' exposure to situations that lead to panic, helping them more effectively manage thoughts and feelings leading to panic, and teaching them how to engage in problem-solving self-talk.

Perhaps the most widely disseminated of the treatments for panic disorder is the one developed by David Barlow of Boston University and Michele Craske of University of California Los Angeles, called panic control treatment (PCT) (Barlow, 2001, 2002; Barlow, Craske, Cerny, & Klosko, 1989). PCT focuses on exposing the client to physiological sensations similar to those that occur during panic. Clients are encouraged to experience the sensations of panic so that they can master them.

So, for example, Shannon, whose disabling panic in the workplace has left her reluctant to seek work, is encouraged in session to imagine being in an anxiety-laden work situation and to breathe in the same way that she does when she has a panic attack. In visiting her worst-case scenario, she is invited to master her fear. In addition to the exposure to situations, thoughts, and feelings that typically lead to panic, PCT includes cognitive examination of the distortions typical in panic, as well as automatic cognitions that go along with them—such as overestimating the level of real threat and dangers during a panic attack. Thus Shannon's dominant thought, that her panic will lead to humiliation and rejection by others, is elicited and examined in the light of her experience. This balanced examination of the evidence points to the fact that Shannon's panic is much more a problem for her than for others; almost all of the times Shannon has had panic attacks, others have been supportive or simply not noticed. Shannon is not only encouraged to remind herself of this clear conclusion, but also to engage in such a rational examination of her other similar beliefs as they come into consciousness and influence her behavior. PCT also includes breath retraining to help people acquire the feeling that they can cope with the signs of impending panic and, eventually, the ability to calm themselves down.

PCT has been frequently studied with impressive results (Barlow, Raffa, & Cohen, 2002). For example, in a large, methodologically rigorous multisite study of this treatment conducted by David Barlow, Jack Gorman, and colleagues, clients were randomly assigned to either PCT, placebo, PCT plus medication, or PCT plus placebo. Treatment was carried out over a three-month period (Barlow, Gorman, Shear, & Woods, 2000). Although all the treatments produced more change than the placebo alone, several findings suggested the superiority of PCT. Adding medications to PCT did *not* demonstrate better outcomes than using PCT alone. And by six months after treatment, there was *greater relapse* for those receiving medication alone or PCT plus medication than for those receiving PCT alone.

Cognitive therapy for anxiety, following the protocol developed by Aaron Beck and colleagues (Beck, 1988; Beck & Weishaar, 1989) and based on correcting cognitive distortions in self-talk, has amassed a similarly impressive record for showing better results than medication in studies of the treatment of panic. In short, the evidence for the effectiveness of PCT and other CBTs for panic disorder vastly outweighs evidence for other approaches. As an example, a recent study by Michael

Addis and colleagues of Clark University found that 43% of those getting cognitive therapy in a managed care setting achieved clinically significant improvement compared to only 19% of those getting other treatments in the same setting (Addis et al., 2004).

OBSESSIVE-COMPULSIVE DISORDER

Just as CBT treatments are coming to be regarded as the treatments of choice for panic disorder, related CBT treatments are emerging as especially potent in treating other anxiety disorders. Because conditioning plays such an important role in causing these difficulties, CBT seems to work uniquely well by teaching clients new skills that "recondition" clients to override the earlier conditioned patterns. Here are a few examples.

Obsessive-compulsive disorder (OCD) includes recurrent obsessions and compulsions that interfere considerably with daily functioning. Obsessions are persistent ideas, thoughts, impulses, or images that are experienced as intrusive and cause marked distress. Compulsions are repetitive behaviors designed to reduce anxiety that become problems in themselves. Examples include people who feel compelled to check and recheck their clothing or that the stove is turned off before leaving the house, thus making them chronically late. CBT treatments for these disorders, including those developed by Edna Foa of the University of Pennsylvania, typically feature exposure to the source of anxiety coupled with the prevention of the obsessive or compulsive behavior and the introduction of some other alternative behavior (Foa & Kozak, 1996).

Maurice, who engages in endless rituals of washing and straightening his clothes, is prevented from engaging in these behaviors and instead is taught to fold his hands while thinking about going to school, a subject about which he has a good deal of anxiety. Self-talk such as that in cognitive therapy is also a frequent component of these treatments. Thus Maurice is helped to examine his belief about what will happen if he does not engage in his compulsive washing. He and the therapist engage in a balanced examination of the chances that his belief that germs will harm him if he does not engage in this ritual is correct. As with panic disorder, he is taught a process of rational examination of his beliefs that is to be used when variants of these beliefs are encountered.

The CBT treatments for OCD are impressively effective (Foa & Franklin, 2001). For example, a multisite study conducted by Foa found that both the exposure program and medication significantly reduced the symptoms of OCD, but the exposure treatment was more effective than medication alone, and the addition of the medication to the exposure treatment did not seem to help (Foa & Franklin, 2001; Foa, Kozak, Steketee, & McCarthy, 1992).

SIMPLE PHOBIA

Exposure-based treatments clearly are the treatment of choice for simple phobias (Barlow, Esler, & Vitali, 1998; Barlow et al., 2002; Nathan & Gorman, 2002). In these treatments, clients are gradually exposed to the feared situation, with clients mastering their fear step by step. Generally, lots of exposure in short duration produces the best results. And new technologies are evolving that are beginning to improve on the impressive results from these treatments. One technology is virtual reality, much like what you might experience in a simulator at Disney World. Virtual reality simulators make for a vivid exposure to feared situations without having to go out of the office to experience those fears. Thus Mike, who is afraid of crossing bridges, experiences in virtual reality the sights and sounds of crossing bridges. These procedures thereby solve the problem of how to create viscerally believable opportunities for exposure in the therapist's office —of a coiling snake, for example, without having to make a trip to the zoo. Although new, virtual reality procedures are emerging as especially effective in recent research (Ruskin, 2005).

Other recent research has begun to look at the use of cognitive enhancing medications in these treatments. Cognitive enhancers are not like traditional psychopharmacological medications. These medications, such as d-cycloserine, simply enhance the ability to learn without affecting feelings directly. Experiments in animals and humans have shown that these drugs lead to better learning of the sorts of classical conditioning paradigms (such as those experienced by Pavlov's dogs) that are at the root of behavioral treatments for phobia. A recent study by Kerry Ressler of Emory University using d-cycloserine showed that using this drug in treatment was more effective in conditioning people to be less afraid of heights and mastering their height phobia, than was traditional behavior therapy conducted without the drug. It is essential here to grasp the use of these medications in such studies (Ressler et al., 2004). These are medications that helps clients learn, not medications that reduce anxiety directly. It continues to be a well-established finding that simple phobias typically do not respond well to medications that reduce anxiety because clients develop less confidence in their abilities at mastery when that mastery is achieved while taking those medications. With those medications, clients are likely to attribute having fewer symptoms to the medication and do not learn new coping behaviors. In contrast, these new cognitive enhancer medications seem to simply open up the client to better learning of reconditioning to not be afraid.

GENERALIZED ANXIETY DISORDER

Individuals with generalized anxiety disorder (GAD) worry much of the time. This tendency to worry too much is the meat and potatoes of many psychotherapy practices, encountered far more often by more therapists than the relatively rarer and more exotic OCD and panic disorder. What is probably not well known by many therapists is that CBT treatment with GAD has been shown to be highly effective (though not quite as effective or as unique an effect as in OCD and panic disorder) (Barlow et al., 2002). In one study conducted by Thomas Borkovec at Penn State University (Borkovec & Costello, 1993), 60% of the clients engaging in a treatment were able to attain a level of functioning in terms of anxiety and worry typical of the general population (a difficult-to-reach criterion for success in almost any treatment of any problem). This treatment included an array of CBT techniques aimed at the rigid behavior and thoughts typical of those with GAD: active self-monitoring to understand the triggers for anxiety; specific training and practice in several relaxation techniques, including progressive muscle relaxation and diaphragmatic breathing; "self control desensitization," in which clients imagine the difficulties they worry about while practicing relaxation; cognitive examination of their beliefs; and having designated worry periods to establish a sense of control over this experience (Borkovec & Ruscio, 2001). A recent meta-analytic review by Kristin Mitte of the University of Jena in Germany (Mitte, 2005) found that, across 65 studies, CBT for GAD worked as well as medication, but without either the side effects or treatment dropout. Dropout rate for medications, Mitte pointed out, was 25%, compared with only 9% for CBT. And she found that studies that directly compared the two found CBT to be superior. Nonetheless, the effort to create even more effective methods continues among CBT researchers since many of those with GAD continue to manifest some continuing difficulty, even with typical CBT treatment. For example, Tom Borkovec has recently expanded his treatment package to include mindfulness techniques and a specific focus on mastering the interpersonal concerns that typify those with GAD (Borkovec & Sharpless, 2004).

CONCLUSION

So what are the implications from this research for us as clinicians? For anxiety disorders, it appears clear that the variants on CBT described here are the treatments of choice at this time. Of course, these methods are not perfect. They don't work for everyone, nor do they produce change in every aspect of a person's life—they are not all-purpose therapy. But when clients specifically want relief from the symptoms of anxiety, these are the treatments (with appropriate variations) they should get. This means that, as responsible therapists, we need to know how to practice these techniques or be prepared to refer these clients to therapists who already do. This does not mean, however, that clients with anxiety problems should see *only* CBT therapists. At the Family Institute at Northwestern, where I practice, clients who may be in more traditional therapies focused on broader life issues, are often referred to an Anxiety Clinic for CBT when they need help with their anxiety symptoms. In short, CBT is not necessarily the only therapy people suffering from anxiety disorders need, but it's hard to argue that their treatment can appropriately exclude evidence-based CBT interventions.

RESOURCES

Barlow, D. H. (Ed.). (2002). *Anxiety and its disorders: The nature and treatment of anxiety and panic* (2nd ed.). New York: Guilford Press.

Nathan, P. E., & Gorman, J. M. (Eds). (2002). *A guide to treatments that work* (2nd ed.). London: Oxford University Press.

REFERENCES

Addis, M. E., Hatgis, C., Krasnow, A. D., Jacob, K., Bourne, L., & Mansfield, A. (2004). Effectiveness of cognitive-behavioral treatment for panic disorder versus treatment as usual in a managed care setting. *Journal of Consulting and Clinical Psychology, 72*(4): 625–635.

Barlow, D. H. (Ed.). (2001). *Clinical handbook of psychological disorders: A step-by-step treatment manual* (3rd ed.). New York: Guilford Press.

Barlow, D. H. (Ed.). (2002). *Anxiety and its disorders: The nature and treatment of anxiety and panic* (2nd ed.). New York: Guilford Press.

Barlow, D. H. (2003). Anxiety and its disorders: The nature and treatment of anxiety and panic. *Journal of Clinical Psychiatry, 64*(3): 345–346.

Barlow, D. H., Craske, M. G., Cerny, J. A., & Klosko, J. S. (1989). Behavioral treatment of panic disorder. *Behavior Therapy, 20*(2): 261–282.

Barlow, D. H., Esler, J. L., & Vitali, A. E. (1998). Psychosocial treatments for panic disorders, phobias, and generalized anxiety disorder. In P. E.

Nathan & J. M. Gorman (Eds.), *A guide to treatments that work* (2nd ed., pp. 288–318). London: Oxford University Press.

Barlow, D. H., Gorman, J. M., Shear, M., & Woods, S. W. (2000). Cognitive-behavioral therapy, imipramine, or their combination for panic disorder: A randomized controlled trial: Correction. *Journal of the American Medical Association, 284*(19): 2450.

Barlow, D. H., Raffa, S. D., & Cohen, E. M. (2002). Psychosocial treatments for panic disorders, phobias, and generalized anxiety disorder. [References]. In P. E. Nathan & J. M. Gorman (Eds.), *A guide to treatments that work* (2nd ed., pp. 301–335). London: Oxford University Press.

Beck, A. T. (1988). Cognitive approaches to panic disorder: Theory and therapy. In S. Rachman & J. D. Maser (Eds.), *Panic: Psychological perspectives* (pp. 91–109). Hillsdale, NJ: Lawrence Erlbaum Associates.

Beck, A. T., & Weishaar, M. E. (1989). Cognitive therapy. In A. Freeman & K. M. Simon (Eds.), *Comprehensive handbook of cognitive therapy* (pp. 21–36). New York: Plenum Press.

Borkovec, T., & Costello, E. (1993). Efficacy of applied relaxation and cognitive-behavioral therapy in the treatment of generalized anxiety disorder. *Journal of Consulting and Clinical Psychology, 61*(4): 611–619.

Borkovec, T. D., & Ruscio, A. M. (2001). Psychotherapy for generalized anxiety disorder. *Journal of Clinical Psychiatry, 62*(Suppl. 11): 37–42.

Borkovec, T. D., & Sharpless, B. (2004). Generalized anxiety disorder: Bringing cognitive-behavioral therapy into the valued present. In S. C. Hayes, V. M. Follette, & M. M. Linehan (Eds.), *Mindfulness and acceptance: Expanding the cognitive-behavioral tradition* (pp. 208–224). New York: Guilford Press.

Foa, E. B., & Franklin, M. E. (2001). Obsessive-compulsive disorder. In D. H. Barlow (Ed.), *Clinical handbook of psychological disorders: A step-by-step treatment manual* (pp. 152–188). New York: Guilford Press.

Foa, E. B., & Kozak, M. J. (1996). Psychological treatment for obsessive-compulsive disorder. In M. R. Mavissakalian & R. F. Prien (Eds.), *Long-term treatments of anxiety disorders* (pp. 285–309). Washington, DC: American Psychiatric Association.

Foa, E. B., Kozak, M. J., Steketee, G. S., & McCarthy, P. R. (1992). Treatment of depressive and obsessive-compulsive symptoms in OCD by imipramine and behaviour therapy. *British Journal of Clinical Psychology, 31*(3): 279–292.

Mitte, K. (2005). Meta-analysis of cognitive-behavioral treatments for generalized anxiety disorder: A comparison with pharmacotherapy. *Psychological Bulletin, 131*(5): 785–795.

Nathan, P. E., & Gorman, J. M. (Eds.). (2002). *A guide to treatments that work* (2nd ed.). London: Oxford University Press.

Ressler, K. J., Rothbaum, B. O., Tannenbaum, L., Anderson, P., Graap, K., Zimand, E., et al. (2004). Cognitive enhancers as adjuncts to psychotherapy: Use of d-cycloserine in phobic individuals to facilitate extinction of fear. *Archives of General Psychiatry, 61*(11): 1136–1144.

Ruskin, P. E. (2005). Virtual reality therapy for anxiety disorders: Advances in evaluation and treatment. *American Journal of Psychiatry, 162*(9): 1772.

Westen, D., Novotny, C. M., & Thompson-Brenner, H. (2004). The empirical status of empirically supported psychotherapies: Assumptions, findings, and reporting in controlled clinical trials. *Psychological Bulletin, 130*(4): 631–663.

10

MINDFULNESS GOES MAINSTREAM: RESEARCH IS PROVING THE VALUE OF AWARENESS PROCESSES

Psychotherapy research has rarely examined interventions that lie outside of the mainstream of practice. And when research centers on these sorts of methods, it's rare that the findings about treatment effectiveness parallel the excitement of clinicians offering these interventions. The integration of mindfulness practice into psychotherapy is a major exception to this trend, with a solid base of research support accumulating. This chapter looks at some major recent trends in research on using mindfulness in psychotherapy.

It seems hard to believe that only about 20 years ago, meditation was still widely considered something practiced only by Zen students, yoga adepts, and New Age esoterics in Birkenstocks. True, in the 1970s, a few outlander physicians, led by Herbert Benson, began studying the power of meditation to evoke a relaxation response that lowered blood pressure and alleviated stress. Still, for a long time, the scientific credibility of meditation as a legitimate healing approach was roughly on the same level as faith healing and exorcism.

Over the past 10 years, however, what began as the outre, even slightly disreputable idea that meditation might actually have a real and empirically measurable impact on mental and physical health has now become almost mainstream. Since the 1970s, dozens of research studies have demonstrated that meditation can reduce anxiety, stress, blood pressure, chronic pain, insomnia, posttraumatic stress disorder symptoms, and substance abuse. It also seems to improve the quality of life.

The practice of mindfulness has been part of many Asian traditions for thousands of years and part of some methods of psychotherapy since the pioneering work of Alan Watts (1963) and others brought Eastern ideas of consciousness into the world of psychotherapy in the 1950s and 1960s. Entire cultures have been profoundly affected by formal and informal exposure to ways of experiencing aimed at increasing mindfulness, such as meditation and yoga, and these methods are now also practiced by millions of Americans.

But, until the last few years, relatively few credentialed, respectable and standard-issue psychotherapists seemed to have discovered meditation for themselves, much less felt prepared to teach their clients how to do it. Hovering for years around the fringy edges of mental health care (along with crystals and aura readings), it is only now beginning to enter the mainstream of psychotherapy practice. These days, more and more workshops and conferences seem to have *mindfulness* or *meditation* in their titles and increasing numbers of therapists are not shy about admitting that, right along with their other favorite modalities, they also teach their clients to sit quietly and follow their breathing.

In spite of increasing support for meditation among practitioners and lots of anecdotal evidence that it works well for many different clients in a variety of circumstances, formal research on the value of incorporating it into the clinical practice of psychotherapy has been relatively sparse. Why should this be? Perhaps the philosophy of detachment, learning to accept and make peace with life as it is, which is often seen to accompany meditation traditions (e.g., Zen Buddhism) seems to conflict with the goal of endless improvement and progress that characterizes Western science and, probably, most psychotherapy models. It is wired into the fabric of our society, business, science, and health care that we aim to improve, to get better, to not be satisfied with the status quo. And the ever-present orienting word for most psychotherapies has been *change* rather than *acceptance*. Or, maybe meditation still seems tainted by its associations with religious and spiritual traditions, and exotic "foreign" traditions. Most likely, the research community is guilty of its own sort of myopia and difficulty thinking outside the box it has created for itself. The biggest, most stultifying box of all is the self-defeating assumption that there must already be some scientifically empirical evidence for the value of an intervention *before* there can be more exploration of its value as an intervention!

But this assumption is indeed nearsighted, because there is a growing body of very exciting research that demonstrates the extraordinary power of mindfulness practice on the way the mind works. Granted, much of this research has not been done in the realm of psychotherapy per se, but some of the evidence for the impact of meditation on the mind and brain is so convincing that even the hardest nosed psychotherapy researcher should be impressed.

In one of the most remarkable partnerships in the history of research, Richard Davidson, a neuroscientist at the University of Wisconsin, collaborated with the Dalai Lama on an astonishingly innovative piece of research investigating the impact of long-term meditation on the mind and brain (Davidson et al., 2003). For this project, the Dalai Lama sent eight of his monks, who had each meditated between 10,000 and 40,000 hours over the preceding 15 to 40 years, to Davidson's laboratory. In a randomized design, comparing the brain waves of these monks with those of novice meditators, Davidson and colleagues found that the monks had substantially higher levels of gamma brain waves, brain activity indicating higher levels of consciousness, than the novices. In addition, the monks' brain waves were also better organized and coordinated than in the controls, indicating that their consciousness seemed to more smoothly invoke a sense of familiarity and openness to experience. Brain activity in the monks was highest in the left prefrontal cortex, the area of the brain that has been associated with happiness. Furthermore, these differences in how the brain functioned remained present even when the monks were not meditating; the years of mindfulness practice seemed to have changed how the brain operated. And as with other dose-response effects, those who had practiced the longest showed the strongest effects.

Other major threads of research are more directly related to psychotherapy. Some studies, for example, have looked at the value of training in mindfulness techniques for increasing happiness and reducing levels of distress and psychopathology. The best known is a series of studies by Jon Kabat-Zinn of the University of Massachusetts Medical Center, who developed and evaluated a program for increasing mindfulness called "mindfulness-based stress reduction" (MBSR)

(Kabat-Zinn, 2003a, 2003b; Kabat-Zinn, Lipworth, & Burney, 1985). Developed originally in the context of exploring its impact on chronic pain, MBSR is an 8- to 10-week course for instruction and practice in mindfulness, which includes an all-day intensive mindfulness session. Participants practice at least 45 minutes per day, 6 days per week. A prominent feature of MBSR training is teaching participants to observe their emotions, sensations, and cognitions, even the unpleasant and painful ones, calmly, dispassionately, and without judgment. Kabat-Zinn's research showed that MBSR led to significant decreases in pain and in the number of medical symptoms reported and reduced psychological distress in participants (Kabat-Zinn, 1984; Kabat-Zinn et al., 1985). Similar findings have emerged in rigorously controlled studies done by Kabat-Zinn and colleagues examining the impact of MBSR on generalized anxiety disorder and depression (Kabat-Zinn, 2003a; Kabat-Zinn, et al., 1992).

What does it mean to be mindful or to do research on mindfulness? How do you take this deeply private, spiritual, and elusive experience and make it the focus of research aimed at studying how these experiences can become part of replicable psychotherapy treatments? Rather than analyzing what is perhaps unanalyzable, researchers studying mindfulness have focused more simply on two core aspects of mindfulness: the value of remaining in the moment and the development of one's ability to accept and go with what is occurring. These sum to maintaining a focus on the present rather than past or future, and on learning to observe and follow one's experience rather than to guide it. Typically, in these efforts, mindfulness is usually defined much the way Kabat-Zinn defines it, as paying attention in a particular way: on purpose, in the present moment, and nonjudgmentally. Such mindful practice is consciously and purposely initiated, but allows experience to unfold without evaluation or criticism. Following from such definitions, researchers have developed a technology for assessing mindfulness, such as the Mindfulness Attention Awareness Scale, developed by Kirk Brown and Richard Ryan (2003) of University of Rochester, and the Kentucky Inventory of Mindfulness Skills, developed by Ruth Baer, Gregory Smith, and Kristen Allen (2004) of the University of Kentucky. Such scales track clients' self-report of their mindful experience such as their ability to remain nonjudgmental. Although such brain technologies as magnetic resonance imaging and electroencephalogram—as used in the Davidson research assessing the monks, described previously—have promise for indicating levels of mindfulness, to date research on the extent to which mindfulness is present remains principally the product of self-reports.

Particularly promising, and unexpected, is a surge in research on mindfulness from cognitive-behavioral therapists, a set of research/practitioners who often seem dismissive of all techniques outside their usual cognitive-behavior therapy (CBT) methodologies and particularly disdainful of so-called humanistic therapies. Yet, a growing number of the most prominent CBT researchers have become convinced of the value of these methods and have come to see them as consistent and complementary with CBT. How can it be that practitioners of such strict, empirically demonstrated, protocol-driven methods are being turned on by something as ephemerally mystical sounding as mindfulness? After all, CBT therapists are typically very concrete and focused on behavior and language, highly active and judgmental in questioning ideas explicitly labeled as "cognitive distortions," a zeitgeist far removed from mindfulness. And unlike the Zen archer, CBT therapists are typically trained to aim their arrows quite precisely.

However, it should be remembered that CBT and mindfulness practice aren't as foreign to each other as they might seem. CBT therapists have always employed techniques, such as relaxation and imagery, that had some overlap with mindfulness practice. Both CBT and mindfulness share the notion of directed awareness about one's inner processes and a focus on how we automatically react to situations and get carried away by our feelings. Furthermore, several decades of pursuing directed change has led some in the CBT movement to come to intimately understand the limits of directed efforts toward change, which does not help everyone and which even leads to active resistance on the part of some clients. Even highly successful CBT treatments such as cognitive therapy for depression do not succeed in helping many clients reach "normal" functioning at the end of treatment. Such findings have led leaders in the CBT movement, such as Steve Hayes (2002, 2004a, 2004b) of the University of Nevada and Andrew Christenson (Christensen, Sevier, Simpson, & Gattis, 2004) of the University of California Los Angeles, to write and speak extensively about the need for self-acceptance and acceptance of others as they are. And, yet another source of connection is that some CBT therapists such as Alan Marlatt and Marsha Linehan have for many years engaged in mindfulness practice in their own lives, long before they brought these methods into their practice of CBT.

One example is a closely related variant of Kabat-Zinn's MBSR developed by John Teasdale and his colleagues in Cambridge, England, that melds mindfulness with cognitive therapy called mindfulness-based cognitive therapy, which has been shown to help reduce recidivism in depression (Teasdale, 2004; Teasdale et al., 2000; Teasdale et al., 2002).

Teasdale and colleagues developed an eight-week program based on Kabat-Zinn's program aimed to help depressed people acquire a sense of detachment from the patterns of thoughts that tend to automatically trigger their depression. Mindfulness-based cognitive therapy includes simple breathing meditations and yoga stretches to help participants become more aware of the present moment, and learning mindfulness meditation that accents allowing distressing and depressive thoughts and feelings to come and go. Teasdale and colleagues found far lower rates of relapse (37%) in depressed patients who had major depressive disorder and received this intervention than those who did not receive this special treatment (who had a relapse rate of 66%). The effect was most pronounced in those who had three or more previous episodes of depression.

In another example of the potential uses of meditation in psychotherapy with a difficult population, Alan Marlatt of the University of Washington examined the impact of a mindfulness practice called Vipassana meditation on the behavior of a prison population (Marlatt, 2002; Marlatt et al., 2004). Prisoners in a minimum security facility in Washington either participated in a 10-day course or simply completed measures receiving the typical regimen in the prison. Marlatt found that even in this highly recidivist population, participating in this program instead of in treatment as usual resulted in reduced levels of arrest, less alcoholism, and less drug use. For example, alcohol use in the meditation group went from 50 days of the last 90 to only 10 days, far fewer days than the control group, and total alcohol and drug use was also much less frequent.

We are also beginning to see mindfulness practice incorporated as one component of multi-method treatments intended for clients with problems notoriously resistant to treatment. Dialectical Behavior Therapy (DBT), for example, originally developed for clients with borderline personality disorder by Martha Linehan of the University of Washington, incorporates mindfulness training as part of a complex treatment strategy. In DBT clients are taught mindfulness skills, such as observing their own emotions, to help them calm down and get some detachment from their own inner turmoil (Bagge & Linehan, 2000; Linehan, 1987, 1993). For this sensitive and very troubled group, the mindfulness training is taught in a more flexible way, with less-demanding expectations for practice than some other more-structured mindfulness instruction programs (Dimidjian & Linehan, 2003; Linehan, 1993). The training is structured in this way to mitigate the difficulties that these clients often have in responding to rigid structures and expectations for performance, as well as in response to the high levels of frustration and powerful troubling affects that these clients can quickly develop. The client is allowed to become comfortable with the techniques in a nondemanding environment so that they can experience the soothing effects and, in this way, gradually increase mindfulness practice. DBT, which makes this mindfulness practice one of several key interventions, has been the subject of several clinical trials that have established it as a well-established treatment for borderline personality disorder, and now the most widely circulated treatment for this difficulty (Linehan, 2000).

Enough research has emerged over the last few years that a meta-analysis of studies specifically testing the impact of mindfulness interventions has recently appeared in the prestigious research journal, *Clinical Psychology*. In that analysis, Ruth Baer (2003) assessed the impact of the summation of all the research on mindfulness on the kinds of problems frequently encountered in psychotherapy, such as depression and anxiety. She found a mean effect size for all these treatments of 0.74, meaning that 74% of those in the groups receiving mindfulness training did better than those receiving the alternative of no treatment or another treatment. This is what is statistically called a "large" effect for these interventions, signifying that in statistical terms the effect is considerable and that the vast majority of those receiving the treatment are helped compared with those not receiving it. And she found these treatments to be highly acceptable to clients: 85% of participants complete these programs.

So where is this research taking us? It seems clear that research has already demonstrated how powerful mindfulness techniques can be in the treatment of pain, anxiety, depression, and even more complex and difficult problems, such as borderline personality disorder. The impact of these methods on those not suffering from emotional problems is equally clear, and mindfulness techniques are increasingly becoming a staple of the movement toward accenting positive psychology led by psychologist Martin Seligman of the University of Pennsylvania (2002). Basic questions still remain about the most useful ways to incorporate these techniques into psychotherapy (particularly, how and when they should be integrated with other techniques) and for which clients these methods are most useful. Furthermore, as Sona Dimidjiian of the University of Washington and Marsha Linehan have pointed out, research so far has focused only on the secular variations on mindfulness, leaving unexplored the role that spirituality has typically played in traditional mindfulness traditions (Dimidjian & Linehan, 2003; Hayes, Follette, & Linehan, 2004). To what extent, if at all, are the beneficial aspects of mindfulness connected to the spiritual or religious meanings ascribed to these practices by traditional cultures? Over the next decade, it will be interesting to see research examining and comparing mindfulness practices both within and outside of the different native contexts in which they originally took root. For now, research has revealed that there is real value, if not fully explored or analyzed, in helping therapists learn mindfulness skills and teach them to their clients.

RESOURCES

Hayes, S. C., Follette, V. M., & Linehan, M. M. (Eds.). (2004). *Mindfulness and acceptance: Expanding the cognitive-behavioral tradition*. New York: Guilford Press.

Kabat-Zinn, J. (2003). Mindfulness-based interventions in context: Past, present, and future. *Clinical Psychology: Science & Practice, 10*(2): 144–156.

REFERENCES

Baer, R. A. (2003). Mindfulness training as a clinical intervention: A conceptual and empirical review. *Clinical Psychology: Science & Practice, 10*(2): 125–143.

Baer, R. A., Smith, G. T., & Allen, K. B. (2004). Assessment of mindfulness by self-report: The Kentucky Inventory of Mindfulness Skills. *Assessment, 11*(3): 191–206.

Bagge, C. L., & Linehan, M. M. (2000). Reasons for living versus reasons for dying: Examining the internal debate of suicide: Commentary. *Suicide & Life-Threatening Behavior, 30*(2): 180–181.

Brown, K. W., & Ryan, R. M. (2003). The benefits of being present: Mindfulness and its role in psychological well-being. *Journal of Personality & Social Psychology, 84*(4): 822–848.

Christensen, A., Sevier, M., Simpson, L. E., & Gattis, K. S. (2004). Acceptance, mindfulness, and change in couple therapy. [References]. In S. C. Hayes, V. M. Follette, & M. M. Linehan (Eds.), *Mindfulness and acceptance: Expanding the cognitive-behavioral tradition* (pp. 288–309). New York: Guilford Press.

Davidson, R. J., Kabat-Zinn, J., Schumacher, J., Rosenkranz, M., Muller, D., Santorelli, S. F., et al. (2003). Alterations in brain and immune function produced by mindfulness meditation. *Psychosomatic Medicine, 65*(4): 564–570.

Dimidjian, S., & Linehan, M. M. (2003). Defining an agenda for future research on the clinical application of mindfulness practice. *Clinical Psychology: Science & Practice, 10*(2): 166–171.

Hayes, S. C. (2002). Acceptance, mindfulness, and science. *Clinical Psychology: Science & Practice, 9*(1): 101–106.

Hayes, S. C. (2004a). Acceptance and commitment therapy and the new behavior therapies: Mindfulness, acceptance, and relationship. [References]. In S. C. Hayes, V. M. Follette, & M. M. Linehan (Eds.), *Mindfulness and acceptance: Expanding the cognitive-behavioral tradition* (pp. 1–29). New York: Guilford Press.

Hayes, S. C. (2004b). Acceptance and commitment therapy, relational frame theory, and the third wave of behavioral and cognitive therapies. *Behavior Therapy, 35*(4): 639–665.

Hayes, S. C., Follette, V. M., & Linehan, M. M. (Eds.). (2004). *Mindfulness and acceptance: Expanding the cognitive-behavioral tradition.* New York: Guilford Press.

Kabat-Zinn, J. (1984). An outpatient program in behavioral medicine for chronic pain patients based on the practice of mindfulness meditation: Theoretical considerations and preliminary results. *ReVISION, 7*(1): 71–72.

Kabat-Zinn, J. (2003a). Mindfulness-based interventions in context: Past, present, and future. *Clinical Psychology: Science & Practice, 10*(2): 144–156.

Kabat-Zinn, J. (2003b). Mindfulness-based stress reduction (MBSR). *Constructivism in the Human Sciences, 8*(2): 73–107.

Kabat-Zinn, J., Lipworth, L., & Burney, R. (1985). The clinical use of mindfulness meditation for the self-regulation of chronic pain. *Journal of Behavioral Medicine, 8*(2): 163–190.

Kabat-Zinn, J., Massion, A. O., Kristeller, J., & Peterson, L. G. (1992). Effectiveness of a meditation-based stress reduction program in the treatment of anxiety disorders. *American Journal of Psychiatry, 149*(7): 936–943.

Linehan, M. M. (1987). Dialectical behavior therapy for borderline personality disorder: Theory and method. *Bulletin of the Menninger Clinic, 51*(3): 261–276.

Linehan, M. M. (1993). *Skills training manual for treating borderline personality disorder.* New York: Guilford Press.

Linehan, M. M. (2000). The empirical basis of dialectical behavior therapy: Development of new treatments versus evaluation of existing treatments. *Clinical Psychology: Science & Practice, 7*(1): 113–119.

Marlatt, G. A. (2002). Buddhist philosophy and the treatment of addictive behavior. *Cognitive & Behavioral Practice, 9*(1): 44–49.

Marlatt, G. A., Witkiewitz, K., Dillworth, T. M., Bowen, S. W., Parks, G. A., Macpherson, L. M., et al. (2004). Vipassana meditation as a treatment for alcohol and drug use disorders. [References]. In S. C. Hayes, V. M. Follette, & M. M. Linehan (Eds.), *Mindfulness and acceptance: Expanding the cognitive-behavioral tradition* (pp. 261–287). New York: Guilford Press.

Seligman, M. E. (2002). Positive psychology, positive prevention, and positive therapy. [References]. In C. R. Snyder & S. J. Lopez (Eds.), *Handbook of positive psychology* (pp. 3–9). New York: Oxford University Press.

Teasdale, J. D. (2004). Mindfulness-based cognitive therapy. [References]. In J. Yiend (Ed.), *Cognition, emotion and psychopathology: Theoretical, empirical and clinical directions* (pp. 270–289). New York: Cambridge University Press.

Teasdale, J. D., Moore, R. G., Hayhurst, H., Pope, M., Williams, S., & Segal, Z. V. (2002). Metacognitive awareness and prevention of relapse in depression: Empirical evidence. *Journal of Consulting & Clinical Psychology, 70*(2): 275–287.

Teasdale, J. D., Segal, Z. V., Williams, J. G., Ridgeway, V. A., Soulsby, J. M., & Lau, M. A. (2000). Prevention of relapse/recurrence in major depression by mindfulness-based cognitive therapy. *Journal of Consulting & Clinical Psychology, 68*(4): 615–623.

Watts, A. W. (1963). *Psychotherapy, East and West.* New York: New American Library.

11

IMPROVING OUR TRACK RECORD: HOW THERAPISTS CAN BETTER MEET THE NEEDS OF THE DISADVANTAGED

Psychotherapy research, much like most other research, tradi-tionally has paid insufficient attention to highly salient variables such as ethnicity and social class. Treatments that are developed and tested with one population may or may not be effective with another. As mental health treatment research moves into the 21st century, we are seeing increasing attention to the question of how well results can be generalized to those from different eth-nicities and social classes. And, as this chapter describes, we are also beginning to be able to learn from research centered on treat-ments that have been specially tailored to the needs of diverse populations and the economically disadvantaged.

Louise and her two children—Joseph, 10, and Anita, 6—live in one of Chicago's poorest housing projects, surrounded by high crime, drug dealers, and violence. Her job as a food service worker pays minimum wage, barely enough to feed her kids. Joseph is in trouble at school constantly, fighting with other kids, talking back to teachers, and playing hooky. Just 25 years old, Louise already feels overwhelmed by life and hopeless that anything will ever change. She spends her evenings staring at the television, sinking deeper into depression. Her older sister, Sally, and their mother have tried without success to help Louise and the kids. Joseph's teachers have urged Louise to set firmer limits, but she just doesn't have the energy. She did go to a conference at the school with Joseph's teachers and school counselors, and after much discussion, they suggested she take the family to the local community mental health clinic for therapy.

Louise called the clinic to make an appointment for the family, as she'd been told to do. But after making the appointment, she began to have second thoughts: Where will she find an extra $5 to pay for the session, when she couldn't pay her bills last week? How will they find transportation to the clinic, and will she and the kids make it back home safely through the neighborhood? And lurking behind all those worries was the nagging fear that she would be blamed for Joseph's behavior. Her mother had told her about people who went to the clinic and lost custody of their children. Still, Louise is determined to be there for the appointment. But when she told the children about going for counseling, they flatly refused, and she had no idea how to get them to attend.

After Louise missed the appointment, the intake worker politely called and encouraged her to try again, but with no success. Louise became more lethargic and depressed, and Joseph spent more and more time in trouble.

The prevalence of stories such as Louise's is confirmed by clinical research, which has established that traditional psychotherapy has a less-than-impressive track record with people in poor communities (Bernal, Bonilla, & Bellido, 1995; Bernal & Scharro-del-Rio, 2001; Miranda et al., 2005). Fortunately, research is finally beginning to offer a picture of what works best for clients whose problems are entangled with dangerous neighborhoods, social isolation, and lack of economic opportunities. In recent years, we have also seen researchers move from asking how therapy works with the poor, a question too general to be useful, to the far more instructive study of how therapy can best have an impact on the specific kinds of problems most likely to affect those living in poverty.

In 1995, 11% of the families in America (36 million people) lived below the poverty level ($15,500 for a family of four) and more than 20% of children lived in poverty. Thirty percent of African Americans, 30% of Hispanics, and 50% of African-American children lived in poverty. Research shows that levels of stress, number of individual psychological problems, marital and family difficulties, and severe mental illness increase as socioeconomic status declines. For example, having a low income increases the likelihood of depression, schizophrenia, anxiety, and psychophysiological distress in adults and psychological distress in adolescents. In Leo Srole and associates' classic 1962 Midtown Manhattan Study, which examined the relationship between socioeconomic status and mental health, lower income individuals were overrepresented among those who had significant difficulties in coping, a finding consistently replicated over the years (Srole, 1962, 1975).

Despite the greater incidence of psychological stress, research assessing mental health treatment shows that poor clients are less likely to use psychotherapy, compared with those with more financial resources. And those who try therapy more frequently drop out before the treatment can be delivered. In a 1984 study, Paul Pilkonis and colleagues found that low-income clients seldom stayed in treatment more than six sessions (Pilkonis, Imber, & Rubinsky, 1984). At the same time, it is extremely important to emphasize that outcome research also shows that those who are able to develop positive alliances with therapists and remain sufficiently long in treatment do as well as higher income clients who stay in therapy (Orlinsky, Grawe, & Parks, 1994). Poverty does not affect clients' ability to benefit from therapy, but rather the likelihood that they will form the kind of therapeutic relationship that encourages them to stay with treatment. This finding is no doubt influenced by the fact that clients in poverty are typically treated by therapists who are beginning their careers and are inexperienced in building a therapeutic alliance. The research also shows that clinicians often expect therapy with poor clients to fail and the negative effect of low therapist expectations is a well-documented empirical finding.

Of course, one must be cautious about overgeneralizing about how poverty influences treatment outcome. Poor, well-educated clients have a much more positive view of therapy than less-educated poor people. Newly divorced mothers with low incomes frequently seek therapy for stress and depression and seem to benefit from it. Social and ethnic groups also differ in their response to psychotherapy, and within specific ethnic groups there is enormous diversity in attitudes. For example, a large-scale study conducted by Stanley Sue and colleagues from the Los Angeles Community Mental Health Services in 1991 found Asian Americans and Mexican Americans much less likely to use services than African Americans or whites (Sue, Fujino, Hu, & Takeuchi, 1991). Other studies, including one conducted by Sue in 1974, have shown African Americans are more likely to drop out before treatment begins or after a few sessions than are poor whites (Sue, McKinney, Allen, & Hall, 1974). Yet researcher Raymond Lorion summarizes the overall finding, replicated again and again about work with low-income clients: "Low-income status contraindicates individual psychotherapy as an intervention" (Lorion, 1978, p. 910). To engage and retain most clients living below the poverty level, therapy needs to be different from traditional office practice.

Researchers have developed and tested approaches to therapy that overcome the most common obstacles to engaging poor clients. Some of their recommendations are

- Offering therapy in clients' homes or neighborhoods
- Reducing costs
- Offering treatments through well-respected community facilities
- Adapting therapy methods to the cultures within a given community

It has been shown that successful treatments for disadvantaged clients typically address multiple levels within the system. The most promising programs combine ingredients from family and individual therapies with ideas drawn from prevention programs, family preservation, and social work. Interventions are aimed at families, individuals, schools, and peer groups.

Howard Liddle, Jose Szapocznik, and Patrick Tolan head large, programmatic research projects that have established, tested, and revised therapy methods targeted at specific populations of economically disadvantaged youth. Liddle, a psychologist at the University of Miami, and his colleagues have developed an approach aimed at urban (largely African American) substance-abusing adolescents and their families (Liddle et al., 2001; Liddle & Diamond, 1991; Liddle & Hogue, 2001). This approach includes elements drawn from structural family therapy, family psycho-education, a developmental perspective on adolescence, and traditional drug abuse therapy. Sessions are typically held in the home. Some meetings are with the entire family, others are with the parents or with the adolescent alone. The therapy first seeks to restore the family's sense of hope through directly engaging their despair about the problem. Subsequent goals focus on helping the family learn about typical patterns in adolescence and drug abuse, on fostering constructive communication, on helping the parents set more effective limits, and on improving the self-image of teenaged family members. Explicit attention is centered on relevant themes within the clients' cultural community, such as anger, rage and alienation. The powerful influence of the teenage peer groups is also addressed.

In a study comparing this approach with cognitive-behavior therapy in a primarily African-American sample in which 55% of the adolescents had been arrested in the previous year, the adolescents receiving multidimensional family therapy used considerably fewer drugs and alcohol and had many fewer symptoms at six-month follow-ups than those receiving cognitive-behavior therapy. Research has also shown that multidimensional family therapy is highly effective in helping parents work in concert in coping with their teenager (Liddle & Hogue, 2001).

Jose Szapocznik, a psychologist at the University of Miami Center for Family Studies, has developed a multisystemic approach combining structural and ecosystemic therapies for intervening with Hispanic families of adolescent delinquents (Beutler & Crago, 1991; Szapocznik et al., 1989; Szapocznik et al., 2002). He was particularly interested in therapeutic engagement tactics, such as in-home visits and using telephone calls to encourage family members to attend the first appointment. In one study, Szapocznik found that an aggressive approach to alliance building engaged 81% of clients, compared with 60% of families treated with a conventional intake process (Blaney et al., 1997; Santisteban et al., 1996; Szapocznik, Perez-Vidal, Brickman, & Foote, 1988; Szapocznik & Williams, 2000).

In their Metropolitan Area Child Study, Patrick Tolan and his colleagues at the University of Illinois at Chicago have developed an intervention for at-risk, inner-city, elementary schoolchildren, identifying those children showing early signs of acting out before these behaviors become major problems (Tolan & McKay, 1996). Tolan and colleagues begin their efforts with a range of interventions to gain the confidence of the children and their parents, including help in dealing with various bureaucracies. The program provides social skills training for the children, behavior-management and instructional-methods training for the teachers, a small-group program on social skills for high-risk children, and a variety of structural and psycho-educational interventions aimed at improving family management of internal and external stressors. The two-year program has been used in 16 urban schools with second- and fifth-grade children. Initial results after seven years of data collection indicate that the interventions reduce later aggression and lead to fewer arrests among the most aggressive group. These results suggest that the engagement of the family is critical to treatment success, especially for high-risk kids in high-risk environments.

With solid data now proving both the relative ineffectiveness of office-bound, traditional therapy, and the success of multilevel interventions for the poor, such as those of Liddle, Szapocznik, and Tolan, the potential of therapy to successfully engage and treat low-income clients who face overwhelming obstacles to traditional participation in psychotherapy is not in doubt. The more that community mental health agencies, therapists, schools, and other local organizations take on the burden of making therapy user-friendly for low-income families, and the more that therapists break down the boundaries between individual, family, and community interventions, the more clients such as Louise and her son will stay in therapy and have successful outcomes.

RESOURCES

Liddle, H. A., & Hogue, A. (2001). Multidimensional family therapy for adolescent substance abuse. [References]. In E. F. Wagner & H. B. Waldron (Eds.), *Innovations in adolescent substance abuse interventions* (pp. 229–261). Amsterdam, Netherlands: Pergamon/Elsevier Science.

Santisteban, D. A., Szapocznik, J., Perez-Vidal, A., Kurtines, W. M., Murray, E. J., & LaPerriere, A. (1996). Efficacy of intervention for engaging youth and families into treatment and some variables that may contribute to differential effectiveness. *Journal of Family Psychology, 10*(1): 35–44.

Tolan, P. H., & McKay, M. M. (1996). Preventing serious antisocial behavior in inner-city children: An empirically based family intervention program. *Family Relations: Journal of Applied Family & Child Studies,* 45(2): 148–155.

REFERENCES

Bernal, G., Bonilla, J., & Bellido, C. (1995). Ecological validity and cultural sensitivity for outcome research: Issues for the cultural adaptation and development of psychosocial treatments with Hispanics. *Journal of Abnormal Child Psychology, 23*(1): 67–82.

Bernal, G., & Scharro-del-Rio, M. R. (2001). Are empirically supported treatments valid for ethnic minorities? Toward an alternative approach for treatment research. *Cultural Diversity & Ethnic Minority Psychology,* 7(4): 328–342.

Beutler, L. E., & Crago, M. (Eds.). (1991). *Psychotherapy research: An international review of programmatic studies.* Washington, DC: American Psychological Association.

Blaney, N. T., Goodkin, K., Feaster, D., Morgan, R., Millon, C., Szapocznik, J., et al. (1997). A psychosocial model of distress over time in early HIV-1 infection: The role of life stressors, social support and coping. *Psychology & Health, 12*(5): 633–653.

Liddle, H. A., Dakof, G. A., Parker, K., Diamond, G. S., Barrett, K., & Tejeda, M. (2001). Multidimiensional family therapy for adolescent drug abuse: Results of a randomized clinical trial. *American Journal of Drug & Alcohol Abuse, 27*(4): 651–688.

Liddle, H. A., & Diamond, G. (1991). Adolescent substance abusers in family therapy: The critical initial phase of treatment. *Family Dynamics of Addiction Quarterly, 1*(1): 55–68.

Liddle, H. A., & Hogue, A. (2001). Multidimensional family therapy for adolescent substance abuse. [References]. In E. F. Wagner & H. B. Waldron (Eds.), *Innovations in adolescent substance abuse interventions* (pp. 229–261). Amsterdam, Netherlands: Pergamon/Elsevier Science.

Lorion, L. P. (1978). Research on psychotherapy and behavior change with the disadvantaged. In S. Garfield & A. Bergin (Eds.), *Handbook of psychotherapy and behavior change.* (pp. 903–938). New York: John Wiley & Sons.

Miranda, J., Bernal, G., Lau, A., Kohn, L., Hwang, W.-C., & LaFromboise, T. (2005). State of the science on psychosocial interventions for ethnic minorities. *Annual Review of Clinical Psychology, 1*(1): 113–142.

Orlinsky, D. E., Grawe, K., & Parks, B. K. (1994). Process and outcome in psychotherapy: Noch einmal. In A. E. Bergin & S. L. Garfield (Eds.), *Handbook of psychotherapy and behavior change* (4th ed., pp. 270–376). Oxford, UK: John Wiley & Sons.

Pilkonis, P. A., Imber, S. D., & Rubinsky, P. (1984). Influence of life events on outcome in psychotherapy. *Journal of Nervous & Mental Disease, 172*(8): 468–474.

Santisteban, D. A., Szapocznik, J., Perez-Vidal, A., Kurtines, W. M., Murray, E. J., & LaPerriere, A. (1996). Efficacy of intervention for engaging youth and families into treatment and some variables that may contribute to differential effectiveness. *Journal of Family Psychology, 10*(1): 35–44.

Srole, L. (1962). Midtown and several other populations. In L. Srole & T. S. Langner, *Mental health in the metropolis: The Midtown Manhattan Study* (pp. 127–156). New York: McGraw-Hill.

Srole, L. (1975). Measurement and classification in socio-psychiatric epidemiology: Midtown Manhattan Study (1954) and Midtown Manhattan Restudy II (1974). *Journal of Health and Social Behavior, 16*(4): 347–364.

Sue, S., Fujino, D. C., Hu, L.-T., & Takeuchi, D. T., (1991). Community mental health services for ethnic minority groups: A test of the cultural responsiveness hypothesis. *Journal of Consulting & Clinical Psychology, 59*(4): 533–540.

Sue, S., McKinney, H., Allen, D., & Hall, J. (1974). Delivery of community mental health services to black and white clients. *Journal of Consulting & Clinical Psychology, 42*(6): 794–801.

Szapocznik, J., Perez-Vidal, A., Brickman, A. L., & Foote, F. H. (1988). Engaging adolescent drug abusers and their families in treatment: A strategic structural systems approach. *Journal of Consulting & Clinical Psychology, 56*(4): 552–557.

Szapocznik, J., Rio, A., Murray, E., Cohen, R., Scopetta, M. A., & Rivas-Vasquez, A., et al. (1989). Structural family versus psychodynamic child therapy for problematic Hispanic boys. *Journal of Consulting & Clinical Psychology, 57*(5): 571–578.

Szapocznik, J., Robbins, M. S., Mitrani, V. B., Santisteban, D. A., Hervis, O., & Williams, R. A. (2002). Brief strategic family therapy. [References]. In F. W. Kaslow (Ed.), *Comprehensive handbook of psychotherapy: Integrative/eclectic* (vol. 4, pp. 83–109). New York: John Wiley & Sons.

Szapocznik, J., & Williams, R. A. (2000). Brief strategic family therapy: Twenty-five years of interplay among theory, research and practice in adolescent behavior problems and drug abuse. *Clinical Child & Family Psychology Review, 3*(2): 117–134.

Tolan, P. H., & McKay, M. M. (1996). Preventing serious antisocial behavior in inner-city children: An empirically based family intervention program. *Family Relations: Journal of Applied Family & Child Studies, 45*(2): 148–155.

12

ADDICTIONS TREATMENT: MYTH VS. REALITY

Many of the most exciting findings in psychotherapy research today center on the treatment of those with specific difficulties or disorders. This chapter focuses on two recent landmark reviews of the research on the treatment of those with substance use disorders that suggest many useful understandings about these difficulties and guidelines for treatment. Highlighting the role that research can play in showing how realities can differ from commonly held beliefs, several of these findings and guidelines contrast with long-held myths about how the treatment of those with substance use disorders is best conducted.

Substance abuse treatment used to bring to mind a no-holds-barred, in-your-face engagement, such as the notoriously confrontational groups of the 1970s and 1980s, often led by tough former addicts, or the Johnson intervention, in which family members and close friends came together to overwhelm the abuser's denial with stories of the harm done and to insist on treatment. It was widely accepted that the best therapists for addicts were former addicts. Many thought intense, confessional 12-step programs, such as Alcoholics Anonymous (AA), were necessary adjuncts to any treatment. Long-term inpatient treatment, which removes addicts from the stresses of everyday life, was considered the treatment of choice for those who could afford it, and still is even today.

Although treatment approaches to substance abuse have continued to evolve, a clear, new picture of what works in addiction treatment hasn't emerged. Clinicians and the public continue to rely on a hodgepodge of old and new approaches, unsure what works when. Fortunately, two recent landmark reviews of the research on adult substance abuse treatment give us a much more coherent picture of what the literature tells us about effective substance abuse treatment, Psychologist Rudolf Moos of the Department of Veterans Affairs and Stanford University, widely considered the dean of researchers in substance abuse disorders, prepared one summary of the research (Moos, 2003). A panel of experts in substance abuse treatment and psychotherapy research, including Peter Nathan of the University of Iowa, Barbara McCrady of Rutgers University, David Haaga of American University, and myself, assembled the second (McCrady, Haaga, & Lebow, 2006). This was part of a larger project to assess principles of change in treating a wide range of clinical problems (Beutler & Castonguay, 2006).

In the last decade, we have seen a prodigious expansion in research on the treatment of adult substance use disorders such as alcoholism and drug addiction. Although these treatments were once conducted primarily in anonymous self-help groups or in expensive inpatient programs, neither of which were much interested in the evaluation of treatment outcomes, the movement of treatment for these disorders into outpatient, day-treatment, and short-term inpatient programs has been accompanied by far greater attention to research on the effectiveness of treatment. The research on substance use disorders now includes many well-crafted studies and even a number of large multisite projects funded by the National Institute of Drug Abuse and the National Institute of Alcohol Abuse and Alcoholism.

For their reviews, the researchers combed through hundreds of studies to distinguish which assumptions about how to treat substance abuse disorders are supported by research and which are empirically unfounded. So what, then, do these reviews tell us about what's effective in the treatment of substance abuse disorders?

The core processes of change for overcoming substance abuse disorders are the same whether addicts participate in psychotherapy self-help programs, or recover without treatment. In each of these contexts, the chemically dependent individual typically builds a sense of hope, gains insight into the harmful nature of addiction, and learns how not only to control addiction but to live a better life. For instance, Tom, who wants to reduce his drinking on his own; Harry, who's in AA; and Steve, who's in outpatient therapy with a therapist who uses motivational interviewing, experience more or less the same process of change. Each was initially unwilling to acknowledge his problem with alcohol; each moved through a process of facing the detrimental effects of alcohol, learning more about its dangers, discovering ways to diminish his exposure to situations in which he was likely to drink, and figuring out ways to say "no" when offered drinks. Each was mired in negative cycles with their families around their alcohol use, and each received considerable support from family members when he stopped drinking. All three negotiated these processes that led to their successful recovery.

Not only are the processes of change the same across groups, so are the stages of change. The research summaries highlight the work by psychologists James Prochaska of the University of Rhode Island and Carlo DiClemente of the University of Maryland, Baltimore (Prochaska & DiClemente, 1986), identifying the predictable stages of change. Although research is beginning to show that stages of change apply in other disorders, most of the research has been done in substance abuse disorders.

In the first stage (precontemplation), addicts typically don't recognize their problems with substances. In the words of singer Tom Waits, "The piano has been drinking, not me." In the next stages, they recognize the problem, but aren't ready to change (contemplation), they take action to try to change (action), and finally they work to maintain the changes they've made (maintenance). Clients typically move back and forth among the stages during treatment. The most effective intervention strategies fit the client's stage of change: giving the client "homework" works best during the action stage, whereas psycho-education and insight therapy are appropriate in the precontemplation stage.

The stages of change point to the special role motivation has in treating clients with substance abuse disorders (Prochaska, DiClemente, & Norcross, 1997). The research reviews suggest that overcoming an addiction to substances requires greater motivation than do many problems. Motivation is important for another reason, too: in substance abuse disorders, clients are more often mandated into treatment by judges, employers, or family members than with most other problems, making motivation a key ingredient in treatment. All the therapies demonstrated to be effective for treating substance abuse either explicitly focus on increasing motivation (for example, William

Miller's Motivational Interviewing [Miller & Rollnick, 2002; Miller, Yahne, & Tonigan, 2003]) or indirectly raise motivation (as in 12-step programs).

Intense treatment of short duration is less successful than treatment that extends over time with little interruption. In a study of 20,000 Veterans Affairs (VA) patients, Moos and colleagues found that patients who received care over longer periods stayed sober longer and functioned better than those in treatment for a shorter period (Moos, Schaefer, Andrassy, & Moos, 2001). The powerful physiological, psychological, and interpersonal effects of addictive substances heighten the likelihood of regressing back into abuse. Longer, more continuous, treatments help overcome the enormous tendency to fall into recidivism.

In a survey of 3,000 VA patients treated for alcoholism, Moos and colleagues found that, no matter what the treatment, only about 20% maintained abstinence at a one-year follow-up (Moos et al., 2001). All the treatments that have been demonstrated to be effective in reducing substance abuse include a major focus on the maintenance of change. Programs that involve clients over long periods of time, such as AA (which finds a role for individuals in treatment even years after abuse has ended), are most effective.

Therapy relationship factors are crucial in treating substance abuse. The research strongly indicates that therapeutic alliances, whether between client and therapist or client and group, are potent curative factors in treatment. Substance abuse treatment requires the same strong relationships as any therapy issue. When clients and therapists form better alliances, clients more readily remain in treatment long enough for it to have an impact, and clients have better short- and long-term outcomes than when alliances are poor. Moos suggests that treatment settings and therapists who establish a strong therapeutic alliance, are oriented toward personal-growth goals, and work with a moderate level of structure achieve the best outcomes.

Contrary to stereotypes, high levels of confrontation seldom result in better treatment outcomes. William Miller and associates found that interventions that include listening and restructuring comments elicit positive response from clients, whereas highly confrontational interventions elicit argumentative responses (Meyers, Miller, Smith, & Tonigan, 2002). A similar pattern emerges over the long term. The multisite Drug Abuse Treatment Outcome Study of more than 2,500 clients found that clients' ratings of the rapport with their therapists were strongly related to their commitment to treatment (Kalman, Longabaugh, Clifford, Beattie, & Maisto, 2000; Longabaugh et al., 2005; Longabaugh, Wirtz, Beattie, Noel, & Stout, 1997). If clients trusted their therapists, they were more likely to engage in treatment in ways that promoted change. There's no evidence within the research on substance abuse that intense confrontation has positive effects (Moos, 2003). Furthermore, the research shows that substance abuse clients who also have personality disorders or anger management problems—those often thought of as most in need of a confrontational approach—respond particularly poorly to high levels of confrontation, frequently becoming oppositional or dropping out of treatment.

Research also shows that high levels of confrontation are *not* as effective in getting clients into treatment as are social support and a quiet, firm attitude toward the substance abuse. In a study comparing methods of engaging unmotivated alcohol abusers, a number of recent studies conducted by Timothy O'Farrell of Harvard Medical School and William Fals-Stewart of the University of New York at Buffalo and their colleagues show positive outcomes when family members are helped to focus on constructive ways to help engage the substance abuser into treatment (Fals-Stewart & Birchler, 2002; Fals-Stewart et al., 2000). And William Miller and his colleagues found that supportive partners who positively reinforced not drinking, increased positive communication, engaged in interests outside the relationship, and encouraged professional treatment had greater positive impact on engagement than the highly confrontational Johnson intervention (Miller, Meyers, & Tonigan, 1999). Whereas only 22% of alcoholics engaged in treatment after the Johnson intervention, 64% engaged with the form approach.

Social support is critical to overcoming addiction and maintaining change. Addicts with supportive social networks, including family members, are more likely to achieve success. Their success is monumentally affected by those around them. According to Moos, "Formal treatment can be a compelling force for change. But it typically has only an ephemeral influence. In contrast, relatively stable factors in peoples' lives, such as informal help and reliable social resources, tend to play a more enduring role" (Rudolf Moos, personal communication, 2003). In therapy, this translates into helping family and friends actively support the changes occurring, through participation in self-help groups as an adjunct to therapy and by helping clients find new support networks that don't support the substance abuse.

Engage and work with family members as a first step in the change process when clients are unmotivated or resist entering treatment. The research strongly indicates that this is a highly effective way to engage those with substance use disorders in treatment when they are initially not ready to enter treatment. Fals-Stewart, O'Farrell, and their colleagues find that initial work that helps spouses to achieve personal differentiation from the substance use and as a support for the person with the substance problem seeking help is especially helpful (Fals-Stewart & Birchler, 2002). Often, the route to successful engagement and treatment begins with family members rather than the person with the substance use problem. O'Farrell and Fals-Stewart also have demonstrated that couples therapy in substance abuse cases achieves better outcomes with the abuse and improves marital satisfaction (Fals-Stewart et al., 2000).

Therapists with a personal history of overcoming substance abuse are no more effective than those without such a history. Both groups fared equally well across the treatment studies. However, research does show that patients treated by those with a clear background in treating addictions have better outcomes than those treated by nonspecialists. For example, in Moos' study of 20,000 patients with substance use disorders, those treated by specialists had longer and more comprehensive care and better outcomes.

No one substance abuse treatment is more successful than others. Among the effective treatments identified by the research review are motivational enhancement therapies, cognitive behavioral treatment, and the 12-step treatments based on the philosophy of AA. Effective treatments are directive and active, provide insight into the harmful nature of addiction, help build life skills, and strengthen important relationships. The research shows 12-step programs to be effective, but no more so than other directive approaches to treatment, such as motivational interviewing. We have yet to see a nondirective treatment shown to be effective.

Perhaps the most important message from these two research reviews is that the general principles of effective therapy still apply for substance abuse disorders. When we encounter therapies that rely on radically different principles of change, we need to remain skeptical until they're demonstrated to be effective, no matter how charismatic the treatment proponents.

RESOURCES

Beutler, L., & Castonguay, L. (Eds.). (2006). *Principles of therapeutic change that work*. New York: Oxford University Press.

Moos, R. H. (2003). Addictive disorders in context: Principles and puzzles of effective treatment and recovery. *Psychology of Addictive Behaviors, 17*(1): 3–12.

REFERENCES

Beutler, L., & Castonguay, L. (Eds.). (2006). *Principles of therapeutic change that work.* New York: Oxford University Press.

Fals-Stewart, W., & Birchler, G. R. (2002). Behavioral couples therapy with alcoholic men and their intimate partners: The comparative effectiveness of bachelor's- and master's-level counselors. *Behavior Therapy, 33*(1): 123–147.

Fals-Stewart, W., O'Farrell, T. J., Feehan, M., Birchler, G. R., Tiller, S., & McFarlin, S. K. (2000). Behavioral couples therapy versus individual-based treatment for male substance-abusing patients: An evaluation of significant individual change and comparison of improvement rates. *Journal of Substance Abuse Treatment, 18*(3): 249–254.

Kalman, D., Longabaugh, R., Clifford, P. R., Beattie, M., & Maisto, S. A. (2000). Matching alcoholics to treatment: Failure to replicate finding of an earlier study. *Journal of Substance Abuse Treatment, 19*(2): 183–187.

Longabaugh, R., Donovan, D. M., Karno, M. P., McCrady, B. S., Morgenstern, J., & Tonigan, J. (2005). Active ingredients: How and why evidence-based alcohol behavioral treatment interventions work. *Alcoholism: Clinical and Experimental Research, 29*(2): 235–247.

Longabaugh, R., Wirtz, P. W., Beattie, M. C., Noel, N., & Stout, R. (1997). Matching treatment focus to patient social investment and support: 18-month follow-up results. [References]. In G. Marlatt & G. R. VandenBos (Eds.), *Addictive behaviors: Readings on etiology, prevention, and treatment* (pp. 602–628). Washington, DC: American Psychological Association.

McCrady, B, Haaga, D., & Lebow, J. (2006) Integration of therapuetic factors in treating substance abuse. In L. Beutler & L. Castonguay (Eds.). *Principles of therapeutic change that work* (pp.341-52). New York: Oxford University Press.

Meyers, R. J., Miller, W. R., Smith, J. E., & Tonigan, J. (2002). A randomized trial of two methods for engaging treatment-refusing drug users through concerned significant others. *Journal of Consulting & Clinical Psychology, 70*(5): 1182–1185.

Miller, W. R., Meyers, R. J., & Tonigan, J. (1999). Engaging the unmotivated in treatment for alcohol problems: A comparison of three strategies for intervention through family members. *Journal of Consulting & Clinical Psychology, 67*(5): 688–697.

Miller, W. R., & Rollnick, S. (2002). *Motivational interviewing: Preparing people for change* (2nd ed.). New York: Guilford Press.

Miller, W. R., Yahne, C. E., & Tonigan, J. (2003). Motivational interviewing in drug abuse services: A randomized trial. *Journal of Consulting & Clinical Psychology, 71*(4): 754–763.

Moos, R. H. (2003). Addictive disorders in context: Principles and puzzles of effective treatment and recovery. *Psychology of Addictive Behaviors, 17*(1): 3–12.

Moos, R., Schaefer, J., Andrassy, J., & Moos, B. (2001). Outpatient mental health care, self-help groups, and patients' one-year treatment outcomes. *Journal of Clinical Psychology, 57*(3): 273–287.

Prochaska, J. O., & DiClemente, C. C. (1986). Toward a comprehensive model of change. In W. R. Miller & N. Heather (Eds.), *Treating addictive behaviors: Processes of change* (pp. 3–27). New York: Plenum Press.

Prochaska, J. O., DiClemente, C. C., & Norcross, J. C. (1997). In search of how people change: Applications to addictive behaviors. [References]. In G. Marlatt & G. R. VandenBos (Eds.), *Addictive behaviors: Readings on etiology, prevention, and treatment* (pp. 671–696). Washington, DC: American Psychological Association.

13

WAR OF THE WORLDS: RESEARCHERS AND PRACTITIONERS COLLIDE ON EYE MOVEMENT DESENSITIZATION AND REPROCESSING (EMDR) AND CRITICAL INCIDENT STRESS DEBRIEFING (CISD)

The clash between researchers and clinicians often is greatest over the utility of new, quite distinct treatments. Treatment developers and practitioners who are early adopters of these treatments typically find these treatments especially effective, whereas researchers tend to be conservative and look for evidence of special effectiveness. This chapter examines the hotly debated conflict that has recently emerged about the impact of two such recently developed treatments: eye movement desensitization and reprocessing (EMDR) and critical incident stress debriefing (CISD).

Nowhere is the gap between researchers and clinicians more evident than in the debate about EMDR and CISD. Researchers have rarely made such a point of singling out treatments for exaggerated claims about their effectiveness as they have with EMDR and CISD. The radically contrasting positions of the enthusiastic clinicians who use these methods for treating posttraumatic effects and the skeptical researchers who evaluate them has led to acrimonious debates in academic journals, Internet chat rooms, and even the *New York Times Magazine*.

Both EMDR and CISD have received an unusual degree of attention from researchers. Little research has been done on the effectiveness of most widely practiced treatments with the exception of cognitive-behavioral therapies, yet researchers have rarely taken aim on treatments unsupported by formal empirical findings and made such a point of singling them out for being ineffective or having deleterious effects. CISD and EMDR, however, have been repeatedly directly attacked by researchers, who claim that these treatments don't work, are basically placebos, or are actually harmful. This remains the case despite the fact that there is more research assessing these treatments than there is about most recently developed therapies (and even many much older ones); research that has been most often initiated by the developers of these treatments.

CISD was developed in the late 1980s by Jeffrey Mitchell, clinical associate professor in the Department of Emergency Health Services at the University of Maryland (Mitchell & Everly, 2000). A highly structured intervention aimed at preventing later symptoms of posttraumatic stress disorder (PTSD) among people who recently experienced trauma, CISD evolved out of Mitchell's experience in fire and emergency medical services. Conducted in a group format 2 to 14 days after a traumatic event, CISD was designed to reduce the long-term emotional fallout among people exposed to trauma by offering an opportunity to verbally process their experiences. During the past 10 years, CISD has been widely used, partly because of growing public concern about trauma, but also because of the simplicity of the method, which can be learned in only a few training sessions. "Debriefing has become a sort of specialized sequitur to the crisis hotline movement of the '70s" (Richard Gist, personal communication, 2003), explains trauma expert Richard Gist of the University of Missouri at Kansas City. Such respected groups as the Red Cross, the Salvation Army, and the National Organization for Victim Assistance use CISD, as do many trauma teams sent to the scenes of natural disasters and accidents.

Despite its widespread application, considerable research indicates that those who receive CISD typically do no better than those who don't, and that a significant number of people treated with CISD do even worse than those who didn't receive any treatment (Gist & Devilly, 2002; Lilienfeld, Lynn, & Lohr, 2003; Lohr, Hooke, Gist, & Tolin,

2003). This negative reaction seems to emerge because, for some people, the very act of focusing on their negative feelings in CISD increases their distress and leads to more difficulties, such as flashbacks, nightmares, and anxiety attacks. According to Gist, "Not only did CISD not deliver much in the way of preventive efficacy, it seemed to inhibit natural resolution for some" (Richard Gist, personal communication, 2003). The Cochrane Collaboration of Great Britain, one of the most prominent gatekeepers in medicine, charged with assessing the effectiveness of procedures ranging from open heart surgery to psychotherapy for depression, evaluated CISD and found it to be without empirical support.

Nevertheless, proponents of CISD remain convinced of its value and continue to promote it. According to George Everly, Mitchell's most frequent collaborator, the critics of CISD have paid disproportionate attention to efficacy trials, in which treatments are studied under controlled conditions, and not enough attention to effectiveness studies, which assess treatments under conditions more typical of ordinary practice. Furthermore, Everly argues, researchers have ignored a crucial feature of CISD—it's a group method, but researchers have been assessing its impact when delivered individually.

Yet there's no avoiding the hard fact that research up to this point indicates that CISD has little positive impact, or at least much less impact than most treatments and leads to deterioration in more clients than other treatments. Gist argues that the wide acceptance of CISD is a prime example of what is called the "Barnum effect": after a treatment seems like a good thing to do, clients tell each other it helped and tend to say they feel better, whether it actually works or not. Because, regardless of the treatment, rates of client satisfaction generally average about 90%, researchers often emphasize that client satisfaction isn't closely related to more rigorously measured treatment outcome. Concludes Gist, "If CISD were a drug, we'd take it off the market" (Richard Gist, personal communication, 2003).

THE FUROR OVER EMDR

The controversy over EMDR is, if anything, even more rancorous than the CISD debate. Introduced by psychologist Francine Shapiro in 1989, EMDR claims to resolve traumatic memories, desensitize stimuli that trigger distress, and teach adaptive coping skills (Shapiro, 2001, 2002b). During EMDR, the therapist guides the client to think about traumatic experiences while engaging the client in some form of bilateral stimulation of the nervous system. Classically, the therapist moves a finger back and forth in front of the client's eyes, although more recently, other forms of stimulation, such as knee tapping or alternating sounds, have replaced the eye movements.

After each set of eye movements, the client rates his or her level of distress and the procedure is repeated until the level of distress is reduced. Shapiro believes that this process of "dual attention" is crucial to EMDR, altering the client's neural pathways and assisting the processing of traumatic memories by the brain. At the same time, EMDR incorporates a variety of other interventions that are typical of cognitive-behavioral and psychodynamic treatments, such as exposure to feared stimuli and the development of more adaptive cognitions regarding the traumatic incident.

Proponents of EMDR point to a growing body of empirical support for its clinical effectiveness. For example, in the January 2002 *Journal of Clinical Psychology*, devoted to research about EMDR, Shapiro asserts that 13 randomized clinical trials have demonstrated its efficacy (Shapiro, 2002a). The American Psychological Association's Division of Clinical Psychology's task force on the Promotion and Dissemination of Psychological Procedures rated EMDR as "probably efficacious" for treating PTSD (Chambless & Ollendick, 2001). But Harvard psychologist and leading EMDR critic Richard McNally (1999), author of *Remembering Trauma*, insists that much of the research in support of EMDR was poorly designed and that the more methodologically superior research indicates that it has less impact than its supporters maintain. EMDR has the dubious distinction of making it onto both researcher Scott Lilienfeld's list of treatments based on pseudoscience (Lilienfeld et al., 2003) and Scott Miller and Mark Hubble's Baloney Watch (http://www.talkingcure.com/baloney.asp?id=97), two efforts that target treatments with exaggerated claims of effectiveness. Researchers also strongly argue that the theories offered by Shapiro and other proponents of EMDR about how the eye movements affect clients at a physiological level are pseudoscience.

Unlike the skeptics about CISD, however, even EMDR's critics concede that it has some clinical impact. What they question is whether it offers anything beyond the more established PTSD treatments. As McNally writes, "Despite repeated attempts, researchers have been unable to obtain any convincing evidence that the defining element of EMDR—eye movement—possesses any therapeutic powers. What is effective in EMDR is not new, and what is new is not effective" (Richard McNally, personal communication, 2003). Others argue that EMDR has little impact beyond the simple relaxation and exposure to traumatic memories invoked during treatment—key elements of numerous other treatments (Lohr et al., 2003). McNally says, "EMDR 'works' in the same way that pink aspirin works. Pink aspirin will certainly relieve headaches. But its efficacy will be due to its analgesic properties, not to the pink food dye" (Richard McNally, personal communication, 2003).

In response, Francine Shapiro argues that much of the research does, in fact, strongly affirm the efficacy of EMDR. But some researchers have left out key components of EMDR, such as some of the cognitive components and free association, ignoring the fact that the treatment doesn't work as well without all of its elements. In effect, such research, she believes, isn't a fair test of EMDR, only of a truncated version of it. She concedes that the research that has compared EMDR with simple exposure methods has typically found equivalent effects, but says that these studies also show that EMDR works more efficiently, showing effects in fewer treatments. She attributes much of the bad press that EMDR has received to attacks from "a small group of prolific coauthors," adding that "their many negative articles have contained a great deal of misinformation, at times even to the point of misreporting data" (Francine Shapiro, personal communication, 2003).

She points to support for the impact of bilateral stimulation among neuropsychologists, including the idea that EMDR has an effect on neural pathways. She also calls attention to the support EMDR has received from a diverse range of well-known therapists, including Bessel van der Kolk, Paul Wachtel, Susan Johnson, and Laura Brown. Psychologist John Norcross of the University of Scranton points to two recent meta-analyses of the clinical research on EMDR that indicate that EMDR and exposure therapies are the most effective therapies for PTSD (Norcross & Shapiro, 2002). He notes that EMDR achieves its effects in fewer sessions than traditional behavior therapies. Summarizing the debate, he concludes,

> Although EMDR has been subjected to 18 or so controlled studies and several meta-analysis, most psychotherapy researchers continue to neglect or outright dismiss its positive outcome data. I believe EMDR is the 'treatment of choice' for PTSD because it is equally as effective as cognitive-behavioral therapy and exposure treatment, and because it does so more rapidly and probably with less client pain. (John Norcross, personal communication, 2003).

LESSONS LEARNED

So what's gone wrong with well meaning efforts that might have been hoped to improve clinical practice and lead to researcher/practitioner collaboration? What accounts for the level of antipathy between researchers and the clinicians who practice these approaches? The key factors appear to include:

- The bold claims made by the developers of these treatments about their impact. These treatments have been touted as breakthrough methods that can change how trauma is experienced.
- The wide dissemination of the treatments among therapists and agencies before the effectiveness of these treatments was tested. The aggressive marketing of these approaches has engendered a strong response. McNally suggests, "Certain EMDR advocates are gifted therapeutic entrepreneurs whose claims and promotional methods have raised eyebrows in the clinical science community. With few exceptions, our field has seldom seen such talents. But extraordinary clinical claims provoke extraordinary scientific scrutiny" (Richard McNally, personal communication, 2003).
- The availability of several research studies that have directly challenged the claims of the proponents of these approaches about their effectiveness and how and when these treatments do have an impact. Such studies are typically not so readily available to challenge a treatment.
- The defensive stance that the proponents of these approaches have assumed in relation to the challenging data, suggesting that these studies are not relevant or must simply be wrong.
- The confrontational language on the part of researchers that has followed the failure of the proponents of these approaches to acknowledge the strength of the findings. Researchers view the proponents of CISD and EMDR as stepping outside of the path of science.
- The very significant financial repercussions for the developers, programs, trainers, and providers who offer these methods if the research data were truly digested. Follow the money. By the same token, researchers who spend a lifetime developing and testing small variations on a treatment see the proponents of these treatments as receiving a great deal of attention and banking the gains that come with it.

Aside from the particulars of the debate about EMDR and CISD, what can we learn from the controversy about creating a more productive relationship between researchers and practitioners? First of all, it must be noted that the proponents of EMDR and CISD have been willing to submit their methods to empirical testing and have thereby run the risk of being "outed" as ineffective, or at least effective for the wrong reasons. Advocates of numerous other approaches as diverse as Jungian therapy, Bowenian therapy, and bioenergetic therapies have yet to make such a commitment to outcome research. Likewise, the researchers involved in this debate have engaged in the rare act of extending beyond the study of their favorite, more easily researched, cognitive-behavioral methods. The efforts and energy brought to this debate by both sides underlines the importance of data that tests the impact of treatment approaches. Where the debate seems to have run aground is in the level of invective and lack of meaningful exchange between the treatment developers and the researcher critics.

If, in this age of clinical accountability, therapy is to maintain its pivotal connection with the scientific tradition of empirical evidence, we practitioners need to become good consumers of research data on treatment models. Most of the problems dealt with in psychotherapy are complex, and we've seen many new approaches make claims of great success only to find that the success was much less evident when the approaches were tested with a wider range of people and over a longer time. Most therapies (and for that matter psychopharmacology) do have a substantial impact, but rarely do treatments end all problems, nor do the solutions last forever (Lambert & Bergin, 1994).

Sometimes, treatments developed for good reasons and offered in a well-meaning way work only to a limited degree—or not at all. Highly stimulating treatments for schizophrenics and their families that raise levels of expressed emotion, once popular on the workshop circuit, and group therapies aimed at acting-out adolescents, which have increasingly proven to be iatrogenic sources for the learning of deviant behaviors, both fall into that category (Dishion & Dodge, 2005; McFarlane & Beels, 1988; McFarlane, Dixon, Lukens, & Lucksted, 2002; Sprenkle, 2002). Therapies that cannot be demonstrated to help must ultimately be replaced by therapies that can be shown to have a greater impact.

The major lesson for researchers in the debates about EMDR and CISD lies in understanding the mindset and working context of clinicians, so they can better communicate their findings to those who should be their primary audience. In their zeal to challenge what they see as overstated claims, researchers need to better understand what makes certain approaches engaging for both clinicians and clients. Conclusions that researchers who aren't based in clinical settings offer about treatments explored only in the rarefied environment of grant-supported research are unlikely to convince practitioners. As Joan Cook and Jim Coyne of the University of Pennsylvania Medical School put it,

> To the envy and dismay of its critics, EMDR has been enthusiastically received by many frontline practitioners. Critics would do well to think long and hard about just why clinicians have so readily seized upon EMDR and integrated it into routine treatment. Certainly we have not seen the same excitement for conventional exposure therapies, despite all the scientific evidence supporting their effectiveness. (Joan Cook & James Coyne, personal communication, 2003).

A model for a more productive approach has been the research on emotion-focused therapy (EFT) conducted by Les Greenberg, Susan Johnson, and their colleagues during the past two decades (Greenberg, 2002; Johnson, 2003). At one time, researchers were so disdainful of experiential methods such as EFT that these methods were used as the control group in research to test the impact of "real" interventions. Nevertheless, Greenberg and Johnson's research has not only established the value of their treatment, but has even led to the incorporation of some of their interventions into some cognitive-behavioral therapies. They built their hypothesis slowly, studying the method and producing research articles before making any claims for its effectiveness. By the time they went public with their research, they had a solid base of controlled studies for establishing the treatment's clinical bona fides. Family therapies have gone through a similar process of testing, honing their methods and only then gaining acceptance among researchers. With EMDR and CISD, however, widespread clinical application and overblown claims came first, way before studies were even attempted.

The experience of these two approaches clearly suggests that, whereas it may command less initial attention, a collaborative relationship between researchers, treatment developers, and practitioners is far more helpful in moving knowledge forward and improving our methods of practice than is mutual distrust and acrimonious debate.

RESOURCES

EMDR: Preliminary investigations and new directions. *Journal of Clinical Psychology* 58(2002): 1451–1531.

Herbert, J. D., Lilienfeld, S. O., Lohr, J. M., Montgomery, R. W., O'Donohue, W. T., Rosen, G. M., & Tolin, D. F. (2000). Science and pseudoscience in the development of eye movement desensitization and reprocessing: Implications for clinical psychology. *Clinical Psychology Review 20*(8): 945–971.

Lohr, J. M., Hooke, W., Gist, R., & Tolin, D. F. (2003). Novel and controversial treatments for trauma-related stress disorders. [References]. In S. O. Lilienfeld, S. J. Lynn, & J. Lohr (Eds.). *Science and pseudoscience in clinical psychology* (pp. 243–272). New York: Guilford Press.

Shapiro, F. (2002). EMDR 12 years after its introduction: Past and future research. *Journal of Clinical Psychology, 58*(1): 1–22.

REFERENCES

Chambless, D. L., & Ollendick, T. H. (2001). Empirically supported psychological interventions: Controversies and evidence. *Annual Review of Psychology, 52*: 685–716.

Dishion, T. J., & Dodge, K. A. (2005). Peer contagion in interventions for children and adolescents: Moving towards an understanding of the ecology and dynamics of change. *Journal of Abnormal Child Psychology, 33*(3): 395–400.

Gist, R., & Devilly, G. J. (2002). Post-trauma debriefing: The road too frequently traveled. *Lancet, 360*(9335): 741–742.

Greenberg, L. S. (2002). *Emotion-focused therapy: Coaching clients to work through their feelings.* Washington, DC: American Psychological Association.

Johnson, S. M. (2003). Emotionally Focused Couples Therapy: Empiricism and art. [References]. In T. L. Sexton, G. R. Weeks, & M. Robbins (Eds.), *Handbook of family therapy: The science and practice of working with families and couples* (pp. 263–280). New York: Brunner-Routledge.

Lambert, M. J., & Bergin, A. E. (1994). The effectiveness of psychotherapy. In A. E. Bergin & S. L. Garfield (Eds.), *Handbook of psychotherapy and behavior change* (4th ed., pp. 143–189). Oxford, UK: John Wiley & Sons.

Lilienfeld, S. O., Lynn, S. J., & Lohr, J. M. (Eds.). (2003). *Science and pseudoscience in clinical psychology.* New York: Guilford Press.

Lohr, J. M., Hooke, W., Gist, R., & Tolin, D. F. (2003). Novel and controversial treatments for trauma-related stress disorders. [References]. In S. O. Lilienfeld, S. J. Lynn, & J. Lohr (Eds.). *Science and pseudoscience in clinical psychology* (pp. 243–272). New York: Guilford Press.

McFarlane, W. R., & Beels, C. (1988). The family and schizophrenia: Perspectives from contemporary research. In E. W. Nunnally, C. S. Chilman, & F. M. Cox (Eds.), *Mental illness, delinquency, addictions, and neglect: Families in trouble series* (vol. 4, pp. 17–38). Thousand Oaks, CA: Sage Publications.

McFarlane, W. R., Dixon, L., Lukens, E., & Lucksted, A. (2002). Severe mental illness. [References]. In D. H. Sprenkle (Ed.), *Effectiveness research in marriage and family therapy* (pp. 255–288). Alexandria, VA: American Association for Marriage and Family Therapy.

McNally, R. J. (1999). EMDR and mesmerism: A comparative historical analysis. *Journal of Anxiety Disorders, 13*(1–2): 225–236.

Mitchell, J. T., & Everly, G. S., Jr. (2000). Critical incident stress management and critical incident stress debriefings: Evolutions, effects and outcomes. In B. Raphael & J. P. Wilson (Eds.), *Psychological debriefing: Theory, practice and evidence* (pp. 71–90). New York: Cambridge University Press.

Norcross, J. C., & Shapiro, F. (2002). Integration and EMDR. [References]. In F. Shapiro (Ed.), *EMDR as an integrative psychotherapy approach: Experts of diverse orientations explore the paradigm prism* (pp. 341–356). Washington, DC: American Psychological Association.

Shapiro, F. (2001). *Eye movement desensitization and reprocessing: Basic principles, protocols, and procedures* (2nd ed.). New York: Guilford Press.

Shapiro, F. (2002a). EMDR 12 years after its introduction: Past and future research. *Journal of Clinical Psychology, 58*(1): 1–22.

Shapiro, F. (2002b). EMDR treatment: Overview and integration. [References]. In F. Shapiro (Ed.), *EMDR as an integrative psychotherapy approach: Experts of diverse orientations explore the paradigm prism* (pp. 27–55). Washington, DC: American Psychological Association.

Sprenkle, D. H. (Ed.). (2002). *Effectiveness research in marriage and family therapy*. Alexandria, VA: American Association for Marriage and Family Therapy.

14

REASSESSING SELECTIVE SEROTONIN REUPTAKE INHIBITORS: SEPARATING HYPE FROM FACT ABOUT ANTIDEPRESSANTS

Arguments about the efficacy of treatments sometimes play out in the marketplace as much as in clinical research and practice. Selective serotonin reuptake inhibitors (SSRIs) have been heavily marketed with extraordinary claims for effectiveness in treating all forms of depression. This chapter looks at the evidence for the impact of SSRIs compared with the evidence for the impact of psychotherapy. The findings discussed provide an example of how research can sometimes point to conclusions that widely differ from popular conceptions.

For the last decade, there's been a spectacularly successful advertising campaign to convince the public that the SSRIs, including Prozac, Zoloft, Celexa, Lexapro, Luvox, and Paxil, have revolutionized the treatment of depression. In response, antidepressant use has doubled and requests for antidepressant treatment have tripled in the last 10 years. Today, 74% of those seeking help with depression in the United States are treated with medication. Incredibly, 28 million Americans have taken an SSRI, including 500,000 children. A full 10% of the elderly now receive antidepressants at any point in time. Researcher James Coyne of the University of Pennsylvania has pointed out that more people fill prescriptions each year for antidepressants than research indicates fit the diagnosis of depression, suggesting the widespread use of these medications for other conditions, even though these uses remain wholly untested (Coyne, Thompson, Palmer, Kagee, & Maunsell, 2000).

Meanwhile, the remarkable growth in use of the SSRIs has paralleled a significant decrease in the use of psychotherapy to treat depression. The proportion of those being treated for major depressive disorder or dysthymic disorder with psychotherapy declined from 71% to 60% over a recent 10-year period.

DEPRESSION AS A DIAGNOSIS

Before exploring the impact of various treatments on depression, it is essential to understand the context for this research. There has been no testing of the impact of medications on the feelings such as sadness, upset, or irritation in the general population. All uses of medication to ameliorate such feelings extend beyond the purposes for which these medications were created and are without any research demonstrating an impact. Antidepressant medications have been tested only in relation to their effect on individuals who meet the criteria for the specific *Diagnostic and Statistical Manual–IV* diagnoses for depression, the conditions they were developed to treat.

The research on depression that we are considering focuses on the treatment of the two principal syndromes in which signs of depression predominate: major depressive disorder and dysthymic disorder. Both of these syndromes feature the presence of such symptoms as depressed mood, diminished pleasure, poor appetite, low energy, low self-esteem, and feelings of hopelessness (and the absence of manic symptoms that would result in a diagnosis of bipolar disorder). Major depressive disorder tends to be more acute and severe, whereas dysthymic disorder tends to be less intense and extend over a longer period. Individuals diagnosed with either syndrome experience something well beyond just feeling sad or reacting to an acute loss.

THE IMPACT OF SSRIs

Do these pills work as advertised for most people? SSRIs have fewer side effects than older generations of antidepressants (the tricyclics), and overdoses tend not to be lethal, making them safer for physicians to prescribe. However, the research provides little support for the notion that these drugs are a breakthrough in the treatment of depression. The key findings of the latest research ("Depressing Research," 2004; Whittington et al., 2004; Wilson & Mottram, 2004) indicate that:

- SSRIs are *no more effective* than the older tricyclic antidepressants, such as Elavil or Tofranil, which have been around for decades. For example, a meta-analysis by several researchers at the Evidence-Based Practice Center at the University of Texas at San Antonio found that the SSRIs help 63% of patients, compared to 60% for tricyclics. So, whereas SSRIs may have fewer side effects, they're no more effective than older generations of drugs, and they're more expensive.
- The impact of SSRIs on depression in children and adolescents is minimal. Recent surveys of treatment research indicate impact no better than placebo.
- Taking SSRIs increases the risk of suicide and suicidal ideation, especially in children and adolescents. Rates of suicidal ideation have been as high as 9% in a trial of Lustral, an SSRI manufactured by Pfizer. This rate is much higher than the rate of suicidal ideation among subjects receiving a placebo.
- Although lacking the side effects of the tricyclics, SSRIs often result in loss of libido, a side effect found in as much as 70% of those taking these medications. Many find this so distressing they discontinue use.
- SSRIs often lead to intense anxiety, lethargy, and distress when medication is discontinued. There's increasing evidence of at least a psychological dependency on these medications, which leads to considerable discomfort when clients stop taking them. This, in turn, makes discontinuing these medications more difficult.

Despite this research, the general public continues to overestimate the effects of the SSRIs. Because the pharmaceutical industry not only spends millions of dollars in advertising, but also funds much of the research on their products, it can largely control the flow of information to the public, which remains unaware of research findings. The *New York Times* recently reported Forest Laboratories' failure to release research showing low levels of impact on children and adolescents for its SSRI Celexa. Under pressure, Forest then released data from a study showing a similar lack of impact for Lexapro, another Forest antidepressant, in children and adolescents. The data demonstrating the small impact and increased risk in children for all SSRIs recently led to a decision by Great Britain's Medicine and Health Care Products Regulatory Agency to warn against prescribing SSRIs for depressed children and adolescents.

Nevertheless, the combined results of all the studies on adults treated with SSRIs do indicate that, though these aren't "wonder drugs," they do help the majority of adult clients with major depressive disorder or dysthymic disorder. Therefore, many professionals and organizations, including the American Psychiatric Association and the American College of Neuropsychopharmacology, argue strongly for the efficacy of SSRIs.

SSRIs VS. PSYCHOTHERAPY

To put the effectiveness of SSRIs into perspective, it's also helpful to compare research on SSRIs with studies of psychotherapy as a treatment for depression. Several forms of brief therapy have been shown to have effects comparable to the SSRIs. The best-established treatment is Cognitive Therapy for Depression (Beck & Young, 1985), a therapy developed by psychiatrist Aaron Beck of the University of Pennsylvania, which focuses on challenging the accuracy of depressive thoughts and building a more optimistic worldview.

Considerable evidence also supports the success of Interpersonal Therapy for Depression (Klerman, Weissman, Rounsaville, & Chevron, 1996), a form of psychodynamic therapy developed by psychiatrist Gerald Klerman and psychologist Myrna Weissman. Behavioral approaches, centered on helping clients become more activated through self-monitoring, scheduling, and self-reward—such as the approach developed by University of Oregon psychologist Peter Lewinsohn (Lewinsohn, Clarke, & Hoberman, 1989)—have also proven effective. Research indicates that approximately 80% of depressed clients are typically helped by each of these therapies, without the side effects and increased risks that accompany medication.

Few studies have directly compared medication and psychotherapy. Such research is expensive and risky for both sides of the controversy. The best known comparative study is the National Institute of Mental Health Treatment of Depression Collaborative Research Program (TDCRP), conducted in the 1980s by psychologist Irene Elkin, now a professor at the University of Chicago (Elkin, 1994; Elkin, Gibbons,

Shea, & Sotsky, 1995; Elkin, Shea, Watkins, & Imber, 1989; Elkin, Parloff, Hadley, & Autry, 1985). This study compared short-term cognitive therapy, interpersonal therapy, and tricyclic medication. The research found all the treatments had comparable impact and concluded that medication and short-term psychotherapy worked equally well in treating dysthymia and depression.

However, the study used many measures and numerous ways of analyzing the sample of clients, leaving a wide range of possible interpretations of the results. Some prominent psychopharmacologists, including psychiatrist Donald Klein (1996, 1999; Klein & Ross, 1993), argue the study supports the superiority of medication, particularly in those with more severe depression. Proponents of psychotherapy, among them Robert DeRubeis of the University of Pennsylvania, rebut that conclusion (DeRubeis & Gelfand, 2000). What's most striking in the TDCRP is that the treatments were comparable in their effectiveness, and even the placebo group improved. Another factor to consider is that the time frame for treatment in these research studies—16 sessions—is more conducive to medication trials than to psychotherapy. The impact of psychotherapy is all the more impressive then, given that clients might still be in early stages of therapy treatment at the study's conclusion.

DEPRESSION AND RELATIONSHIPS

Recent studies of the treatment of depression have also suggested a special place for couple therapy. Typically, one-half to two-thirds of depressed individuals who are married also have distressed intimate relationships, pointing to these relationships as an obvious target for intervention. Two major studies have found couple therapy to have an impact comparable with individual therapy on depression, with the impact especially marked for those who are in distressed relationships (Jacobson, Dobson, Fruzzetti, Schmaling, & Salusky 1991; O'Leary & Beach, 1990). And in these studies, only the couple therapy improves the distressed relationships. Based in these findings, psychologists Maya Gupta, James Coyne, and Steven Beach (Gupta, Coyne, & Beach, 2003) have suggested that for many people with depression what may be needed may be a new kind of couple therapy: one that deals with the difficulty of involving partners of depressed clients in therapy and possibly that does not depend on the participation of both partners.

CHRONIC DEPRESSION

Another research finding not generally publicized is the fact that a substantial number of depressed clients in these studies (20%–30%) don't improve, no matter what treatment they receive. And among those who do improve, there are high rates of recurrence. The risk of repeated episodes of depression exceeds 85% over a period of 10–15 years. Individuals who have one episode of major depressive disorder typically experience four major episodes of approximately 20 weeks' duration during their lifetime, in addition to other symptoms of depression, such as intense sadness and low energy, during the periods of remission (Westen, Novotny, & Thompson-Brenner, 2004)

Although some therapists and researchers think these findings about treatment failure suggest a need for better medications and more effective short-term psychotherapies, this ignores the data on the nature of depression itself. Others argue that high incidence of recurrence may simply be a risk of depression and that no treatment may fully eradicate the problem. In a landmark research study examining depressive symptoms over time, James Coyne and his colleagues Michael Klinkman and Thomas Schwenck found the patterns in depression to be more like chronic disorders, such as asthma, than like acute disorders that are amenable to targeted interventions, such as appendicitis (Coyne, Thompson, Klinkman, & Nease, 2002). Coyne and colleagues suggest depression is a chronic condition and that effective intervention should focus on the factors that bring on and intensify depression, much like the lifelong treatment of diabetes. However, the acute-disorder model is the one driving most psychopharmacological intervention for depression today.

CONCLUSION

Based on the recent research on the treatment of depression, it's clear that the health care establishment, the general population, and mental health providers need to broaden their view of depression and its treatment. This won't be easy, because short-term decisions provide immediate gratification. To the depressed client, taking a pill to feel better soon is easier than engaging in therapy. To the health care system, dispensing pills is cheaper, faster, and more profitable than therapy. What's missing from these approaches is the recognition of the long-term psychological and economical consequences of these short-term solutions. From a financial standpoint, the cost of taking an antidepressant over a lifetime is much greater than the cost of psychotherapy offered as needed to fit the ecology of depression. When the psychological benefits that result only from therapy, such as increased emotional maturity, improved relationships, and greater life skills, are added to the equation, the value of medication to the depressed patient and to society pales in comparison with the efficacy of psychotherapy.

The research on the treatment of depression is far out of keeping with the depictions in the ubiquitous advertisements we see for antidepressants. Even on the playing field of research designs which are better suited to drugs and which constrain psychotherapy, enough data have already accrued to argue strongly for psychotherapy as at least equally effective as medication even in simply accomplishing the goals of symptom reduction. And in children and adolescents, psychotherapy is clearly the safest and most effective treatment for depression. But, of course, who receives what treatment is a matter not just of what works but of other factors, such as the marketing of those treatments to the public. The pharmaceutical industry is powerful and has deep pockets. We can hope that this will be a place where the data triumphs and the trend toward using antidepressants as *the* primary treatment for depression will reverse course.

RESOURCES

Elkin, I., Shea, M., Watkins, J. T., & Imber, S. D., (1989). National Institute of Mental Health Treatment of Depression Collaborative Research Program: General effectiveness of treatments. *Archives of General Psychiatry, 46*(11): 971–982.

Healy, D. (2004). *Let them eat Prozac: The unhealthy relationship between the pharmaceutical industry and depression.* New York: New York University Press.

REFERENCES

Beck, A. T., & Young, J. E. (1985). Depression. In D. H. Barlow (Ed.), *Clinical handbook of psychological disorders: A step-by-step treatment manual* (pp. 206–244). New York: Guilford Press.

Coyne, J. C., Thompson, R., Klinkman, M. S., & Nease, D. E., Jr. (2002). Emotional disorders in primary care. *Journal of Consulting & Clinical Psychology, 70*(3): 798–809.

Coyne, J. C., Thompson, R., Palmer, S. C., Kagee, A., & Maunsell, E. (2000). Should we screen for depression? Caveats and potential pitfalls. *Applied & Preventive Psychology, 9*(2): 101–121.

Depressing research. (2004). *Lancet, 363*(9418): 1335.

DeRubeis, R. J., & Gelfand, L. A. (2000). Medications versus cognitive behavior therapy for severely depressed outpatients: Mega-analysis of four randomized comparisons: Reply. *American Journal of Psychiatry, 157*(6): 1025–1026.

Elkin, I. (1994). The NIMH Treatment of Depression Collaborative Research Program: Where we began and where we are. In A. E. Bergin & S. L. Garfield (Eds.), *Handbook of psychotherapy and behavior change* (4th ed., pp. 114–139). Oxford, UK: John Wiley & Sons.

Elkin, I., Gibbons, R. D., Shea, M., & Sotsky, S. M., (1995). Initial severity and differential treatment outcome in the National Institute of Mental Health Treatment of Depression Collaborative Research Program. *Journal of Consulting & Clinical Psychology, 63*(5): 841–847.

Elkin, I., Parloff, M. B., Hadley, S. W., & Autry, J. H. (1985). NIMH treatment of Depression Collaborative Research Program: Background and research plan. *Archives of General Psychiatry, 42*(3): 305–316.

Elkin, I., Shea, M., Watkins, J. T., & Imber, S. D., (1989). National Institute of Mental Health Treatment of Depression Collaborative Research Program: General effectiveness of treatments. *Archives of General Psychiatry, 46*(11): 971–982.

Gupta, M., Coyne, J. C., & Beach, S. R. H. (2003). Couples treatment for major depression: Critique of the literature and suggestions for some different directions. *Journal of Family Therapy, 25*(4): 317–346.

Jacobson, N. S., Dobson, K., Fruzzetti, A. E., Schmaling, K. B., & Salusky, S. (1991). Marital therapy as a treatment for depression. *Journal of Consulting & Clinical Psychology, 59*(4): 547–557.

Klein, D. F. (1996). Preventing hung juries about therapy studies. *Journal of Consulting and Clinical Psychology, 64*(1): 81–87.

Klein, D. F. (1999). Studying the respective contributions of pharmacotherapy and psychotherapy: Toward collaborative controlled studies. In S. Weissman & M. Sabshin (Eds.), *Psychiatry in the new millennium* (pp. 217–235). Washington, DC: American Psychiatric Association.

Klein, D. F., & Ross, D. C. (1993). Reanalysis of the National Institute of Mental Health Treatment of Depression Collaborative Research Program General Effectiveness Report. *Neuropsychopharmacology, 8*(3): 241–251.

Klerman, G. L., Weissman, M. M., Rounsaville, B., & Chevron, E. S. (1996). Interpersonal psychotherapy for depression. In J. E. Groves (Ed.), *Essential papers on short-term dynamic therapy* (pp. 134–148). New York: New York University Press.

Lewinsohn, P. M., Clarke, G. N., & Hoberman, H. M. (1989). The coping with depression course: Review and future directions. *Canadian Journal of Behavioural Science, 21*(4): 470–493.

O'Leary, K., & Beach, S. R. (1990). Marital therapy: A viable treatment for depression and marital discord. *American Journal of Psychiatry, 147*(2): 183–186.

Westen, D., Novotny, C. M., & Thompson-Brenner, H. (2004). The empirical status of empirically supported psychotherapies: Assumptions, findings, and reporting in controlled clinical trials. *Psychological Bulletin, 130*(4): 631–663.

Whittington, C. J., Kendall, T., Fonagy, P., Cottrell, D., Cotgrove, A., & Boddington, E. (2004). Selective serotonin reuptake inhibitors in childhood depression: Systematic review of published versus unpublished data. *Lancet, 363*(9418): 1341–1345.

Wilson, K., & Mottram, P. (2004). A comparison of side effects of selective serotonin reuptake inhibitors and tricyclic antidepressants in older depressed patients: A meta-analysis. *International Journal of Geriatric Psychiatry, 19*(8): 754–762.

15

OUTING THE UNPROVEN: A NEW JOURNAL EXPOSES THERAPIES THAT DON'T WORK

There are many therapies outside of the mainstream that make strong claims about their effectiveness. How are we to know what the evidence says about these treatments? This chapter describes a new journal devoted to examining such treatments and distinguishing those that work from pseudoscience.

Scott Lilienfeld has a mission: to make the practice of psychotherapy more scientific and eliminate approaches that have been demonstrated to be ineffective. An associate professor of psychology at Emory University and past president of the Society for the Science of Clinical Psychology, he argues that the mental health field is beset by an increasing proliferation of questionable tools and treatments made popular by radio psychologists, best-selling authors, and sensational media stories.

To promote science-based practice, Lilienfeld and other prominent researchers have founded an organization, the Council for Scientific Mental Health Practice, which in 2002 published the first issue of a journal, *The Scientific Review of Mental Health Practice*, subtitled *Objective Investigations of Controversial and Unorthodox Claims in Clinical Psychology, Psychiatry, and Social Work*. The journal is principally devoted to outing questionable methods. Lilienfeld is its editor and the editorial board includes such clinical research luminaries as David Barlow of Boston University, Aaron Beck of the University of Pennsylvania, Donald Klein and Robert Spitzer of Columbia University, and Arnold Lazarus of Rutgers University.

Aggressively challenging unsubstantiated methods, the first issue of the journal touches on whether all psychotherapies have the same impact (conclusion: they don't), the effectiveness of treatments for autism (conclusion: some work; many are shams), and an assessment of neurotherapy, a biofeedback technique used in treating children with attention-deficit disorder (conclusion: it doesn't work).

Lilienfeld believes identifying and ridding the field of unvalidated or scientifically unsupported methods is important because such methods undermine the general public's confidence in the mental health professions, lead individuals to forgo effective treatments, and in some instances, can actually be harmful. He's most concerned about methods that have been demonstrated to do harm. Widely circulated methods he cites as frequently harmful include those described below.

GROUP TREATMENTS FOR ADOLESCENT CONDUCT DISORDERS, DELINQUENCY, AND SUBSTANCE ABUSE

Several different investigators, who hoped such groups would be a source of support and a catalyst for positive change, have found them to have just the opposite effects. While assessing behavioral treatment, Thomas Dishion of the Oregon Research Institute found such groups more likely to help their members augment their antisocial skills and burrow further into a deviant subculture than to help them improve their functioning (Dishion & Dodge, 2005). Scott Henggeler found exactly the same result while assessing his Multi-Systemic Therapy, an intense treatment that works to help the adolescent engage more constructively with teachers, family members, and friends (Henggeler, Schoenwald, Borduin, Rowland, & Cunningham, 1998). Henggeler includes virtually every therapy format in this powerful and effective multi-systemic approach, but actively avoids the adolescent group format. Yet, as Lilienfeld highlights, such therapy groups remain the foundation of many treatment programs.

THE RORSCHACH
COMPREHENSIVE SYSTEM OF ASSESSMENT

The Rorschach, the classic technique of showing inkblots to people and having them suggest what they see, has never been demonstrated to achieve any purpose other than separating the actively psychotic from those who are not. Still, it remains a part of much psychological assessment. Lilienfeld is particularly concerned that the Rorschach Comprehensive System—the most widely circulated system of assessing responses—tends to overpathologize clients (Lilienfeld, Wood, & Garb, 2000). Lilienfeld believes the use of this system leads therapists to label many people as having mental illnesses who don't have them.

CRITICAL INCIDENT STRESS DEBRIEFING

This method features having people exposed to traumatic situations talk about their experiences just after the traumatic event. Lilienfeld points to several studies that have shown that, for many, this method leads to more negative effects than having no treatment at all (Lilienfeld, Lynn, & Lohr, 2003d; Lohr, Hooke, Gist, & Tolin, 2003). A recent review by Cochrane Collaboration, one of the major gatekeepers of evidence-based medicine, found it to be without empirical support and to pose some risk to those receiving it.

OTHER TREATMENTS

The journal also focuses on methods that have no documented research demonstrating effectiveness. Lilienfeld cites a large-scale study by psychologist Ronald Kessler and colleagues (Kessler et al., 2003), showing that individuals with a recent history of anxiety attacks or severe depression availed themselves of unsubstantiated complementary and alternative mental health treatments more often than they undertook conventional treatments.

The list of therapies Lilienfeld identifies as without scientific support include facilitated communication for infantile autism, suggestive techniques for memory recovery (e.g., hypnotic age-regression), energy therapies (e.g., Thought Field Therapy), and New Age therapies (e.g., rebirthing, reparenting, past-life regression, Primal Scream therapy, and neurolinguistic programming). He says the evidence suggests that any positive effects that eye movement desensitization and reprocessing (EMDR) might generate have nothing to do with the eye movements, and that what EMDR offers is accomplished more effectively by other treatments, such as cognitive-behavioral treatment for posttraumatic stress (Herbert et al., 2000; Lilienfeld, Fowler, Lohr, & Lynn, 2005; Lilienfeld, Lynn, & Lohr, 2003a–d).

The Scientific Review of Mental Health Practice each month adds to these lists of harmful or ineffective methods, points to self-help methods without foundation, and calls attention to poorly validated psychiatric diagnoses. But Lilienfeld and his journal doesn't focus exclusively on questionable methods. A part of each issue of the journal is devoted to highlighting methods with proven research support, particularly those only recently tested.

CONCLUSION

So what are we to make of this effort? We can take comfort in having a *Consumer Reports* that assesses controversial mental health claims. The journal expands the range of inquiry about mental health treatment, which typically is limited in academic journals to the evaluation of only a few methods, such as variants of cognitive behavior therapy. This allows for commentary on the status of a wider range of treatments, and ultimately should result in more and better efforts to assess less traditional treatments.

Expanding the net of what's examined also serves the goal of consumer protection. In a field in which the promulgation of new models merely requires someone to develop an approach and have the charisma and audacity to disseminate it, placing novel methods under the microscope helps.

A few concerns: Lilienfeld's organization and its journal are new and clearly in an early stage of development. It is only beginning to acquire a constituency for readership and submission. As a refereed academic journal, it can have content that's only as good as the articles that are submitted to it. As a young journal, it can be expected to have only a small number of submissions.

More specifically, where will the articles in support of nontraditional therapies come from? A circular feedback loop limits evaluation of many treatments: because they haven't been studied, research evaluating them is particularly difficult to fund, so questions about the effectiveness of many treatments are never asked. Although the journal performs a service in showing that scientific-sounding treatments such as neurotherapy are without research support, it would help to see the journal highlight more nontraditional therapies that show promising results in research evaluation. Possible candidates include therapy methods drawing on meditation and imagination (Kabat-Zinn, 2003; Lazarus, 1990).

The journal's purpose also becomes clouded when it publishes articles such as the one that questions whether all therapies impact on the whole to the same degree. This article presents in an unquestioning way one side of a heated debate among researchers. (For the other side of this argument, see Bruce Wampold's recent book *The Great Psychotherapy Debate* [Wampold, 2001]). The editors need to make it clear to readers when the journal is presenting debatable conclusions and when the evidence for the author's position is overwhelming.

All told, these are minor concerns. We can look to Lilienfeld and his journal to promote the extension of inquiry about methods in mental health treatment beyond the narrow range of treatments that typically come to be evaluated, to examine controversies in the field, and to question methods that gain favor without research support. In the field of mental health treatment, in which the acceptance of nearly everything can easily become the norm, Lilienfeld's organization and journal provides a loud and challenging voice.

RESOURCES

(2002). *The Scientific Review of Mental Health Practice, 1*(1).

REFERENCES

Dishion, T. J., & Dodge, K. A. (2005). Peer contagion in interventions for children and adolescents: Moving towards an understanding of the ecology and dynamics of change. *Journal of Abnormal Child Psychology, 33*(3): 395–400.

Henggeler, S. W., Schoenwald, S. K., Borduin, C. M., Rowland, M. D., & Cunningham, P. B. (1998). *Multisystemic treatment of antisocial behavior in children and adolescents*. New York: Guilford Press.

Herbert, J. D., Lilienfeld, S. O., Lohr, J. M., Montgomery, R. W., O'Donohue, W. T., Rosen, G. M., & Tolin, D. F. (2000). Science and pseudoscience in the development of eye movement desensitization and reprocessing: Implications for clinical psychology. *Clinical Psychology Review, 20*(8): 945–971.

Kabat-Zinn, J. (2003). Mindfulness-based stress reduction (MBSR). *Constructivism in the Human Sciences, 8*(2): 73–107.

Kessler, R. C., Demler, O., Jin, R., Walters, E. E., Berglund, P., Koretz, D., et al. (2003). Treatment of depression by mental health specialists and primary care physicians: Reply. *Journal of the American Medical Association, 290*(15): 1992.

Lazarus, A. A. (1990). Can psychotherapists transcend the shackles of their training and superstitions? *Journal of Clinical Psychology, 46*(3): 351–358.

Lilienfeld, S. O., Fowler, K. A., Lohr, J. M., & Lynn, S. J. (2005). Pseudoscience, nonscience, and nonsense in clinical psychology: Dangers and remedies. [References]. In R. H. Wright & N. A. Cummings (Eds.), *Destructive trends in mental health: The well-intentioned path to harm* (pp. 187–218). New York: Routledge.

Lilienfeld, S. O., Lynn, S. J., & Lohr, J. M. (2003a). Pseudoscience is alive and well. *Scientific Review of Mental Health Practice, 2*(2): 107–110.

Lilienfeld, S. O., Lynn, S. J., & Lohr, J. M. (Eds.). (2003d). *Science and pseudoscience in clinical psychology*. New York: Guilford Press.

Lilienfeld, S. O., Lynn, S. J., & Lohr, J. M. (2003b). Science and pseudoscience in clinical psychology: Concluding thoughts and constructive remedies. [References]. In S. O. Lilienfeld, S. J. Lynn, & J. M. Lohr (Eds.), *Science and pseudoscience in clinical psychology* (pp. 461–465). New York: Guilford Press.

Lilienfeld, S. O., Lynn, S. J., & Lohr, J. M. (2003c). Science and pseudoscience in clinical psychology: Initial thoughts, reflections, and considerations. [References]. In S. O. Lilienfeld, S. J. Lynn, & J. M. Lohr (Eds.), *Science and pseudoscience in clinical psychology* (pp. 1–14). New York, NY: Guilford Press.

Lilienfeld, S. O., Wood, J. M., & Garb, H. N. (2000). The scientific status of projective techniques. *Psychological Science in the Public Interest, 1*(2): 27–66.

Lohr, J. M., Hooke, W., Gist, R., & Tolin, D. F. (2003). Novel and controversial treatments for trauma-related stress disorders. [References]. In S. O. Lilienfeld, S. J. Lynn, & J. M. Lohr (Eds.), *Science and pseudoscience in clinical psychology* (pp. 243–272). New York: Guilford Press.

Wampold, B. E. (2001). *The great psychotherapy debate: Models, methods, and findings*. Mahwah, NJ: Lawrence Erlbaum Associates.

16

THE MESSENGER IS THE MESSAGE: THE EFFECTIVENESS OF TREATMENT STILL DEPENDS ON WHO DELIVERS IT

Psychotherapy research typically focuses on the treatment and the clients, but rarely on the psychotherapist. Yet therapies are only delivered through a therapist and research shows that therapists differ in the relationships they are able to build with clients and in their effectiveness. This chapter centers on the largest and most comprehensive effort to study psychotherapists, an effort that helps us understand who therapists are and the ways they practice most effectively

Psychotherapy researchers typically focus exclusively on different clinical interventions while ignoring the psychotherapists who make use of them. It's as if treatment methods were like pills, in no way affected by the person administering them. Too often researchers regard the skills, personality, and experience of the therapist as side issues, features to control to ensure that different treatment groups receive comparable interventions.

However, studies that do take into account the therapists' relational skills and personal styles have found that these qualities have a greater impact on outcome than the treatments they offered. In fact, comparative studies of different treatments often show more variation within a group getting one kind of treatment than between groups getting two different kinds of treatment (Lambert & Barley, 2001). And the largest proportion of this outcome variance, it's now well known, stems from relationship factors (Wampold, 2001). In fact, the National Institute of Mental Health Treatment of Depression Collaborative Research Program found that even the effectiveness of psychopharmacology is significantly influenced by the "bedside manner" of the physician dispensing the medication (Krupnick, Elkin, Collins, & Simmens, 1994).

And yet, surprisingly, little research has been performed on psychotherapists themselves, even though their individual characteristics are probably the single most important factor in therapy's success or failure. Without having a clear idea of who and what psychotherapists are as a group—their personal traits, professional training, personal and professional experience of therapy, clinical orientations, and how they develop over time—it is difficult to fully understand their clinical impact.

Now, at last, there's some serious, long-range research being conducted on psychotherapists. David Orlinsky, a professor of psychology at the University of Chicago and a founder of the Society for Psychotherapy Research, has launched an international research project to determine what therapists bring to the therapeutic encounter, personally and professionally, and what their experience of the therapeutic process is at different stages in their careers (Ackerman et al., 2001; Ambühl, Orlinsky, Cierpka, & Buchheim, 1995; Smith & Orlinsky, 2004).

Long before there were narrative therapies, Orlinsky, along with long-time collaborator Ken Howard of Northwestern University, intensely studied the views of clients and therapists session by session over the course of therapy in a project described in the book, *Varieties of Psychotherapeutic Experience*. In that study, Orlinsky and Howard found a complex set of interactions between the way clients' and therapists' experience therapy. These interactions involved the clients' and therapists' sense of collaboration and shared positive experience, which determined the impact of the therapy (Howard, Orlinsky, & Hill, 1968; Orlinsky & Howard, 1967a, 1967b). Now, working on a shoestring budget outside the limits imposed by government funding and with an international group of coinvestigators that included

M. Helge Rønnestad of the University of Oslo, Hansruedi Ambühl of the University of Bern, Ulrike Willutzki of Ruhr-University of Bochum, Jean-Francois Botermans of Catholic University of Louvain, Manfred Cierpka of University of Heidelberg, John Davis of the University of Warwick, and Marcia Davis of North Warwickshire Health, Orlinsky developed an extensive questionnaire to assess how therapists experience therapy, training, and their own lives (Frank et al., 1992; Orlinsky, Ambühl et al., 1999; Orlinsky, Rønnestad et al., 1999). That questionnaire asked about such obvious factors as discipline, employment setting, years of experience, orientation and training, but also delved into therapists' self-perceptions at the beginning their careers and how they changed over time, the kinds of clients they saw, their degree of satisfaction in their work, their views of themselves as therapists, their coping strategies, their difficulties, and their degree of satisfaction in their own lives.

To date, 8,000 therapists from 30 countries have completed the questionnaire. The largest numbers of respondents are from the United States, Germany, South Korea, Norway, and Great Britain. The study provides the best snapshot we have of what therapists around the world are like. The clinical experience of this sample ranges from less than 1 year to more than 50 years, with therapists averaging 11 years in practice. Some 44% of the therapists have either a part-time or full-time private practice. Slightly more than 50% of the therapists are female. They range in age from 21 to 91 years old, with a mean age of 42.

In terms of preferred modality, nearly 60% of these therapists rely strongly on psychodynamic concepts in their work with patients, about 30% rely strongly on humanistic/existential orientations, 20% are strongly influenced by cognitive and cognitive-behavioral approaches, and 20% by systemic theories. More than 75% of the respondents had experienced therapy themselves at least once in their lives and more than 25% were in personal therapy.

PATTERNS OF PRACTICE

Examining how therapists generally experience the process of doing therapy themselves, Orlinsky and his colleagues identified two distinct states of mind and work: "healing involvement" and "stressful involvement." In healing involvement, therapists experience themselves as feeling personally committed, affirming, fully engaged with a high level of empathy, having good communication skills, and enjoying a sense of conscious "flow" during sessions. They feel effective, and they can deal with difficulties constructively when they arise. By contrast, in stressful involvement, therapists experience themselves as feeling bored and anxious during sessions and as having difficulties with clients, which they tend to deal with unconstructively by avoiding engagement.

Most of us can recognize both these states in our own practices: we know that feeling of being alive, engaged, and productive, and we've also felt that other state, often expressed as the fervent wish, "I hope they don't make their session today!" But, clearly, if we're doing a good job and generally enjoy our work, we feel more dedicated than we do detached.

Although all therapists experience some proportion of each of these states, Orlinsky and his colleagues found that the amount of time therapists spend in each state produces four distinct practice patterns: effective practice (characterized by much healing involvement and little stressful involvement), challenging practice (with much healing involvement but also much stressful involvement), distressing practice (with high stressful involvement and little healing involvement), and disengaged practice (with little stressful involvement but also little healing involvement). Half the therapists in the study emerge as in "effective practice," a quarter in "challenging practice," and a small but significant minority described themselves in "disengaged" (1 in 6) and "distressed" practice (1 in 10). Thus most therapists have a predominantly positive experience of their clinical work, but nearly 30% experience themselves as stressed or disengaged in their work—a significant number by any standards.

In their recently published book, Orlinsky and his Norwegian colleague Helge Rønnestad (2005) also examine therapists over their professional life cycle. Their findings on this subject include the following:

- Therapists at all levels of experience value their continuing development and show high levels of current growth. For most therapists, growth is a lifetime task. And if therapists don't feel they're moving forward, they're susceptible to becoming disengaged or distressed practitioners.
- As they become more experienced, therapists come to feel increasing levels of healing involvement and lower levels of stressful involvement. Thus the number of therapists reporting effective practice grew from about 40% among novices to 65% among experienced therapists. The therapists reporting distressed and disengaged practice declined from 20%–25% percent among novices to 3%–11% among experienced therapists. Beginners experience the highest levels of stressful involvement.
- High levels of theoretical breadth, variety of caseloads, and current experiences of growth increase healing involvement and

effectiveness. Clearly, remaining effective as a therapist is a function of renewal and change, not mere repetition of methods of practice over time. And a sense of improving over time also depends on the breadth and depth of case experiences.

DIRECTIONS

Based on the findings of what differentiates therapists who experience their careers positively from those who don't, Orlinsky and Rønnestad offer a number of suggestions for the training and development of therapists, including the following:

- Because the relationship between therapist and client is so important for effective therapy, therapists should be selected for academic programs, in part, because they have good interpersonal skills. This criterion is often ignored by training programs, which base their selection of candidates primarily on school performance.
- Therapists should receive a foundation of training in a clear method of practice. Such a foundation seems to reduce the levels of stressful practice for therapists, which is the bane of existence for many clinicians early in their careers.
- Therapists should broaden their own base of practice as their careers progress. Having a variety of different types of clients and professional experiences, as well as expanding one's repertoire of methods and interventions, promotes the sense of personal renewal and professional growth that's essential to building and maintaining effective practice.
- Therapists should be mindful of the stress that inevitably accompanies their career choice and monitor as well as limit the number of highly distressing clients in their caseloads. They also should always maintain strong personal and professional support networks among family, friends, and colleagues to mitigate stress and burnout.

Of course, the sources for these data are therapists themselves. Can we as therapists trust ourselves to report accurately about our experiences? The answer appears to be "yes." A long line of research studies of therapist, client, and observer reports about therapy is unambiguous on the subject. Research has also shown that therapists do see therapy somewhat differently than do clients and observers. Their perspective is unique, though typically honestly reported (Beutler, Machado, & Neufeldt, 1994).

In outcome studies, they also tend to be most pessimistic about outcomes of the three perspectives about progress in psychotherapy.

Orlinsky and colleagues have provided a unique view into the minds and experiences of psychotherapists, and clearly psychotherapists themselves are the best source of information about their own experiences, just as clients are. What emerges most strongly from their study is a reminder from the world of research that psychotherapy is most of all a human activity, and shouldn't be confused with that kind of treatment described by Alan Gurman as "technolotry"—the worship of technique over everything else. Orlinsky and Rønnestad say, "Therapists did not experience themselves as detached technicians dispassionately administering treatment procedures but rather as healers working with the heart as well as the mind" (Orlinsky & Rønnestad, 2005). The traditional image of the psychotherapist as neutral, recently further implied in the context of some technique-oriented evidence-based practice, is clearly at odds with how most therapists experience themselves, and is typical of only a minority who experience themselves as relatively ineffective.

RESOURCES

Orlinsky, D. E., & Rønnestad, M. H. (2005). *How therapists develop: A study of therapeutic work and professional growth.* Washington, DC: American Psychological Association.

REFERENCES

Ackerman, S. J., Benjamin, L. S., Beutler, L. E., Gelso, C. J., Goldfried, M. R., Hill, C., et al. (2001). Empirically supported therapy relationships: Conclusions and recommendations of the Division 29 Task Force. *Psychotherapy: Theory, Research, Practice, Training, 38*(4): 495–497.

Ambühl, H., Orlinsky, D., Cierpka, M., & Buchheim, P. (1995). Changing patterns in theoretical orientation in the development of psychotherapists. *Psychotherapie Psychosomatik Medizinische Psychologie, 45*(3–4): 109–120.

Beutler, L. E., Machado, P. P. P., & Neufeldt, S. A. (1994). Therapist variables. In A. E. Bergin & S. L. Garfield (Eds.), *Handbook of psychotherapy and behavior change* (4th ed., pp. 229–269). Oxford, UK: John Wiley & Sons.

Frank, J. D., Luborsky, L., Wallerstein, R. S., Howard, K. I., Orlinsky, D. E., Bergin, A. E., et al. (1992). Historical developments in research centers. [References]. In D. K. Freedheim & H. J. Freudenberger (Eds.), *History of psychotherapy: A century of change* (pp. 391–449). Washington, DC: American Psychological Association.

Howard, K. I., Orlinsky, D. E., & Hill, J. A. (1968). The patient's experience of psychotherapy: Some dimensions and determinants. *Multivariate Behavioral Research Special Issue.* (pp. 55–72). New York: Lawrecne Erlbaum.

Krupnick, J. L., Elkin, I., Collins, J., & Simmens, S., (1994). Therapeutic alliance and clinical outcome in the NIMH Treatment of Depression Collaborative Research Program: Preliminary findings. *Psychotherapy: Theory, Research, Practice, Training, 31*(1): 28–35.

Lambert, M. J., & Barley, D. E. (2001). Research summary on the therapeutic relationship and psychotherapy outcome. *Psychotherapy: Theory, Research, Practice, Training, 38*(4): 357–361.

Orlinsky, D. E., Ambühl, H., Rønnestad, M. H., Davis, J., Gerin, P., Davis, M., et al. (1999). Development of psychotherapists: Concepts, questions, and methods of a collaborative international study. *Psychotherapy Research, 9*(2): 127–153.

Orlinsky, D. E., & Howard, K. I. (1967a). Dimensions of conjoint experiential process in psychotherapy relationships. *Proceedings of the Annual Convention of the American Psychological Association, 2,* 251–252.

Orlinsky, D. E., & Howard, K. I. (1967b). The good therapy hour: Experiential correlates of patients' and therapists' evaluations of therapy sessions. *Archives of General Psychiatry, 16*(5): 621–632.

Orlinsky, D. E., & Rønnestad, M. H. (2005). *How therapists develop: A study of therapeutic work and professional growth.* Washington, DC: American Psychological Association.

Orlinsky, D. E., Rønnestad, M. H., Ambühl, H., Willutzki, U., Botersman, J.-F., Cierpka, M., et al. (1999). Psychotherapists' assessments of their development at different career levels. *Psychotherapy: Theory, Research, Practice, Training, 36*(3): 203–215.

Smith, D. P., & Orlinsky, D. E. (2004). Religious and spiritual experience among psychotherapists. *Psychotherapy: Theory, Research, Practice, Training, 41*(2): 144–151.

Wampold, B. E. (2001). *The great psychotherapy debate: Models, methods, and findings.* Mahwah, NJ: Lawrence Erlbaum Associates.

Part III

*Research Focused on or Relevant
to Couple and Family Therapy*

17

FAMILY THERAPY SCORECARD: RESEARCH SHOWS THE FAMILY APPROACH IS OFTEN THE TREATMENT OF CHOICE

Ultimately, the impact of a therapy is determined by outcome research assessing effectiveness. This chapter, focused on two pivotal reviews of the literature, summarizes the findings from the research on outcome in couple and family therapy.

Say "family therapy" and many therapists, particularly those trained in the heyday of the movement of the 1970s and 1980s, will conjure up images of brilliant innovators such as Salvador Minuchin challenging an overcontrolling mother, Carl Whitaker arm wrestling with a disengaged father, or Virginia Satir nurturing an entire household into lowering its guard. However, two comprehensive reviews of research on family therapy compiled under the auspices of the American Association of Marriage and Family Therapy (AAMFT) suggest that in the 50 or so years since therapists first began seeing families in treatment, the science of couples and family therapy has moved well beyond its originators' footsteps. Both *Effectiveness Research in Marriage and Family Therapy*, edited by Doug Sprenkle (2002, 2003), and *The Effectiveness and Efficacy of Marital and Family Therapy*, edited by William Pinsof and Lyman Wynne (1995b), consist of state-of-the-art reviews of outcome research assessing the effectiveness of family therapy across a range of clinical problems.

THE IMPACT OF COUPLE AND FAMILY THERAPY

First and foremost, there is now overwhelming evidence that treatment does have positive affect on the lives of clients, with hundreds of studies demonstrating that couple and family therapy leads to differences that make a difference. With many recent state-of-the-art studies featuring methods much improved over early research, there is now little question about the basis for the findings.

William Shadish and colleagues (Sprenkle, 2002), using a statistical technique called meta-analysis that compares the size of the impact of treatment in a typical study with changes in untreated groups, found couples and family therapy to have an "effect size" comparable to both successful medical treatments and individual psychotherapy. But in marked contrast with the older vision of family therapies, most of the current approaches summarized by Shadish freely mix individual, couple, family, and group session formats. Confrontation in these therapies is rare. Most emphasize carefully nurturing therapeutic alliances with family members. Exotic techniques, such as paradoxical interventions, are nowhere in sight. Gone also is the attention to consulting-room drama. The kind of family therapy being researched is grounded in change over time, rather than in single, eventful interventions.

In this context, "family" therapy might best be thought of as an umbrella term for systemic approaches that take into account clients' networks of intimate relationships, whereas leaving room for many different approaches. The family intervention strategies reviewed in the AAMFT volumes typically combine structural, strategic, cognitive, behavioral, and systemic elements. The heated ideological debates that once defined the family field have largely given way to an overarching pragmatism about what works best with what type of problem.

Yet although educating professionals about new methods of practice, the AAMFT reviews also provide powerful empirical support for the core theoretical assumptions of the family therapy pioneers, including the importance of understanding the wider systemic context for change, rather than just focusing on the individual, and the value of including family members in the treatment of the "identified patient." Spouses' active involvement in treatment has emerged as a crucial intervention in treating problems such as alcohol and substance abuse, depression, and anxiety disorders. The critical importance of involving parents is underscored in most of the treatments reviewed for child and adolescent difficulties, as is the involvement of family members with clients suffering from severe mental illness and physical disorders.

FAMILY THERAPY AS TREATMENT FOR SPECIFIC PROBLEMS

Particular types of family and couples therapy have demonstrated their effectiveness as treatments for a broad array of problems traditionally considered "individual psychopathologies," including several major *Diagnostic and Statistical Manual of Mental Disorders* (*DSM*) Axis I disorders of great concern to public health policy makers as well as workaday clinicians.

A strong base for effectiveness has been demonstrated in treating families with schizophrenic members, depression in women with marital problems, alcoholism, adolescent conduct disorders and drug abuse, and a range of child disorders, including conduct disorder and autism. Numerous couples and family therapies—including those for adult alcoholism, adult and childhood depression, childhood conduct disorder, and childhood attention deficit disorder—have sufficient research support to qualify as empirically supported therapies. In addition, several treatments have been shown to be effective in reducing the difficulties surrounding physical illnesses. These therapies include pediatric illnesses such as diabetes, asthma, cancer, and cystic fibrosis; chronic diseases in adults such as hypertension and diabetes; and dementia in the elderly. And common patterns of couples conflict are also treated effectively. Some family treatments have shown such clear results that they can be regarded as treatments of choice for several specific problems. These treatments include couples therapy for marital problems and some depression, psycho-educational therapy for families with a schizophrenic member, and structural and behavioral therapy for conduct disorders.

To highlight some specific examples, couple and family therapies have been shown to considerably impact each of the following problem areas.

Severe Mental Illness

A resounding body of research now points to the vastly superior outcomes achieved by family-based therapies for treating adult schizophrenia and bipolar disorder when compared with treatment with other psychotherapies or with psychopharmacology alone. Several variations on family psycho-education for working with schizophrenia—originally developed by Ian Falloon and Michael Goldstein at the University of California Los Angeles (Falloon, 1988), Carol Anderson at the University of Pittsburgh (1977), and William McFarlane at the University of Vermont (2002)—have proven to be much more effective in reducing patient rehospitalization, symptoms, and distress, and in improving family functioning. David Miklowitz at the University of Colorado has demonstrated similar results with bipolar disorder (Miklowitz, 1996; Miklowitz et al., 2004). Each of these approaches begins with psycho-education and uses strategies for reducing the high affect and criticism aimed at the person with the disorder, an occurrence that researchers have termed *expressed emotion*. Other key aspects of these approaches are direct efforts to build coping skills in the patient, to increase the availability of therapists for crisis intervention, and to garner family involvement in assuring compliance with medication regimens.

Adolescent Substance Abuse and Delinquency

Four distinct family therapies with strong empirical support have been shown to be superior to the alternatives of generic outpatient therapy, day treatment, hospitalization, and individual drug and alcohol counseling. Each is becoming widely used in treatment programs around the country.

Functional family therapy, developed by Jim Alexander of the University of Utah and Tom Sexton of Indiana University (Alexander & Sexton, 2002), melds strategic and behavioral methods in a three-stage model, beginning with creating a positive therapy alliance, teaching communication, parenting, and problem-solving skills, and then helping generalize positive change developed within the family to other systems.

Multi-systemic therapy, developed by Scott Henggeler of the Medical University of South Carolina (Henggeler, Schoenwald, Borduin, Rowland, & Cunningham, 1998), targets interventions in multiple systems. This approach integrates individual, structural, and behavioral family therapy, along with a focus on the other key systems in the lives of the adolescents. Therapy is intensive; therapists have small caseloads, working with the systems the adolescent is involved in and managing crises as they unfold.

Multidimensional family therapy, developed by Howard Liddle at the University of Miami Medical School (Rowe, Liddle, McClintic, & Quille, 2002), combines a developmental perspective with behavioral and structural family therapy. The therapist works with the teenager alone and with the parents to enhance the connection between parents and children and improve parenting skills. Sessions with parents and children are aimed at changing interaction patterns.

Brief strategic therapy, developed by Jose Szapocznik at the University of Miami Medical School (Szapocznik & Williams, 2000), is a variation on structural family therapy, based on system, structure, and strategy. Key interventions include joining, diagnosis of family interactional patterns, restructuring, working in the present, reframing, and working with boundaries and alliances. Much of the work in this approach is done in clients' homes.

Distressed Marriages

The only therapies that have been found effective for relationship difficulties are those involving conjoint couple treatment. Of those with empirical support, a variety of theoretical perspectives and techniques is represented. The common element, besides the conjoint approach, seems to be the introduction of new behaviors, cognitions, and emotions into the couples' system, with the idea that they will generate a positive feedback loop, leading to change.

Behavioral marital therapy, a cognitive-behavioral therapy developed by Robert Weiss and others, is the oldest and most researched of these approaches (Weiss, 1975). It is organized around teaching communication and problem-solving skills, and having couples renegotiate their behavioral exchanges.

Emotion-focused couples therapy, developed by Susan Johnson and Leslie Greenberg (Greenberg, 2002; Greenberg & Johnson, 1988; Johnson, 2003), is an experiential therapy focused on emotion and attachment. The emphasis is on couples helping each other work through early attachment injuries and replacing old maladaptive emotional schema with more relationship-affirming meanings.

Insight-oriented couples therapy, developed by Doug Snyder (2002), focuses on identifying the origins of relationship themes for each partner and using this understanding to change current relationship patterns.

Integrative behavioral couples therapy, developed by Andrew Christenson and Neil Jacobson (Christensen & Jacobson, 2000; Christensen, Sevier, Simpson, & Gattis, 2004), adds an emphasis on acceptance derived from humanistic approaches to the skill-building and contracting focus of behavioral couples therapy. Couples are helped to recognize the polarizing patterns in their relationship, while achieving more realistic attitudes about the possibilities of changing each other and developing their individual capacities for self-care.

Depression

In their review of couples therapy and depression, Stacey Prince and Neil Jacobson (1995) conclude that "conjoint marital therapy on an out-patient basis may be as effective as individual treatment for a specific subset of depressed patients: those who are also experiencing marital distress" (p. 388). However, couple therapy is not an effective means of treating depression in individuals whose marital relationship is not troubled. Similarly, treating depression with individual treatment does not resolve marital difficulty.

ALL HAVE NOT WON, AND SO NOT ALL SHALL HAVE PRIZES

Outcome research is limited to a few family therapy approaches. There is much more evidence for the positive impact of cognitive-behavioral, structural, psycho-educational, and problem-oriented integrative approaches on certain problems than for other approaches. Some very prominent and historically influential approaches to couple and family therapy remain untested, including the Bowen approach, strategic, narrative, solution-focused, object-relations, psychodynamic, intergenerational, and a plethora of other approaches that claim special effectiveness with specific groups of clients. Approaches for which there is no relevant research may work as well or even better than those already tested, but this remains to be demonstrated, and the primary onus for establishing the effectiveness of these methods rests on their proponents.

ONE-DIMENSIONAL, ONE-SIZE-FITS-ALL THERAPY IS THE WAVE OF THE PAST

Several of the couple and family treatments that have proved effective have a highly integrative character, bringing together concepts and interventions from various schools of treatment and bridging family, couple and individual sessions, and sometimes even actively involve larger systems, such as juvenile justice. Although grounded in theory, these methods are pragmatic, flexible, and responsive to the particular problems and circumstances of each case. For example, Howard Liddle's (Liddle et al., 2001) work with adolescent substance abusers and their families has origins in principles of systems theory, structural family therapy, and adolescent development, but is adapted to the specific realities of working with this treatment population. Such integrative treatment has also been shown to be effective in the treatment of schizophrenia, alcoholism, depression, and physical illness. Including family therapy clearly improves efficacy, but the most effective treatments combine a range of methods.

This new emphasis on integrative treatment is one of the unmistakable signs that the field of family therapy is moving away from the simplistic ideas that all effective therapy must involve sessions with the whole family, and toward an approach that includes multiple organizing concepts, methods of intervention, and types of sessions (Lebow, 1997). Involvement of the family is an essential ingredient in the treatment of many problems, but not the only one. What is emerging is the value of couples and family therapy as one salient aspect of effective integrative treatment. With many problems, family therapy clearly enables far better outcomes when offered as part of a multicomponent treatment, but it is not sufficient to produce optimal results by itself. Practicing clinicians should be urged to incorporate these validated methods into their therapeutic repertoires with appropriate cases, and training programs should be urged to incorporate these methods into their curricula.

FAMILY THERAPY HELPS ENGAGE
THE DIFFICULT TO ENGAGE

If a treatment is not acceptable, clients are unlikely to participate, and therefore significant impact is unlikely. A powerful research finding transcending specific problems is the positive impact that involving families has on engagement and continuation in treatment. Research has shown that including families in therapy increases the participation of alcoholics, adolescent substance abusers, delinquents, and schizophrenics. When clients aren't motivated to change at the onset of treatment, as is the case, for example, with many alcohol or substance abusers, the reviews highlight the fact that family therapy is often the *only* effective path toward change. In fact, some of the most successful treatments in alcohol and substance abuse begin with helping the spouse or family members cope with the problem and then working to engage the partner in treatment (O'Farrell & Fals-Stewart, 2000).

MAINTAINING CHANGE

A disheartening trend that emerges from the research is the tendency of treatment effects to dissipate over time. Alcoholism, depression, and marital distress have been found to have high rates of recurrence in follow-up several years later. What this says about treatment is a matter of debate. Some have argued that this finding points to the limited power of our treatments. It could also be argued that it would be truly extraordinary for the kinds of brief treatments that are the subject of most research studies to relieve problems for all time. Further, problem recurrence does not necessarily point to a failing of earlier treatment, but to a need to search for ways to improve the durability of change. Some research has begun to indicate that there are intervention strategies that produce more durable change. One example is Snyder and Wills's (Snyder, Wills, & Grady-Fletcher, 1991) demonstration of very low problem-recurrence with the addition of insight as part of couples therapy for distressed relationships and the reduction of recidivism in schizophrenia through reducing stress and anticipating crises in the psycho-educational treatment (McFarlane, Dixon, Lukens, & Lucksted, 2003). The clinical lesson is that the effects of treatment may not endure, even when they appear to be striking, and that we should take measures to make them last longer.

Such sobering findings bring into focus Neil Jacobson's call (Jacobson & Truax, 1991) not to oversell our work. Research indicates couple and family therapy is not as a wonder cure, but is as a solid set of treatments that help most clients. As Jacobson has pointed out, in few individual or family treatments do more than 50% of clients attain levels of functioning that meet the most ambitious criteria for success (i.e., coming to look no different from the general population in the area of the presenting problem). What is required is a kind of rational reading of the research. There is substantial support for many treatments, little for others. Maintenance of change emerges as a significant problem, as is true in individual psychotherapy.

GENDER, CULTURE, AND DIVERSE FAMILY FORMS

Despite the increased attention to these dimensions of family life over the past 15 years, there is almost no research to illuminate questions such as how best to deal with problems most specific to African-American or Latino families, or treatment issues with gay and lesbian clients. The extent to which there is research on treatments in diverse populations is growing (Bernal, Bonilla, Padilla-Cotto, & Perez-Prado, 1998; Bernal & Scharro-del-Rio, 2001), but until proven otherwise, questions about how well treatments will generalize to other populations remain.

IGNORANCE IS NOT BLISS

Even with this impressive array of research, there is still a lot we don't know. Most research has focused on a few treatments and their impact on *DSM* conditions, partly because it is hard to get funding for anything else. And yet, as noted earlier, we have virtually no data concerning the impact of several major methods. In general, we depend too much on the diligent efforts of those studying behavioral treatments to tell us about how well generic aspects of couples and family therapy work with too many specific groups of patients. Ironically, we also have little research assessing the impact of family therapy on the problems that most directly fall in the family domain, such as intergenerational communication and conflict, and difficulties with family of origin. And despite the focus of most research being on the impact of therapy on diagnosable conditions (because of the much greater opportunities for funding of this type of research), research remains sparse on a wide range of important problems, such as anxiety and depression in children. We have limited knowledge about the impact of family therapy under naturalistic conditions as opposed to controlled laboratory conditions, and we also are only beginning to learn how the complex processes of couples and family therapy relate to outcome.

It should also be noted that much of the research conducted so far has taken place away from the major training and treatment centers of family therapy, where many of the most influential treatment models have been developed. Pinsof and Wynne (Pinsof & Wynne, 1995a) state in their summary article in their volume:

> Well over half of the marital and family treatments covered in this special issue that have demonstrated efficacy are provided by therapists who would not define themselves as marital and/ or family therapists. Additionally, most of the research has been conducted by researchers who would not define themselves as working within the field of marital and family therapy research (p. 610).

The strong evidence for the efficacy of couples and family interventions is more the product of the innate power of involving family in treatment than any programmatic effort to demonstrate the effectiveness of the major family therapies. Fortunately, there is a related positive factor that emerges with this problem: although it is discouraging that serious attempts to evaluate clinical outcomes have not been made in some major schools of family therapy, the fact that so much of the existing research has been done by outsiders suggests that experimenter bias may have been minimized in many of these studies, reinforcing the robustness of the findings.

ONE FINAL CAVEAT

Research findings do not replace clinical wisdom, but they do augment and help shape such knowledge to inform practice. Research is only one of several ways of knowing. Although it is fortunate that research has assumed an increasingly prominent place in family therapy, it is unfortunate that some of the motivation has been the anxiety of practitioners' protecting their pocketbooks. We should not be so naive as to believe that these summaries will send clinicians running to get retrained in demonstrably effective therapy methods that may be quite different from those they call on every day. The most powerful effect of recent treatment outcome research will probably be on the training of the next generation of family and couples therapists.

Nonetheless, the resounding message from these reviews is that we already know a great deal, and that much of what we know suggests that couple and family therapies are potent methods of treatment. These reviews demonstrate how far couple and family therapy have moved from being renegade therapies challenging the establishment to becoming some of the most empirically supported treatments for numerous disorders and difficulties. And even though the specific treatment methods of the pioneers of family therapy have not been much in focus in the studies of contemporary researchers, the importance they placed on understanding social systems and family relationships is now firmly established within the mental health field.

RESOURCES

Pinsof, W. M., & Wynne, L. C. (1995). Effectiveness research in marital and family therapy [Special issue]. *Journal of Marital & Family Therapy, 21*(4): 339–618.

Sprenkle, D. H. (Ed.). (2002). *Effectiveness research in marriage and family therapy.* Alexandria, VA: American Association for Marriage and Family Therapy.

REFERENCES

Alexander, J. F., & Sexton, T. L. (2002). Functional family therapy: A model for treating high-risk, acting-out youth. [References]. In F. W. Kaslow

(Ed.), *Comprehensive handbook of psychotherapy: Integrative/eclectic,* (vol. 4, pp. 111–132). New York: John Wiley & Sons.

Anderson, C. M. (1977). Family intervention with severely disturbed inpatients. *Archives of General Psychiatry, 34*(6): 697–702.

Bernal, G., Bonilla, J., Padilla-Cotto, L., & Perez-Prado, E. M. (1998). Factors associated to outcome in psychotherapy: An effectiveness study in Puerto Rico. *Journal of Clinical Psychology, 54*(3): 329–342.

Bernal, G., & Scharro-del-Rio, M. R. (2001). Are empirically supported treatments valid for ethnic minorities? Toward an alternative approach for treatment research. *Cultural Diversity & Ethnic Minority Psychology, 7*(4): 328–342.

Christensen, A., & Jacobson, N. S. (2000). *Reconcilable differences.* New York: Guilford Press.

Christensen, A., Sevier, M., Simpson, L. E., & Gattis, K. S. (2004). Acceptance, mindfulness, and change in couple therapy. [References]. In S. C. Hayes, V. M. Follette, & M. M. Linehan (Eds.), *Mindfulness and acceptance: Expanding the cognitive-behavioral tradition* (pp. 288–309). New York: Guilford Press.

Falloon, I. R. (1988). Behavioral family management in coping with functional psychosis: Principles, practice, and recent developments. *International Journal of Mental Health, 17*(1): 35–47.

Greenberg, L. S. (2002). *Emotion-focused therapy: Coaching clients to work through their feelings.* Washington, DC: American Psychological Association.

Greenberg, L. S., & Johnson, S. M. (1988). *Emotionally focused therapy for couples.* New York: Guilford Press.

Henggeler, S. W., Schoenwald, S. K., Borduin, C. M., Rowland, M. D., & Cunningham, P. B. (1998). *Multisystemic treatment of antisocial behavior in children and adolescents.* New York: Guilford Press.

Jacobson, N. S., & Truax, P. (1991). Clinical significance: A statistical approach to defining meaningful change in psychotherapy research. *Journal of Consulting & Clinical Psychology, 59*(1): 12–19.

Johnson, S. M. (2003). Emotionally Focused Couples Therapy: Empiricism and art. [References]. In T. L. Sexton, G. R. Weeks, & M. Robbins (Eds.), *Handbook of family therapy: The science and practice of working with families and couples* (pp. 263–280). New York: Brunner-Routledge.

Lebow, J. (1997). The integrative revolution in couple and family therapy. *Family Process, 36*(1): 1–17.

Liddle, H. A., Dakof, G. A., Parker, K., Diamond, G. S., Barrett, K., & Tejeda, M. (2001). Multidimiensional family therapy for adolescent drug abuse: Results of a randomized clinical trial. *American Journal of Drug & Alcohol Abuse, 27*(4): 651–688.

McFarlane, W. R. (2002). *Multifamily groups in the treatment of severe psychiatric disorders.* New York: Guilford Press.

McFarlane, W. R., Dixon, L., Lukens, E., & Lucksted, A. (2003). Family psychoeducation and schizophrenia: A review of the literature. *Journal of Marital & Family Therapy, 29*(2): 223–245.

Miklowitz, D. J. (1996). Psychotherapy in combination with drug treatment for bipolar disorder. *Psychopharmacology Bulletin 32*(4): 613–621.

Miklowitz, D. J., George, E. L., Axelson, D. A., Kim, E. Y., Birmaher, B., & Schneck, C. (2004). Family-focused treatment for adolescents with bipolar disorder. *Journal of Affective Disorders, 82*(Suppl. 1): S113–S128.

O'Farrell, T. J., & Fals-Stewart, W. (2000). Behavioral couples therapy for alcoholism and drug abuse. *Behavior Therapist, 23*(3): 49–70.

Pinsof, W. M., & Wynne, L. C. (1995a). Effectiveness research in marital and family therapy [Special issue]. *Journal of Marital & Family Therapy, 21*(4): 339–618.

Pinsof, W. M., & Wynne, L. C. (1995b). The efficacy of marital and family therapy: An empirical overview, conclusions, and recommendations. *Journal of Marital & Family Therapy, 21*(4): 585–613.

Prince, S. E., & Jacobson, N. S. (1995). A review and evaluation of marital and family therapies for affective disorders. *Journal of Marital & Family Therapy, 21*(4): 377–401.

Rowe, C., Liddle, H. A., McClintic, K., & Quille, T. J. (2002). Integrative treatment development: Multidimensional family therapy for adolescent substance abuse. [References]. In F. W. Kaslow (Ed.), *Comprehensive handbook of psychotherapy: Integrative/eclectic* (vol. 4, pp. 133–161). New York: John Wiley & Sons.

Snyder, D. K. (2002). Integrating insight-oriented techniques into couple therapy. In J. H. Harvey & A. Wenzel (Eds.), *A clinician's guide to maintaining and enhancing close relationships* (pp. 259–275). Mahwah, NJ: Lawrence Erlbaum Associates.

Snyder, D. K., Wills, R. M., & Grady-Fletcher, A. (1991). Long-term effectiveness of behavioral versus insight-oriented marital therapy: A 4-year follow-up study. *Journal of Consulting & Clinical Psychology, 59*(1): 138–141.

Sprenkle, D. H. (Ed.). (2002). *Effectiveness research in marriage and family therapy.* Alexandria, VA: American Association for Marriage and Family Therapy.

Sprenkle, D. H. (2003). Effectiveness research in marriage and family therapy: Introduction. *Journal of Marital & Family Therapy, 29*(1): 85–96.

Szapocznik, J., & Williams, R. A. (2000). Brief strategic family therapy: Twenty-five years of interplay among theory, research and practice in adolescent behavior problems and drug abuse. *Clinical Child & Family Psychology Review, 3*(2): 117–134.

Weiss, R. L. (1975). Contracts, cognition, and change: A behavioral approach to marriage therapy. *Counseling Psychologist, 5*(3): 15–26.

18

MARITAL PREPARATION AND ENRICHMENT PROGRAMS DOCUMENT THEIR VALUE

Skill-building programs aimed at enhancing marriages and pre-venting problems have become increasingly popular in recent years. They serve a parallel function to couples therapy, enhancing relationships and teaching many of the same skills taught in therapy. This chapter looks at these programs and the evidence for their effectiveness.

Sandy and Tom have known each other for three years and feel very much in love. They met while attending law school, where they immediately discovered they shared strong interests in biking, camping, and traveling. They have a lot of fun together and have planned a lavish wedding and honeymoon. Nonetheless, a skeptical clinical observer might see some signs of trouble. The two of them rarely discuss their expectations about their marriage and the future. Moreover, when emotionally loaded issues come up, they frequently fall into the classic pursuer-withdrawer pattern, with Sandy initiating the discussion and Tom heading for the exit as soon as possible (Fruzzetti & Jacobson,

1990). Their arguments frequently include a wide variety of below-the-belt tactics: Sandy falls into name-calling and bringing up many issues from the past, Tom typically becomes defensive, stops listening, and shifts the focus to criticizing how critical Sandy can be. Not surprisingly, their conflicts typically escalate and rarely result in satisfying resolution.

It's way too early for Tom and Sandy to see themselves as potentially at risk for divorce, yet when Sandy heard a local community mental health center advertise a weekend workshop called the Prevention and Relationship Enhancement Program (PREP), a psycho-educational course in how to make a relationship more satisfying (Renick, Blumberg, & Markman, 1992; Stanley, Blumberg, & Markman, 1999), she managed to convince Tom to sign up with her.

The last 10 years have been a boom time for programs such as PREP that teach specific skills needed for effective communication, problem solving, and conflict resolution and are designed to increase couples' self-awareness and encourage self-disclosure of feelings, mutual empathy, and intimacy. Much of the vast enthusiasm for these preventive programs has come from clergy and community education organizations, and they have remained largely outside the purview of marriage and family therapists, even though they cover much of the territory practitioners typically navigate in couples therapy. But with the mounting evidence that these methods help create more satisfying relationships that last longer and the increasing interest of the public, it seems time for therapists to learn more about them. In fact, given the limits imposed by managed care on traditional practice, some observers are arguing that teaching psycho-educational courses, rather than treating couples and families case by case, is the wave of the future (Halford, Markman, Kline, & Stanley, 2003). But from the viewpoint of the researcher, the question is just how successful these programs are and whether they are an effective alternative to psychotherapy.

Of the almost 40 relationship-enhancement programs that have been developed so far, most have their empirical roots in the ground-breaking studies conducted by researchers like John Gottman (1994, 1998), Robert Weiss (1978), Howard Markman (Markman, Duncan, Storaasli, & Howes, 1987), Frank Fincham (1997), and others, which have provided an empirical foundation for understanding both what makes marriages work and what factors underlie their dissolution. We now have a substantial body of research that has identified both the basic skills associated with satisfying marriages and the skill deficits that typically accompany unhappy relationships. The differences are clear: satisfied couples know how to resolve their differences, whereas dissatisfied couples do not. Although both happy and unhappy couples have arguments, unhappy couples are far more likely to engage in a wide range of destructive fight tactics, including personal attack, dredging up the past, losing focus and name-calling. Satisfied couples are better able to speak clearly with each other and listen empathically. Additionally, as John Gottman has highlighted, distressed couples are far more likely to resort to the "four horsemen of the apocalypse," behaviors highly predictive of later divorce: criticism, defensiveness, withdrawal, and contempt (Gottman, 1999; Gottman & Notarius, 2000). Satisfied couples also have many more positive than negative exchanges and have better problem-solving skills (Weiss & Heyman, 1997). In contrast, dissatisfied couples are much more likely to experience negatively escalating arguments and become stuck in repetitively harmful patterns.

Related research has tracked the problems appearing early in relationships that lead to serious long-term difficulties (Gottman, 1998). Poor communication early on directly predicts relationship dissatisfaction later, particularly the inability to surface painful feelings, find some mutually acceptable way to discuss them, and reach a resolution to the problem. How the male partner handles conflict is particularly important in predicting the trajectory of a heterosexual relationship (Gottman, 1998). In general, men tend to be less competent in relationship skills than women, and when they handle conflict poorly, deterioration in the relationship is more likely than when women do so.

Relationship preparation and enrichment programs are based on the idea that mastering certain skills will lead to more satisfying and enduring relationships. Tom and Sandy learned a great deal during their PREP course. As they listened to lectures and watched videotapes of couples, they learned about problematic patterns for handling conflict. Sandy soon realized that she was a classic pursuer and that in her frustration, she often resorted to personal attack. Tom could see his tendency to withdraw and to end conversations by simply not responding. Both Tom and Sandy saw that this pattern needed to change. Perhaps because their relationship was still strong, it was not hard for each to see his or her own contribution to their problems as a couple.

They learned the "speaker–listener technique," in which one partner speaks and the other repeats what he or she has heard, and then responds (Stanley, Markman, Blumberg, & Eckstein, 1997). They also learned how to give specific constructive feedback, state and negotiate expectations, identify hidden agendas, improve problem-solving skills, increase commitment, focus on the physical relationship and sexuality, develop spiritual values, and use the right skills at the right time. They were given homework to practice the techniques they learned when conflicts occurred between the meetings. An argument one evening centered on Tom's monopolization of the television remote control and Sandy's complaint that she rarely had control over the family television. Although the conversation soon descended into the familiar pattern of attack and withdrawal, they were able to call on their newfound skills and began to take turns speaking and listening, which led to a satisfactory compromise. The conversation then moved on to consider other, similar situations that involved distributing control. Tom and Sandy agreed that in these activities, one person would be primarily designated as being in charge but the other's feelings always would be considered. By the end of the weekend, Tom and Sandy were satisfied that they had learned some skills that could make a real difference in their future relationship.

Despite their common focus on relationship skills, there are also significant differences among the many couples' communication programs. Relationship Enhancement (Guerney, 1988), for example, developed by psychologist Bernard Guerney and associates, teaches many of the same skills as PREP, but with a more experiential emphasis. Psychologist David Olson and colleagues have created programs called PREPARE and ENRICH 2000 that make much more use of assessment scales for determining compatibilities and areas of relationship difficulty (Olson & Olson, 1999). The Practical Application of Intimate Relationship Skills program, developed by social worker Lori Gordon, is a more extensive, 4- to 5-month, 120-hour psycho-educational course that includes skills training, but features a greater emphasis on developing an in-depth knowledge of the self, especially how past experiences can disrupt present-day relationships. Other popular programs include The Minnesota Couples Communication Program, developed by psychologist Sherrod Miller and his colleagues; Training in Marital Enrichment, developed by psychologists Don Dinkmeyer and Jon Carlson; Growing Together, developed by sociologist Preston Dyer and educator Genie Dyer; the Marriage Survival Kit, developed by psychologist John Gottman; Getting the Love You Want, developed by pastoral counselor Harville Hendrix; and Marriage Savers, developed by clergyman Mike McManus (Crohn, Markman, Blumberg, & Levine, 2000; Floyd, Markman, Kelly, Blumberg, & Stanley, 1995; Halford & Markman, 1997; Widenfelt, Markman, Guerney, & Behrens, 1997). Perhaps the most widely known and oldest program is Marriage Encounter, developed within the Catholic Church, which features structured discussion of such topics as intimacy, sexuality, and spirituality, but lacks the skills-building focus of the other programs.

So just how successful are these programs in transforming relationships? Howard Markman, Scott Stanley, and colleagues have followed the heterosexual participants in PREP for more than 12 years in the Denver Family Development Study, and have convincingly demonstrated that those who participated in PREP before marriage have maintained richer, more stable relationships than those who did not (Renick et al., 1992). In fact, PREP couples maintained, or even improved, their levels of relationship satisfaction after the program, whereas couples who did not participate became less satisfied over time. PREP couples, as compared with couples who did not receive PREP, had one-third the likelihood of breaking up, consistently showed better communication and reported fewer instances of physical violence (Markman, Renick, Floyd, & Stanley, 1993). In a study in Germany, 4% of PREP couples had divorced at a five-year follow-up, whereas 24% of couples who received either the more traditional Marriage Encounter or no premarital counseling divorced within five years (Hahlweg, Markman, Thurmaier, Engl, & Eckert, 1998). There is considerable evidence that marriage preparation and enrichment programs, in general, are highly effective and satisfying for participants. In a comprehensive evaluation of the 85 studies available, marriage and family therapist Paul Giblin and colleagues conducted a meta-analysis of these programs' typical impact and found that couples who participate in a program are 66% more likely to be better off than couples who do not participate (Achenbach, 1999; Giblin, 1986, 1996; Giblin & Combs, 2003). Giblin's analysis also revealed that these programs appear to affect what people actually *do* in relationships rather than just influencing relationship satisfaction. Couples' behaviors actually change as a result of the programs. Because women are typically better than men at relationship skills before attending, the programs have more direct impact on men.

The research literature is still uncertain about whom these programs help the most. In his meta-analysis, Giblin found more impact on younger, less educated, recently married, and more distressed couples, all of whom appear to have had more to learn. No statistical relationship was found between outcome and years of marriage, income, or religion. The programs did not appear to differ substantially in their effectiveness, although programs of 12 hours or more did better than those of briefer duration. Across programs, typical participants tended to be better educated than average. Based on this finding and some of his own data, psychologist Thomas Bradbury (Bradbury & Fincham, 1990) has suggested that, contrary to Giblin's findings, these programs primarily work with a highly select set of couples and may not be as effective with less educated groups from different backgrounds. However, program researchers such as Markman insist that they find the programs just as effective across a wide range of participants.

How are these programs similar or different from couples therapy? In contrast to the highly individualized approach of most couples therapy, these brief, time-limited programs use a group format and teach generic skills. Couples who enroll are basically satisfied with their relationships and do not, typically, describe themselves as having substantial difficulties. Usually, they are seeking enrichment, education, and new skills, not immediate help with a marital crisis.

Why then is there a need for more expensive clinical approaches when these psycho-educational programs have so great an impact? Ultimately, the answer to this question has to do with matching the right intervention with the right clients. Preparation and enrichment programs demonstrate their greatest impact on those who are most likely to enroll in them—primarily heterosexual young people who are substantially satisfied with their relationships. However, it has yet to be demonstrated that these programs are effective with the more severely troubled couples who typically seek therapy. For couples who are on the verge of breaking up or have other substantial difficulties, couples therapy is the only intervention established as effective. Further, Giblin found in his meta-analysis that the positive effects of enrichment programs on participants were considerably smaller than those typically experienced in couples therapy.

Nonetheless, the limitations of psycho-educational programs should not diminish their distinct contribution. It seems most useful to think of therapy and psycho-education as overlapping and often complementary approaches with different emphases and strengths. Clearly, both couples therapists and the leaders of couples preparation and enrichment programs have a great deal to learn from one another.

RESOURCES

Gottman, J. M. (1994). *What predicts divorce? The relationship between marital processes and marital outcomes.* Hillsdale, NJ: Lawrence Erlbaum Associates.

Halford, W., Markman, H. J., Kline, G. H., & Stanley, S. M. (2003). Best practice in couple relationship education. *Journal of Marital & Family Therapy,* 29(3): 385–406.

Renick, M. J., Blumberg, S. L., & Markman, H. J. (1992). The Prevention and Relationship Enhancement (PREP): An empirically based preventive intervention program for couples. *Family Relations: Interdisciplinary Journal of Applied Family Studies,* 4(2): 141–147.

REFERENCES

Achenbach, T. M. (Ed.). (1999). Developmental taxonomy. In W. K. Silverman & T. H. Ollendick (Eds.), *Developmental issues in the clinical treatment of children* (pp. 31–43). Needham Heights, MA: Allyn & Bacon.

Bradbury, T. N., & Fincham, F. D. (1990). Preventing marital dysfunction: Review and analysis. In F. D. Fincham & T. N. Bradbury (Eds.), *The psychology of marriage: Basic issues and applications* (pp. 375–401). New York: Guilford Press.

Crohn, J., Markman, H. J., Blumberg, S. L., & Levine, J. R. (2000). *Fighting for your Jewish marriage: Preserving a lasting promise.* San Francisco: Jossey-Bass.

Fincham, F. D. (1997). Understanding marriage: From fish scales to milliseconds. *Psychologist, 10*(12): 543–547.

Floyd, F. J., Markman, H. J., Kelly, S., Blumberg, S. L., & Stanley, S. M. (1995). Preventive intervention and relationship enhancement. In N. S. Jacobson & A. S. Gurman (Eds.), *Clinical handbook of couple therapy* (pp. 212–226). New York: Guilford Press.

Fruzzetti, A. E., & Jacobson, N. S. (1990). Toward a behavioral conceptualization of adult intimacy: Implications for marital therapy. In E. A. Blechman (Ed.), *Emotions and the family: For better or for worse* (pp. 117–135). Hillsdale, NJ: Lawrence Erlbaum Associates.

Giblin, P. (1986). Research and assessment in marriage and family enrichment: A meta-analysis study. *Journal of Psychotherapy & the Family, 2*(1): 79–96.

Giblin, P. (1996). Marriage and family enrichment: A process whose time has come (and gone?). *Family Journal: Counseling and Therapy for Couples and Families, 4*(2): 143–151.

Giblin, P., & Combs, M. P. (2003). Marital enrichment in clinical practice. In G. P. Sholevar (Ed.), *Textbook of family and couples therapy: Clinical applications.* Washington, DC: American Psychiatric Press.

Gottman, J. M. (1994). *What predicts divorce? The relationship between marital processes and marital outcomes.* Hillsdale, NJ: Lawrence Erlbaum Associates.

Gottman, J. M. (1998). Psychology and the study of the marital processes. *Annual Review of Psychology, 49*: 169–197.

Gottman, J. M. (1999). *The marriage clinic: A scientifically based marital therapy.* New York: W. W. Norton & Co.

Gottman, J. M., & Notarius, C. I. (2000). Decade review: Observing marital interaction. *Journal of Marriage & the Family, 62*(4): 927–947.

Guerney, B. G. (1988). Family relationship enhancement: A skill training approach. In L. A. Bond & B. M. Wagner (Eds.), *Families in Transition: Primary Prevention Programs That Work.* Beverly Hills: Sage Publications.

Hahlweg, K., Markman, H. J., Thurmaier, F., Engl, J., & Eckert, V. (1998). Prevention of marital distress: Results of a German prospective longitudinal study. *Journal of Family Psychology, 12*(4): 543–556.

Halford, W., & Markman, H. J. (Eds.). (1997). *Clinical handbook of marriage and couples interventions*. New York: John Wiley & Sons.

Halford, W., Markman, H. J., Kline, G. H., & Stanley, S. M. (2003). Best practice in couple relationship education. *Journal of Marital & Family Therapy, 29*(3): 385–406.

Markman, H. J., Duncan, W., Storaasli, R. D., & Howes, P. W. (1987). The prediction and prevention of marital distress: A longitudinal investigation. In K. Hahlweg & M. J. Goldstein (Eds.), *Understanding major mental disorder: The contribution of family interaction research* (pp. 266–289). New York: Family Process Press.

Markman, H. J., Renick, M. J., Floyd, F. J., & Stanley, S. M. (1993). Preventing marital distress through communication and conflict management training: A 4- and 5-year follow-up. *Journal of Consulting & Clinical Psychology, 61*(1): 70–77.

Olson, D. H., & Olson, A. K. (Eds.). (1999). *PREPARE/ENRICH program: Version 2000*.

Renick, M. J., Blumberg, S. L., & Markman, H. J. (1992). The Prevention and Relationship Enhancement (PREP): An empirically based preventive intervention program for couples. *Family Relations: Interdisciplinary Journal of Applied Family Studies, 41*(2): 141–147.

Stanley, S. M., Blumberg, S. L., & Markman, H. J. (1999). Helping couples fight for their marriages: The PREP approach. In R. Berger & M. T. Hannah (Eds.), *Preventive approaches in couples therapy* (pp. 279–303). Philadelphia: Brunner/Mazel.

Stanley, S. M., Markman, H. J., Blumberg, S. L., & Eckstein, D. (1997). The speaker/listener technique. *Family Journal: Counseling & Therapy for Couples & Families, 5*(1): 82–83.

Weiss, R. L. (1978). The conceptualization of marriage from a behavioral perspective. In T. J. Paolino & B. S. McCrady (Eds.), *Marriage and marital therapy: Psychoanalytic, behavioral and systems theory perspectives* (pp. 165–239). Oxford, UK: Brunner/Mazel.

Weiss, R. L., & Heyman, R. E. (1997). A clinical-research overview of couples interactions. In W. Halford & H. J. Markman (Eds.), *Clinical handbook of marriage and couples interventions* (pp. 13–41). New York: John Wiley & Sons.

Widenfelt, B. V., Markman, H. J., Guerney, B., & Behrens, B. C. (1997). Prevention of relationship problems. In W. Halford & H. J. Markman (Eds.), *Clinical handbook of marriage and couples interventions* (pp. 651–675). New York: John Wiley & Sons.

19

WHAT REALLY MAKES COUPLES HAPPY? A CONTROVERSY DIVIDES THE WORLD OF MARITAL RESEARCHERS

Researchers don't always agree with one another, even when look-ing at the same research. The cause may be ambiguous findings in a study that are open to interpretation or, sometimes, questions arising from the threats to validity from methodological problems in a study. This chapter describes such a difference of opinion about the meaning of findings between two outstanding groups of family researchers: John Gottman and his collaborators, and Scott Stanley, Tom Bradbury, and Howard Markman. Their debate is instructive, not only for what it tells us about marital processes, but also for understanding the kinds of methodological issues raised. It provides an example of how science progresses through an iteration between findings and discussion of the meaning of those findings, followed up with further research that sheds more light on the question in focus.

John Gottman is the most widely respected and recognized marriage researcher in the world today. Over the past four decades, he has been responsible for a watershed change in the impact of research findings on couples therapy, illuminating crucial features that distinguish happy from unhappy couples and provide clues for creating and maintaining better marriages. In his "love lab" Gottman has investigated questions of such fundamental importance (for example, can we predict which couples will divorce and which will be happy?) and his research methods have been so innovative (including recording couples' moment-by-moment physiological responses to each other) that his work has captured the imagination not only of fellow researchers, but of clinicians, the media, and the general public.

Among Gottman's principal contributions have been the identification of "the four horsemen" of marital discord (criticism, defensiveness, contempt, and stonewalling) and a new, fifth horseman (belligerence), which are identifiable predictors of divorce and dissatisfaction (Gottman, 1994, 1999). He has also enumerated a parallel set of essential caring processes that lead to what he terms "positive sentiment override" and relationship success (Gottman, 1998). Gottman's research has led him to propose a theory of how successful and unsuccessful marriages evolve, along with a clinical model for intervention to help marriages become satisfying.

Some of Gottman's recent work was challenged, however, in an article in the February 2000 issue of the *Journal of Marriage and the Family* by another respected group of younger marital researchers, including Scott Stanley, Thomas Bradbury, and Howard Markman (2000), a former student of Gottman's. Stanley and Markman are the principal developers of the Prevention and Relationship Enhancement Program (PREP), one of the most prominent methods of marital preparation and enrichment, which was based, in part, on findings from Gottman's research (Stanley, Blumberg, & Markman, 1999). PREP's approach and the research supporting it have received a great deal of media attention, often presented in tandem with Gottman's as cornerstones of the emerging science of marriage. Now, citing invalid conclusions and faulty methodology in Gottman's research, Stanley and his fellow researchers have sparked a debate about their work and Gottman's.

THE GOTTMAN STORY

The debate was set off by the publication by Gottman with his colleagues James Coan, Sybil Carrere, and Catherine Swanson (1998) of an article in the February 1998 *Journal of Marriage and the Family* reporting on a longitudinal study of marital happiness. In the study, Gottman's team observed 179 newlywed couples as they discussed relationship problems in Gottman's love lab. The team took physiological measures assessing arousal during the discussions, videotaped the couples, and coded the behaviors and affects they displayed. Gottman's team then followed up with the couples over 4–6 years. They sorted the couples into three groups: the 17 couples who divorced, the 20 couples who emerged as most happily married, and the 20 couples who emerged as the most unhappily married. The remaining couples did not fall into any of these groups and were not part of the study. The study looked at the degree to which these couples' interaction patterns as newlyweds predicted the success of their marriages. The study's goal was to test how well common notions of what is crucial in marriage predicted which couples would emerge as happily married, dissatisfied but still married, or divorced.

Gottman and his team reported a number of provocative findings from their study. Perhaps most challenging to conventional wisdom was the failure of some patterns that have frequently been cited as crucial to marital success to have any value in predicting marital happiness.

- The amount of anger displayed in the premarital interactions did not predict the success of marriages. Couples who emerged later as happy were as likely to express anger in the discussions as those who turned out to have less successful marriages. Gottman and colleagues concluded that the amount of harm caused by anger in marriage is overrated.
- The extent to which couples responded in kind to anger in their interactions also did not predict marital success. Gottman and associates concluded that it is characteristic of all marriages, even happy, stable ones, for people to react negatively when facing negativity.
- The extent to which the couples used active listening early in marriage also did not predict their subsequent success; in fact, almost no one used active listening in their discussions. Gottman and colleagues concluded active listening has little utility in successful marriages.

In contrast to the failure of these predictors, several other premarital interaction patterns were highly predictive of who would emerge as happy, dissatisfied, or divorced. Patterns predicting success included the following:

- Couples showing each other positive affect while discussing a difficult issue.
- Husbands being influenced by their wives and not escalating an argument when presented with negativity.
- Wives raising concerns in a way that does not trigger strong feelings in their husbands.
- Wives using humor to soothe their husbands.
- Partners ending conflicts with a return of positive feeling.
- The absence of defensiveness, contempt, and belligerence between partners.

Although some of these findings were concerned with aspects of interaction that had rarely previously been studied, all these findings were consistent with Gottman's earlier research. He has developed an approach to marital therapy, based in part on these findings, that counsels couples to expect conflict, but to develop a "gentle" approach toward it (Gottman, 1999, 2004). Gottman suggests that such an approach includes allowing for humor and positive connection during conflict and, in the most typical scenario, for women to start discussions in a softer way and men to accept influence and not escalate conflicts.

THE CRITIQUE

In the February 2000 *Journal of Marriage and the Family*, Stanley, Bradbury, and Markman took issue with a number of the Gottman team's conclusions (2000). They argued that the pernicious effects of anger accrue and that the power of negative exchanges should not be underestimated, pointing to other research that indicates that a disproportionate number of troubled couples fall prey to these patterns. Although Gottman maintained active listening does not occur much in successful marriages, and may even be harmful in some situations, Stanley and colleagues pointed to a long history of research showing the value of active listening, particularly in slowing the escalation of conflicts. They suggested that although active listening may not occur very often without mindfulness and practice, it is an essential skill in resolving unproductive arguing. Stanley, Bradbury, and Markman also disagreed about the meaning of the finding that couples do better when husbands accept influence from wives and wives raise concerns to husbands gently. They argued that the Gottman team made an unwarranted leap from the actual data, which centered on how much one partner's emotions affected the other's (i.e., whether one becomes angry when the other does), giving the misleading label of "influence" to behavior that was not about influence as it is ordinarily understood, but rather about catching the other's feeling state.

Most of all, they pointed to a number of methodological failings that open up the possibility that at least some of the Gottman group's conclusions may be overstated or even incorrect. They claimed that Gottman and his associates made several technical errors that could explain some of their results. These include the following:

- Suggest that analyzing only the most and least happy marriages diminished the generalizability of the study and increased the likelihood that impressive findings would emerge.
- Question whether the three groups of couples that were formed for comparison purposes based on their later marital happiness were comparable to one another as newlyweds. If the groups were not comparable, those differences might account for the differences in marital success, rather than those patterns the Gottman group found important.
- Question the format of the study that made it inevitable that the wives would initiate the interactions, thereby failing to take into account situations in which husbands initiate conversation.
- Question the timing for assessing the physiological responses.
- Question the conclusions about anger because the study narrowly defined what constitutes anger.
- Argue that the study's small, unrepresentative population makes suspect broad generalizations to couples beyond those in the study.

In their rejoinder, also in the February 2000 *Journal of Marriage and the Family*, Gottman and his team replied to each of Stanley, Bradbury, and Markman's criticisms (Carrere, Buehlman, Gottman, Coan, & Ruckstuhl, 2000; Gottman, Carrere, Swanson, & Coan, 2000). They argue that the central findings of this study now have emerged in several different studies Gottman has conducted. They explain that they were precisely interested in the differences between the most and least happy couples, but also went on to point out that when they add the mid-range couples in the analysis, essentially the same results emerge. To the objection that the groups were initially not comparable, they argued that they did the proper analyses and the groups did not differ from one another in their personal characteristics. The format of the study, they claimed, in which the women began the discussions, replicated the most typical way couples communicate: women initiate, men respond. They suggested that to look at situations in which men initiate communication would merely be to look at atypical situations, which tells us little.

CONCLUSION

In spite of this recent disagreement, Gottman and Stanley, Bradbury, and Markman do agree about a number of things. They agree that couples therapy should be strongly informed by science and that there is great value in helping couples learn the skills needed in marriage. They agree on the pernicious effects of the "four horsemen" in marriage. They also see eye to eye about the importance of positive connection and of creating and maintaining a high enough ratio of positive-to-negative experience to generate marital satisfaction.

But what do we make of the debate? Although the Gottman team does a fine job of responding point by point to the concerns raised, the multiple threats to validity pointed out by Stanley, Bradbury, and Markman clearly indicate that the findings of the latest Gottman study must be replicated before we accept them as a true, accurate, and widely applicable picture of marriage. This is particularly the case when we consider the more radical findings that question widely circulated results of other marital therapy research; for example, Gottman's assertion that anger is benign or that active listening is not necessary and may be counterproductive for successful marriages.

The exchange between the Gottman and Stanley groups points to something exciting going on in the world of marital therapy research that directly tests our most important assumptions about marriage and couple therapy. Whether we are concerned with the clinical impact of positive exchanges, anger, or active listening, there is a growing body of research that will ultimately offer empirical evidence on matters that have been long debated only in the arena of beliefs. Findings such as the pernicious effects on marriage of Gottman's "four horsemen," the need for a sufficiently high ratio of positive-to-negative experience in marriage, and the importance of what Gottman calls "positive sentiment override" (a strong positive feeling within a marriage that can help withstand the vicissitudes of everyday life) have already been sufficiently well demonstrated that they should inform all approaches to couples therapy. Other provocative findings, such as many of those in the Gottman, Coan, Carrere, and Swanson study, are not yet ready to stand as foundations for practice, but at present have greatest import in the ideas they stimulate and the hypotheses they suggest—hypotheses that no doubt will be tested in future research.

RESOURCES

Gottman, J. M. (1999). *The marriage clinic: A scientifically based marital therapy.* New York: W. W. Norton & Co.

Gottman, J. M., Carrere, S., Swanson, C., & Coan, J. A. (2000, February). Reply to "From basic research to interventions." *Journal of Marriage & the Family, 62*(1): 265–273.

Gottman, J. M., Coan, J., Carrere, S., & Swanson, C. (1998, February). Predicting marital happiness and stability from newlywed interactions. *Journal of Marriage & the Family, 60*(1): 5–22.

Stanley, S. M., Bradbury, T. N., & Markman, H. J. (2000, February). Structural flaws in the bridge from basic research on marriage to interventions for couples. *Journal of Marriage & the Family, 62*(1): 256–264

REFERENCES

Carrere, S., Buehlman, K. T., Gottman, J. M., Coan, J. A., & Ruckstuhl, L. (2000). Predicting marital stability and divorce in newlywed couples. *Journal of Family Psychology, 14*(1): 42–58.

Gottman, J. M. (1994). *What predicts divorce? The relationship between marital processes and marital outcomes.* Hillsdale, NJ: Lawrence Erlbaum Associates.

Gottman, J. M. (1998). Psychology and the study of the marital processes. *Annual Review of Psychology, 49*: 169–197.

Gottman, J. M. (1999). *The marriage clinic: A scientifically based marital therapy.* New York: W. W. Norton & Co.

Gottman, J. M., Carrere, S., Swanson, C., & Coan, J. A. (2000, February). Reply to "From basic research to interventions." *Journal of Marriage & the Family, 62*(1): 265–273.

Gottman, J. M., Coan, J., Carrere, S., & Swanson, C. (1998, February). Predicting marital happiness and stability from newlywed interactions. *Journal of Marriage & the Family, 60*(1): 5–22.

Gottman, J. S. (Ed.). (2004). *The marriage clinic casebook.* New York: W. W. Norton & Co.

Stanley, S. M., Blumberg, S. L., & Markman, H. J. (1999). Helping couples fight for their marriages: The PREP approach. In R. Berger & M. T. Hannah (Eds.), *Preventive approaches in couples therapy* (pp. 279–303). Philadelphia: Brunner/Mazel.

Stanley, S. M., Bradbury, T. N., & Markman, H. J. (2000, February). Structural flaws in the bridge from basic research on marriage to interventions for couples. *Journal of Marriage & the Family, 62*(1): 256–264.

20

EMERGING EVIDENCE IN THE RESEARCH ABOUT DIVORCE

Approximately half of married couples divorce. Thus, research on divorce and its repercussions and prevention has vast importance for society and psychotherapy. Yet the research on divorce provides a prime example of how research findings can be poorly represented in the media, especially when it deals with values and when some of it combines questionable methodology and powerful findings. This chapter looks at what research tells us about the impact of divorce, the prediction of divorce, and about the impact of therapy and prevention programs on divorce.

Over the past decade, a movement of "marriage savers"—therapists, marriage-education programs, and religious and secular pro-marriage organizations has been pushing back against what many feel is a divorce culture run amok. To cement their case against divorce, many marriage savers—particularly social conservatives—quote liberally and publicly from what they present as "definitive" research on the damaging effects of broken marriages on individual spouses, families, and, most of all, the ill-fated "children of divorce." You would never know, listening to this often polemicized use of evidence, that the social science research on divorce actually presents a far more nuanced—and far less pessimistic—picture. What, then, does the research about divorce tell us?

THE IMPACT OF DIVORCE

To understand the controversy about the impact of divorce, it's helpful to take a look at the history of research into the issue. Perhaps the most famous of the early research were the longitudinal studies of Judith Wallerstein (Wallerstein, 1984, 1987; Wallerstein & Blakeslee, 1989; Wallerstein, Corbin, & Lewis, 1988; Wallerstein & Lewis, 2004) now of the Judith Wallerstein Center for the Family in Transition in California. In the early 1970s, Wallerstein first conducted a study in which she interviewed a sample of 131 children and their parents from middle-class, white, urban, Northern California families that recently had gone through a divorce (Wallerstein & Kelly, 1974, 1975, 1980). In the years following, she interviewed the children of these divorces at several junctures in their lives into young adulthood (only 93 of the original 131 children were reinterviewed at the 25-year mark). In their initial study, Wallerstein and her then-collaborator, Joan B. Kelly, found a range of reactions of the children in their sample just after the divorce. Some seemed to be handling the disruption without major emotional difficulty, but some children were struggling with depression, school difficulties, and other psychopathology.

After the first study of these children, Kelly (who came to doubt Wallerstein's premise that children were "scarred for life" by divorce) left the project. Over the next 20 years, Wallerstein alone conducted three further follow-ups of the children from these divorces and came to increasingly dark conclusions about the long-term effects of divorce (Wallerstein & Blakeslee, 1989; Wallerstein, Lewis, & Blakeslee, 2002). By the time she had produced her last follow-up study in 2001, Wallerstein believed that divorce was not only harmful to children when it happened, but it also led to what she termed a "sleeper effect" that crippled these children's ability to form romantic relationships as adults. Her view was adopted wholesale by socially conservative, self-defined "family values" proponents and widely trumpeted as proving beyond a doubt that virtually all children whose parents divorce suffer traumatic and lasting emotional injury.

Yet the methodology underlying Wallerstein's famous study is today considered primitive by most social science researchers. In the first place, she is criticized for basing her conclusions on interviews with a small sample of divorced families representing only one particular kind of family—urban, middle class, and Caucasian. The study, critics contend, is thereby low in what is called external validity, the ability to represent the general population.

A more serious objection is that Wallerstein's version of the effects of divorce may not accurately represent even the population she studied. There was never a control group (now virtually *de rigueur* in this kind of study)—that is, a set of comparable individuals at the same juncture in life who had not experienced divorce in their family. Thus it is impossible to know how many of the difficulties Wallerstein observed in the children of divorce might also hold true for those whose parents did *not* get divorced.

Additionally, Wallerstein's data-gathering methods have been challenged. Rather than being the dispassionate observer, she clearly developed relationships with many of the children of divorce she followed and encouraged them to read her books. Some critics suggest she actively cocreated with them the idea that they were irreparably damaged by their parents' divorce. In sum, the threats to validity render the Wallerstein reports a good read, but poor science.

Wallerstein's study did have the positive effect of spurring some of the most prominent social science researchers in America to carefully check out whether her findings applied to other populations as well. Of the many projects that have assessed the impact of divorce on families, most prominent have been those conducted by Mavis Hetherington (Hetherington, 1979, 1990; Hetherington & Kelly, 2003), of the University of Virginia, who followed divorced families over time; Christine Buchanan, Eleanor Maccoby, and Sanford Dornbusch (1996), of Stanford University, who examined the effects of divorce on adolescents; Constance Ahrons (Ahrons & Tanner, 2003), of the University of Southern California, who examined the effects on the adult partners over time; and Robert Emery (Laumann-Billings & Emery, 2000), of the University of Virginia, who examined the feelings of young adults whose parents had divorced when they were children.

So what does this better research tell us? A great deal, as it turns out—but it is a far more complex and hopeful story than Wallerstein's research suggests.

1. For almost everyone experiencing divorce, there are indeed short-term negative consequences. Both children and adults show more role strain, a greater number of emotional and behavioral difficulties, and, in Mavis Hetherington's provocative words, a feeling of not "being me"—that is, of experiencing and acting in ways that the person doesn't typically act and feel (Hetherington & Kelly, 2003).

2. But, after this initial period of one to two years, most family members in divorced families do well and cannot be distinguished on measures of functioning, symptoms, or happiness from families that did not go through divorce. That is, most of those in divorced families don't suffer from depression, anxiety, school or work problems, or grave disruptions in their lives.

3. Rates of problems in families, both in children and adults, who have gone through divorce remain higher over time than in non-divorced families, but only *slightly* higher (e.g., about 25% in children from divorced families vs. 10%–15% in other children). The vast majority of children whose parents divorce, even when they have problems, fall within the normal range on all measures of functioning and symptoms.

4. There is no specific evidence that family members who go through divorce are any worse off than those headed by an unhappily married couple who stay married. To determine what impact divorce *per se* has on family members, the divorced sample typically is compared with samples that include both with happily married parents and undivorced but unhappily married parents. Even the percentage of family members in divorced families who have slightly more difficulty than those in nondivorced families may be inflated in the research findings reported, because the former have been compared with all undivorced families, happy and unhappy alike. That is, it's hard to sort out how much of their difficulty stems from divorce and how much simply from living in a family headed by spouses in a troubled, conflict-loaded marriage.

5. Indeed, *high conflict in marriage* is a major risk factor (and many researchers would say the greatest risk factor) both for children of parents whose marriages last over time and for children of parents who divorce (Grych & Fincham, 1999). It is not known whether high conflict is worse for children when it is an aspect of the divorcing family (either before or after the divorce) or when it is chronically present in marriages that remain intact. High conflict, in either context, hurts everyone.

6. Even though children from divorced families do not necessarily do worse, or do only slightly worse on average, in life than those whose parents stay together, children of divorce almost universally experience emotional suffering at the time of the divorce and have strong feelings about the event long afterward. When Robert Emery surveyed college students at the University of Virginia about their experiences with divorce in their families (Laumann-Billings & Emery, 2000), he found that even these academically successful young people typically told stories of family life filled with pain. For example, nearly 50% believed they had a harder childhood than others (compared with 14% among adults whose parents' marriages remained intact) and 28% wondered if their fathers loved them (compared with 10% among adults whose parents had not divorced).

7. According to some researchers, one group of children is worse off after divorce than they were when their parents were together. These are children who had never witnessed any signs of overt unhappiness or conflict between their parents before the divorce and for whom the earlier family life had been smooth and easy. Sociologist Paul Amato (2001) of the University of Nebraska and author with Ross Thompson of *The Postdivorce Family*, for example, consider these children of low-conflict parents particularly vulnerable. Others, however, including Constance Ahrons, point out that we simply don't know how their lives would have progressed if their parents had stayed together—there are no studies that directly compare how these children do when unhappily married parents divorce and when they do not, nor is it possible to project how those unhappy marriages would evolve over time.

In sum, divorce is undoubtedly painful, but, on the other hand, we simply do not know whether it's better or worse for children if their parents divorce than if they stay together in an unhappy marriage. There are indications, however, that the happiness of children has less to do with the simple fact of divorce—whether it happens or not—than with the nature of their family life—whether it is basically stable, calm, without open conflict and emotional turmoil, or whether there is a lot of fighting, anxiety, and depression. It is certainly possible that children of divorced parents, who grow up in a peaceful, stable, financially secure environment without a lot of parental conflict, may well be better off than children living with parents who don't divorce but do fight all the time.

PREDICTING WHO WILL DIVORCE

Another line of research with direct implications for the practice of psychotherapy is predicting who will divorce. It has been possible for some time to predict which marriages will be happy and which will be unhappy—by looking at factors like the ratio of positive-to-negative interactions, presence of spousal violence, psychopathology in one or both spouses, communication skills (or lack thereof), and level of shared expectations. But, until the last decade, it was true that predicting which couples would actually stay together and which would divorce was impossible—there were just too many seemingly random variables.

John Gottman's (Gottman, 1999; Gottman & Notarius, 2000) path-breaking research, however, has radically changed this view by uncovering the particular factors that do foreshadow divorce. What Gottman and his collaborator Richard Levenson (1992, 1999, 2000, 2002a, 2002b) isolated as predictors were not aspects of individual personality, but certain processes engaged in by the couple. Gottman and Levinson found that the presence in the marriage of what they termed the "four horsemen" (patterns of criticism, defensiveness, contempt, stonewalling, and a recently added fifth, belligerence) are very strong signs that a divorce is on its way. It appears, for example, that when one partner treats the other with contempt or stonewalling—treating him or her as if he or she weren't present, worth listening to, or worthy of respect, the marriage is probably on its way to ending. Surprisingly, Gottman found that the extent to which couples argued was unrelated to whether they divorced. Instead, what mattered was how couples treated each other, especially during arguments. Gottman describes how these patterns of mutual mistreatment (one or more of the five horsemen) tend to produce what he calls a "cascade" effect—a downward spiral of worse and worse behavior by both spouses, leading with a kind of inevitability to divorce.

Gottman's insights are invaluable to clinicians, arming them with the kind of empirically validated information they can use with great effect with couples on a slippery slope. In my own practice, I will directly point out to clients who show one of Gottman's "horsemen" how their behavior corresponds to patterns that research has shown lead to the demise of marriage. Hearing that their behavior has been definitively linked to divorce can be a loud wake-up call for couples, making them more aware of what they are doing and promoting a real sense of urgency about changing how they treat each other.

PREVENTING DIVORCE

A great deal, maybe most, marital therapy is conducted with couples hovering on the tipping point of getting divorced. With the frequency of divorce now around 50% of marriages in our society, a fundamental goal of marital therapy and the plethora of marriage education and enrichment programs available is to help keep couples together in at least reasonably satisfactory marriages. And yet, very little actual research has been done to answer the simplest, most fundamental questions looking at the impact on divorce of both marital therapy and marital preparation and enrichment programs: Can or do these therapeutic and educational interventions actually reduce the frequency of divorce? As yet, the large sample sizes and lengthy follow-up over time required to examine these questions, coupled with the limited funds available to study these interventions, have left us with few relevant studies. It has been established that both marital therapy and marital preparation/enrichment are effective in improving relationship skills and marital satisfaction, but the impact on divorce is still unknown.

And we have not even begun to have research that examines the kinds of complex questions that are compelling for the future direction of the marital therapy field and which often today become the focus of discussion: Do marital therapies do a better job of improving marriages and keeping couples together when they demonstrate an active bias in favor of staying married or when they assume a posture of strict neutrality about what the couple does? According to the marriage preservers, the answer is obvious—the more a therapist "fights" for the marriage, the better chance the marriage has. But, as yet, there is no research clearly demonstrating this position.

Nonetheless, to the extent there is such research, there are some encouraging findings. Kurt Hahlweg, Howard Markman, and their colleagues (Hahlweg, Markman, Thurmaier, Engl, & Eckert, 1998) showed that, after taking a six-session Couples Learning program, 9% of the recipients divorced after three years compared with 22% in the control group who had not taken the course. In another study, Andrew Christenson of the University of California–Los Angeles and the late Neil Jacobson of the University of Washington and their colleagues studied the impact on couples' intentions to divorce of two treatments—traditional behavioral marital therapy and a version of behavioral therapy accentuating acceptance of one's partner called Integrative Behavior Couple Therapy (Christensen et al., 2004; Jacobson, Christensen, Prince, Cordova, & Eldridge, 2000). They found that both treatments decreased clients' thoughts about divorce to a level matching that of typical nondistressed couples, even though many couples in this study began treatment with a high level of marital dissatisfaction and were close to ending their marriages. An interesting finding in the Christensen study was that changes in couples' thoughts about divorce most often came early in treatment (before the 12th session), suggesting that changes, if they were going to occur at all, happened earlier rather than later in the therapy.

Thus it seems that at least some marital therapies and some education programs do have an impact on rates of divorce. Yet, the research is still too limited to give us much insight into the complex questions of when marriages can and cannot be improved, when the therapist's commitment to preserving the marriage is most helpful, or when divorce might be the best choice for everyone in a family. If researchers can find the money to do the research (and for whatever reason there is almost no such money available to study marital therapy aimed at distressed marriages), these are among the questions that need examination.

CONCLUSION

In summary, we know a lot more about marriage and divorce than we did even 10 years ago, and this knowledge has real clinical value, particularly in educating our clients about what behavior ruins marriages—so maybe they can stop doing it—and, if that fails, what to expect to experience during and after a divorce.

However, research can accurately depict only some of the realities of divorce: what it is, why it happens, and how it might be averted. Research cannot tell us about what we as individuals value. Some value the preservation of marriage above all. Others value individual happiness more or think in terms of promoting what they see as best for long-term family development, even if it involves remarriage. We need to continue debating these fraught issues about competing values. But, the debates, if they are to have any substantive meaning, must be informed by good, relevant research rather than by the biased reporting of questionable "findings" from inadequate studies that serve a particular social, moral, or political agenda. As clinicians and citizens, by becoming informed consumers of this research, we can begin to separate solid, rational arguments from moralistic exhortation.

RESOURCES

Amato, P. R. (2001). Children of divorce in the 1990s: An update of the Amato and Keith (1991) meta-analysis. *Journal of Family Psychology, 15*: 355–370.

Gottman, J. M., & Levenson, R. W. (1992). Marital processes predictive of later dissolution: Behavior, physiology, and health. *Journal of Personality & Social Psychology, 63*: 221–233.

Grych, J. H., & Fincham, F. D. (1999). The adjustment of children from divorced families: Implications of empirical research for clinical intervention. In R. M. Galatzer-Levy & L. Kraus (Eds.), *The scientific basis of child custody decisions* (pp. 96–119). New York: John Wiley & Sons.

Hetherington, E. M. (1979). Divorce, a child's perspective. *American Psychologist, 34*: 851–858.

Hetherington, E. M., & Kelly, J. (2003). For better or for worse: Divorce reconsidered. *Journal of Child Psychology and Psychiatry, 44*: 470–471.

REFERENCES

Ahrons, C. R., & Tanner, J. L. (2003). Adult children and their fathers: Relationship changes 20 years after parental divorce. *Family Relations: Interdisciplinary Journal of Applied Family Studies, 52*: 340–351.

Amato, P. R. (2001). Children of divorce in the 1990s: An update of the Amato and Keith (1991) meta-analysis. *Journal of Family Psychology, 15*: 355–370.

Buchanan, C. M., Maccoby, E. E., & Dornbusch, S. M. (1996). *Adolescents after divorce.* Cambridge, MA: Harvard University Press.

Christensen, A., Atkins, D. C., Berns, S., Wheeler, J., Baucom, D. H., & Simpson, L. E. (2004). Traditional versus integrative behavioral couple therapy for significantly and chronically distressed married couples. *Journal of Consulting & Clinical Psychology, 72*: 176–191.

Gottman, J. M. (1999). *The marriage clinic: A scientifically based marital therapy.* New York: W. W. Norton & Co.

Gottman, J. M., & Levenson, R. W. (1992). Marital processes predictive of later dissolution: Behavior, physiology, and health. *Journal of Personality & Social Psychology, 63*: 221–233.

Gottman, J. M., & Levenson, R. W. (1999). Rebound from marital conflict and divorce prediction. *Family Process, 38*: 287–292.

Gottman, J. M., & Levenson, R. W. (2000). The timing of divorce: Predicting when a couple will divorce over a 14-year period. *Journal of Marriage & the Family, 62*: 737–745.

Gottman, J. M., & Levenson, R. W. (2002a). Generating hypotheses after 14 years of marital followup; or, How should one speculate? A reply to DeKay, Greeno, and Houck. *Family Process, 41*: 105–110.

Gottman, J. M., & Levenson, R. W. (2002b). A two-factor model for predicting when a couple will divorce: Exploratory analyses using 14-year longitudinal data. *Family Process, 41*: 83–96.

Gottman, J. M., & Notarius, C. I. (2000). Decade review: Observing marital interaction. *Journal of Marriage & the Family, 62*: 927–947.

Grych, J. H., & Fincham, F. D. (1999). The adjustment of children from divorced families: Implications of empirical research for clinical intervention. In R. M. Galatzer-Levy & L. Kraus (Eds.), *The scientific basis of child custody decisions* (pp. 96–119). New York: John Wiley & Sons.

Hahlweg, K., Markman, H. J., Thurmaier, F., Engl, J., & Eckert, V. (1998). Prevention of marital distress: Results of a German prospective longitudinal study. *Journal of Family Psychology, 12*(4): 543–556.

Hetherington, E. M. (1979). Divorce, a child's perspective. *American Psychologist, 34:* 851–858.

Hetherington, E. M. (1990). Coping with family transitions: Winners, losers, and survivors. *Annual Progress in Child Psychiatry & Child Development,* 221–241.

Hetherington, E. M., & Kelly, J. (2003). For better or for worse: Divorce reconsidered. *Journal of Child Psychology and Psychiatry, 44*(3): 470–471.

Jacobson, N. S., Christensen, A., Prince, S. E., Cordova, J., & Eldridge, K. (2000). Integrative behavioral couple therapy: An acceptance-based, promising new treatment for couple discord. *Journal of Consulting & Clinical Psychology, 68*(2): 351–355.

Laumann-Billings, L., & Emery, R. E. (2000). Distress among young adults from divorced families. *Journal of Family Psychology, 14*(4): 671–687.

Wallerstein, J. S. (1984). Children of divorce: Preliminary report of a ten-year follow-up of young children. *American Journal of Orthopsychiatry, 54:* 444–458.

Wallerstein, J. S. (1987). Children after divorce: Wounds that don't heal. *Perspectives in Psychiatric Care, 24:* 3–4.

Wallerstein, J. S., & Blakeslee, S. (1989). *Second chances: Men, women, and children a decade after divorce.* New York: Ticknor & Fields.

Wallerstein, J. S., Corbin, S. B., & Lewis, J. M. (1988). Children of divorce: A 10-year study. In E. M. Hetherington & J. D. Arasteh (Eds.), *Impact of divorce, single parenting, and stepparenting on children* (pp. 197–214). Hillsdale, NJ: Lawrence Erlbaum Associates.

Wallerstein, J. S., & Kelly, J. B. (1974). The effects of parental divorce: The adolescent experience. In E. J. Anthony & C. Koupernik (Eds.), *The child in his family: Children at psychiatric risk* (pp. 202–219). Oxford, UK: John Wiley & Sons.

Wallerstein, J. S., & Kelly, J. B. (1975). The effects of parental divorce: Experiences of the preschool child. *Journal of the American Academy of Child Psychiatry, 14:* 600–616.

Wallerstein, J. S., & Kelly, J. B. (1980). *Surviving the Break-Up.* New York: Basic Books.

Wallerstein, J. S., & Lewis, J. M. (2004). The unexpected legacy of divorce: Report of a 25-year study. *Psychoanalytic Psychology, 21*: 353–370.

Wallerstein, J. S., Lewis, J., & Blakeslee, S. (2002). The unexpected legacy of divorce: A 25 year landmark study. *Journal of the American Academy of Child & Adolescent Psychiatry, 41*: 359–360.

21

NOT QUITE THE BRADY BUNCH: RESEARCH ON REMARRIAGE FAMILIES

Sometimes, research focused on describing a problem, a charac-teristic in an individual, or a family type has as much relevance for psychotherapists as does research on psychotherapy. Remar-riage families have many special features that must be recognized and responded to in effective practice with these families. This chapter centers on research that has contributed significantly to our understanding of remarriage families.

Ashley and Tad each had strong opinions about how they wanted life to be in the remarriage family they were forming. They wanted their relationship to be able to flourish and not be impeded by the presence of their children from previous marriages. Ashley also had a strong desire for Tad's children, Jimmy and Hank, to feel as close to her as they did to their mother, and for her child, Amy, to feel like Tad was just like a father. In the wake of two years of disappointment, Tad and Ashley came to see a couples' therapist on the verge of divorce. Both Ashley and Tad resented their lack of intimate time together. Tad was disappointed with Amy's lack of response to his directives. Ashley resented the way Tad appeared to favor his boys. This led to stormy fights, during which they argued about the children relentlessly.

Therapists who work with members of remarriage family systems encounter stories like that of Tad and Ashley on a regular basis. A marriage begins with great hope, only to be followed by a period of enormous stress, which shakes the very fabric of the relationship. The statistics are sobering (Emery, 1999). Approximately one-half of all marriages end in divorce. Among those who divorce, approximately one-half of women and three-quarters of men remarry within five years and more than half of these remarrying adults have children from previous marriages, making the remarriage family a very common family form. Changes accrue quickly. Almost one-quarter of children whose parents remarry will gain a stepsibling in the first 18 months after remarriage. Yet, the divorce rate for remarriage couples is more than 60%, and remarriage couples are twice as likely to divorce early in marriage as first-marriage couples. The result is that half of children whose parents divorce and remarry will have their parents redivorce. When asked, these redivorcing couples point to conflicts over children as the major source of difficulty.

As prominent therapists who specialize in remarriage families, Emily and John Visher (Neighbor, Beach, Brown, Kevin, & Visher, 1958; Visher & Visher, 1993), Anne Bernstein (1989, 1994, 1999), Scott Browning (1987), and Froma Walsh (1991) have cogently argued that hope should not be deflated by these statistics. Remarriage families often thrive. If family members are realistic in their expectations and committed to a process of working through issues, life in the remarriage family can be happy and very satisfying. Studies consistently show that children from remarriage families, as a group, are just as happy and well adjusted as those from first marriages (Hetherington et al., 1999). The research further shows that couples who succeed in making remarriages last are just as happy with their marriages as those in first marriages.

But how do you make a remarriage family work? We have the good fortune to have available the findings from a number of excellent research projects aimed at answering this question. These studies have tracked the development of remarriage families for many years and that can help us better understand these families and develop tools for our work with them. A prime example is the recent publication by psychologist James Bray, professor of family medicine at Baylor College of Medicine, of the results of a nine-year study that compared 100 stepfamilies in which children lived with their mother with 100 nuclear families (Bray, 1993, 1994a, 1994b, 1995, 1999a, 1999b; Bray & Berger, 1992). Bray's study, along with others such as that of psychologist Mavis Hetherington of the University of Virginia, suggests that there are distinct patterns in how life evolves in these families, as well as clearly better and worse ways to deal with the inevitable issues that emerge (Bray & Kelley, 1999). As therapists, we can add much to our understanding and to our repertoire of interventions by grasping the norms that apply to these families, the ways of relating that are experienced most positively, and the ways in which families are most successful in dealing with the inevitable issues which appear. What then do these studies tell us?

Remarriage represents a difficult transition but not necessarily one with dire long-term consequences. The research shows that the vast majority of families experience great stress and upheaval, particularly in the first two years. The contrast with first marriages is striking. Instead of a honeymoon period, these families must immediately face many complex and difficult relationships issues. Family cohesion begins at a low level. It is vital to keep in focus, as Mavis Hetherington has suggested, that families going through the transition of remarriage inevitably have already gone through multiple difficult transitions of divorce or death. Complex and painful feelings are probably inevitable.

Nonetheless, the research of Hetherington, Bray, and numerous others shows that children in remarriage families function as well as other children and have no more problems than other children, and that those remarriages that do last have the same levels of marital satisfaction as first marriages. Remarriages also have been shown to offer new opportunities, not the least of which is that they often resolve the financial pressures that often are the bane of postdivorce life.

Remarriage families must attend to multiple tasks that may compete for attention. Remarriage families must simultaneously work to build a marriage, create a relationship between a stepparent and children, work out boundary issues with the other biological parent, and adapt the bond between the biological parent and children to the new situation. How do you build marital intimacy while also attending to the feelings of children about the changes occurring and losing time with their biological parent?

In marked contrast to first marriages, marital happiness and the happiness of children in remarriage families do not have a strong connection. In fact, a striking finding in the research on remarriage families is that, at times, marital happiness is lower when attachments to children are stronger and children are happier. Competition for precious resources such as time and interest are powerful forces in these families.

Typical patterns in the styles of remarriage families. Bray was able to divide remarriage families in which mothers lived with their children into readily discernable types, which he termed matriarchal, neotraditional, and romantic. The neotraditional family engages in a gradual process of building a shared sense of connection and mutual responsibility. Neotraditional families are characterized by close step-parent child bonds that develop in parallel with the marital bonds, and these families ultimately look most like nuclear families.

Chuck and Gina Brown and Gina's two children from her previous marriage are an example of a neotraditional family. Chuck and Gina nurture their own relationship. Chuck spends considerable time with the children and is highly invested in their activities, yet does not confuse his role with that of their father. When conflicts emerge, the family tries to problem solve so that gratifications and frustrations are equally distributed.

Life in the matriarchal family is quite different. In the matriarchal remarriage family, mothers retain most of the decision-making power, especially about the children. In these families, the stepfather's primary concern remains being a companion and support to his wife. These men show limited interest in parenting.

In the Steiglitz family, Joe and Trudy are very close and connected, but Joe rarely connects with the children and never is involved directly in resolution of their problems or in limit setting. Trudy remains highly connected with her children and with Joe, and is clearly the hub around which the family is organized.

The romantic stepfamily has the greatest sense of urgency to become a nuclear family. Couples in these families look to have intense relationships and be closely connected with children, often with a sense that these goals can instantaneously be achieved. In these families, the other biological parent is often the object of much criticism and conflict. Given the many adaptations needed in remarriage family life, Bray has found that romantic families are most at risk for relationship difficulties and child–stepparent problems. Ashley and Tad offer an example of the romantic family after the fall of unmet expectations.

Unrealistic expectations that do not account for the vicissitudes of life in the remarriage family set the scene for the emergence of difficulty. Cohesion in remarriage families generally tends to be lower than in the families of first marriages. Bonds between stepparents and children grow over time, but typically do not reach the levels of first marriages. The parenting norm for stepfathers is a laissez-faire style.

These findings need not be a cause for disappointment, but instead can be seen as a reality of this family's life form. Just because a child prefers to spend time with her biological parent instead of a stepparent does not mean that the family is failing.

Clear developmental epochs in the life of the remarriage family. Bray found that stepfamilies have their own natural lifecycle that includes several transition points at which families are thrown into temporary crisis. The first two years of remarriage are a time of great stress, low cohesion, and the emergence of many issues. Bray found that families did not start to think and act like a family until the third year, a time when, if the family was successful in its adaptation, stability began to emerge. This stability lasted until the young children in his sample of families entered adolescence, when conflict and high levels of stress reappeared. The stresses on these families are severe enough during this time that 20% of adolescents in remarriage families relocate to the home of the other parent.

Special strains on stepmothers. Research shows that stepparenting is not an equal playing field for men and women (Bernstein, 1994). Women's socialization and cultural expectations cause them to assume much more of a hands-on, connected approach to their relationships with stepchildren, whereas men tend to gravitate to greater distance and more of a laissez-faire position. Ironically, this greater involvement by women leads to the development of more instances of difficulty in relationships between a stepmother and children than with stepfathers. This difference is most pronounced in girls.

Remarriage doesn't affect the involvement of the noncustodial parent. In most of the samples studied, remarriage doesn't tend to change the involvement of the noncustodial parent or hinder the relationship between that parent and the children. The fear that a parent will be replaced is a relatively rare phenomenon. Nor does having a strong bond with the nonresidential parent hinder the development of stepparent–child relationships. In contrast, the remarriage of noncustodial parents (who most often are fathers) tends to result in a marked reduction in their involvement with their children.

Relevance for psychotherapy. So what should we do as therapists given these findings (Bernstein, 1989)? First, we can provide psychoeducation to help remarriage families understand typical patterns for this family form. Many family members feel lost in the array of feelings that accrue when exposed to the many tasks that need to be negotiated. Information that such feelings are not unusual, and knowledge that the first two years are almost necessarily turbulent can help set a frame for coping.

We can also help a family understand which of Bray's family types they resemble, and then help them assess how to work on the issues that are likely to emerge within the particular family type to which they have gravitated. Romantic families require special focused intervention to help them adapt their beliefs to their life circumstance.

We also can help families understand the normative pathways for development in these families and patterns that are most effective at various points in the life cycle. For example, we can suggest ways for including stepparents in the lives of children that appear to work best: beginning with the stepparent helping the other parent monitor a child's behavior, and only later moving into having real authority and responsibility for discipline.

As Bray suggests, ultimately, flexibility becomes an essential characteristic in these families, and we can work toward such flexibility. Having helped families understand the ecology of their lives and how it relates to norms of this family life form, we can move on to explore the many obstacles to flexibility and adaptation, be they in family-of-origin issues, issues of loyalty to biological parents, poor communication, or individual psychodynamics. What is clear is that, as Bray suggests, remarriage family life can present opportunities to build at least as good a life and perhaps a better life than the one that, preceded it, as well as opportunities for all to grow, if the norms are understood and developmental tasks are negotiated.

RESOURCES

Bray, J. H., & Kelley, J. (1999). *Step-families: Love, marriage and parenting in the first decade.* New York: Broadway Books.

Visher, E. B., & Visher, J. S. (1993). Remarriage families and stepparenting. In F. Walsh (Ed.), *Normal family processes* (2nd ed., pp. 235–253). New York: Guilford Press.

REFERENCES

Bernstein, A. C. (1989). *Yours, mine, and ours: How families change when remarried parents have a child together.* New York: Charles Scribners Sons.

Bernstein, A. C. (1994). Women in stepfamilies: The fairy godmother, the wicked witch, and Cinderella reconstructed. In M. P. Mirkin (Ed.), *Women in context: Toward a feminist reconstruction of psychotherapy* (pp. 1–27). New York: Guilford.

Bernstein, A. C. (1999). Reconstructing the Brothers Grimm: New tales for stepfamily life. *Family Process, 38*(4): 415–429.

Bray, J. H. (1993). Developmental issues for long-term stepfamilies. *Family Journal: Counseling & Therapy for Couples & Families, 1*(4): 361–364.

Bray, J. H. (1994a). Assessment issues with stepfamilies. *Family Journal: Counseling & Therapy for Couples & Families, 2*(2): 163–166.

Bray, J. H. (1994b). What does a typical stepfamily look like? *Family Journal: Counseling & Therapy for Couples & Families, 2*(1): 66–69.

Bray, J. H. (1995). Children in stepfamilies: Assessment and treatment issues. In D. K. Huntley (Ed.), *Understanding stepfamilies: Implications for assessment and treatment* (pp. 59–71). Alexandria, VA: American Counseling Association.

Bray, J. H. (1999a). From marriage to remarriage and beyond: Findings from the Developmental Issues in Stepfamilies Research Project. In E. Hetherington (Ed.), *Coping with divorce, single parenting, and remarriage: A risk and resiliency perspective* (pp. 253–271). Mahwah, NJ: Lawrence Erlbaum Associates.

Bray, J. H. (1999b). Stepfamilies: The intersection of culture, context, and biology. *Monographs of the Society for Research in Child Development, 64*(4): 210–218.

Bray, J. H., & Berger, S. H. (1992). Stepfamilies. In M. E. Procidano & C. B. Fisher (Eds.), *Contemporary families: A handbook for school professionals* (pp. 57–80). New York: Teachers College Press.

Bray, J. H., & Kelley, J. (1999). *Step-families: Love, marriage and parenting in the first decade.* New York: Broadway Books.

Browning, S. W. (1987). *Preference prediction, empathy, and personal similarity as variables of family satisfaction in intact and stepfather families.* Berkeley: California School of Professional Psychology.

Emery, R. E. (1999). *Marriage, divorce, and children's adjustment* (2nd ed.). Thousand Oaks, CA: Sage Publications.

Hetherington, E., Henderson, S. H., Reiss, D., Anderson, E. R., Bridges, M., Chan, R. W., et al. (1999). Adolescent siblings in stepfamilies: Family functioning and adolescent adjustment. *Monographs of the Society for Research in Child Development, 64*(4): 222–235.

Neighbor, J., Beach, M., Brown, D. T., Kevin, D., & Visher, J. S. (1958). An approach to the selection of patients for group psychotherapy. *Mental Hygiene New York, 42*: 243–254.

Visher, E. B., & Visher, J. S. (1993). Remarriage families and stepparenting. In F. Walsh (Ed.), *Normal family processes* (2nd ed., pp. 235–253). New York: Guilford Press.

Walsh, F. (1991). Promoting healthy functioning in divorced and remarried families. In A. S. Gurman & D. P. Kniskern (Eds.), *Handbook of family therapy* (vol. 2, pp. 525–545). Philadelphia: Brunner/Mazel.

22

METHODS OF RELATIONAL ASSESSMENT

One vital function of research is to help develop and validate reliable and valid measures of individual, couple, and family functioning. These measures can then serve as the foundation for measurement in research and as a source of information in clinical assessment. This chapter describes relational diagnosis and some of the best measures available to assist with this task.

There has been a significant breakthrough in relational diagnosis and assessment in the past decade. Before this time, flowing from an ideology focused on the individual, the tradition of assessment in mental health almost exclusively focused on describing disorders and personality characteristics within individuals. Systems assessing disorders, such as the *Diagnostic and Statistical Manual of Mental Disorders (DSM)–IV* of the American Psychiatric Association and the International Statistical Classification of Diseases-9, as well as systems assessing dimensions of pathology and personality, such as the Minnesota Multiphasic Personality Inventory-R and Thematic Apperception Test, have been predicated on the assumption that description is best offered at the level of the person in isolation.

A relational viewpoint contrasts with this notion. Although allowing that description at the level of the individual may assume importance, relational diagnosis emphasizes the dimensions of interaction that emerge across individuals. A relational viewpoint suggests that much of what is most essential is manifested in the ongoing processes between people.

DEVELOPMENT OF THE RELATIONAL VIEW

There is both a broader and more limited version of the relational viewpoint. In the broader versions of the relational viewpoint that were most prominent early in the history of family therapy, the relational perspective was offered as a radical contrast to the individual view. The first generation of family therapists attributed powerful properties to the systems in which people lived, viewing them as the essential determinant of individual thoughts, feelings, and behavior. From this vantage point, the occurrences at the level of the individual were insignificant, and therefore clinicians did not need to be concerned with an individual's depression, anxiety, or schizophrenia. Individual personality and disturbance, and, accordingly, individual assessment, was seen as superfluous. What mattered from this view were the roles individuals filled and how their behavior played out in interactional cycles. This could best be addressed through assessment of interactions.

This bold new paradigm helped direct attention toward relational assessment and diagnosis. However, the complete rejection of individual assessment was not warranted. The radical position taken stemmed from ideology, not the data about families. Indeed, the brilliant ideas about systemic impacts were developed without a well-validated method for assessing interactional processes. Assessment depended on the eye of the observer and therefore remained subject to considerable bias. Those who could not see the presence of powerful individual factors did not notice their impact. But what remained was the brilliant insight about the impact and significance of relationships. Many years of family research have confirmed and reconfirmed the power of this influence.

Recently, a more mature science-based view of relational diagnosis presents systems assessment not as a complete rejection of individual assessment, but as an additional dimension for assessment, one that is equally as important as individual assessment. A complete understanding must consider both interactional factors and family and other system processes. This vantage point is now most common among family therapists, with the more radical position rejecting individual diagnosis and assessment falling into disfavor. The present vantage point allows that individual functioning is significant, but that individual functioning is inevitably interwoven in a circular process with interactional processes.

From this perspective, interactional views and assessment should always be part of our diagnostic view, and our measures should always assess the interactional factors regardless of the issue being assessed. We need to know both how individuals function and how the systems in which they live function, regardless of the problem under study. A contemporary version of the relational viewpoint also suggests that there are a number of conditions and difficulties for which relational diagnosis assumes greater importance than individual diagnosis. For example, the evidence overwhelmingly suggests that couple satisfaction and its flip side, marital maladjustment, are far more a product of what occurs in the relationship process between individuals than of the particular characteristics of the individuals.

The development of the relational viewpoint has led to efforts to describe pathology from a relational perspective. At one level, this has led to the development of relational nomenclatures, describing interaction patterns that are problematic. Just as the *DSM IV* offers the criteria for individual diagnosis, a similar list of criteria can be offered for problematic relational patterns, be they marital difficulties, triangulation between parents and children, or family violence. Such criteria have been summarized in relation to a number of common interpersonal difficulties in a seminal book edited by Florence Kaslow (1997). Analogous to this form of diagnosis is the recent development of measures of interpersonal processes. The relational viewpoint has led to a series of methods for assessing relationships.

DIMENSIONS OF RELATIONAL MEASURES

Sources of Report

Measures of interpersonal processes can be classified by their source. There are measures in which clients report their own views of their interpersonal processes, termed self-report measures. The strength of self-report measures lies in their inclusion of the individual's views of his or her experience. Additionally, they are based on all the information about family life available to the individual. Clearly, they provide the best route to assessing the inner experience of those involved in an interaction or interactional pattern. However, self-report measures also offer the possibility for considerable distortion of the processes that are occurring. For example, a depressed spouse may label and rate all the processes in a marriage with an overly negative viewpoint, providing a distorted view of what is occurring in the relationship.

An alternative source of data are reports in which family members rate one another. Here, bias about self may be removed, but bias toward others and toward family processes remains a distinct possibility.

A third source of data comes from more objective raters who have less stake in the labeling of ongoing family processes. Such raters can be expected to be less affected by bias. However, these individuals inevitably base ratings on small samples of observed behavior, and research has shown some bias occurs even when there is little connection to the subject. Thus each of these methods for rating interactional processes has benefits and liabilities.

Another observer measure moves away from ratings and toward more objective counts of behavior. These methods are typically invoked in laboratory interactional tasks, in which families are observed and their processes are rated on various indices. The most elaborate versions of these methods, such as those invoked in the marital studies of John Gottman (1999) include videotaping interactional sequences and micro-encoding the behavior on various dimensions on a second-by-second basis. These methods have the advantage of great objectivity. However, these measures also carry the disadvantages of having to be based on small samples of interaction created in atypical settings, most often laboratories. No matter how much effort is made to make these settings proximate situations in which behavior is not observed, the results remain susceptible to subject reactivity to the study environment, which may cause the subjects to subtly alter their behavior. The limited time frame during which the information to be rated is acquired in these efforts also creates a likelihood of capturing atypical patterns.

Range of Focus

Another important distinction across relational measures is their range of focus. Some interactional measures are limited to describing the whole family. Such measures capture the big picture, but also carry the disadvantage that they must be some average of the processes studied within smaller units within the family. For example, a "disengaged" family may actually include two members who are quite close. Other measures focus more specifically on sub-systems. Measures may center on the couple relationship or only on parent–child dyads. Such measures can tap a dimension of family experience more precisely but are more limited in scope.

Naturalistic vs. Laboratory Measures

Measures can also be differentiated between those that examine family systems in the context of situations specially created to assess interactions and naturalistic observation of families in their native contexts. Measures that are predicated on specially created interaction tasks have the advantage of pulling for precisely the patterns that one is looking to examine. Along with assuring the presence of the phenomenon of interest, these assessment devices also are very efficient in the use of client and observer time. In contrast, naturalistic measures offer a view of the family in its own environment and are therefore less likely to be altered by the research. But they necessitate longer periods to study interaction (to elicit the kind of phenomenon under study) and much greater expense.

Levels of Abstraction

Measures also differ in the complexity of the construct that they are designed to address. Some measures are designed to assess simple concepts, whereas others are designed to assess the most complex concepts. This dimension has assumed particular importance among relational measures because of the innate complexity of many systems' concepts. These circumstances have often forced a choice between measures that could easily be validated assessing constructs of little interest (e.g., how much individuals in a family talk) and measures assessing very complex variables that had low reliability and validity; e.g., family structure). Fortunately, recent measure development has achieved a constructive balance that has allowed for complexity of constructs and construct validation of instruments.

SPECIFIC MEASURES

There clearly is no one best set of measurement techniques. Instead, we have a range of measures that assess interaction from different perspectives. To achieve a comprehensive representation of interaction, there is a need for what Campbell and Fiske (1959) termed a multitrait, multimethod matrix, including various types of measures from diverse sources to assess myriad aspects of interaction. In research and clinical work, careful instrument selection is vital because using the measure or measures that tap the aspects of interaction of greatest interest in a particular endeavor is key. In these choices, selecting reliable and valid measures is especially important. In the history of relational diagnosis, measures have varied considerably in their validation.

Today, we are fortunate to have many fine measures for assessing relational process. Here are a few of the best, limited to those that do not require complex coding of behavior and those that can readily be utilized by clinicians in practice.

Couple Measures

The Locke-Wallace Marital Adjustment Test

This instrument (Locke & Wallace, 1959) is a short self-report questionnaire consisting of 15 items asking couples about areas of agreement and disagreement, followed by a series of items asking about diverse aspects of the relationship, such as whether they would marry again or confide in their partner.

The Weiss-Cerreto Marital Status Inventory

This brief self-report instrument (Weiss & Cerreto, 1980) measures the extent to which a married individual is considering dissolution of the marriage or has taken action toward obtaining a divorce.

Dyadic Adjustment Scale

The Dyadic Adjustment Scale (Spanier, 1976) is a 32-item self-report inventory designed to measure the severity of relationship discord in couples. Scores range from 0 to 151, with higher values indicating more favorable adjustment. Items load on four factors: dyadic consensus, dyadic cohesion, dyadic satisfaction, and affectional expression.

Marital Satisfaction Inventory-R

As with the Locke-Wallace Marital Adjustment Test and Dyadic Adjustment Scale, this couple self-report instrument (Snyder & Aikman, 1999) is intended to provide an overall indication of relationship satisfaction. Additionally, subscales tap a range of specific dimensions of couple functioning. The Marital Satisfaction Inventory-R is a 150-item true-false self-report measure, including a global distress measure and subscales assessing affective communication, problem-solving communication, aggression, time together, disagreement about finances, sexual dissatisfaction, role orientation, family history of distress, dissatisfaction with children, and conflict over child rearing.

The Positive and Negative Quality in Marriage Scale

This scale offers a simple measure for assessing positive and negative quality in marriage (Fincham & Linfield, 1997). Based in theory that there are readily differentiated positive and negative aspects to couple relationships, this six-item scale directly inquires about these dimensions of relationship.

The Areas of Change Questionnaire

The Areas of Change Questionnaire (Weiss, Hops, & Patterson, 1973) is a 34-item self-report measure listing specific areas of marital functioning and asking the degree to which change is desired from their partners in each area. It represents the most widely used instrument for tapping areas in which couples desire change.

Conflict Tactics Scale

The Conflict Tactics Scale (Straus, 1979) is the most widely used instrument for assessing physical aggression in marriage as well as types of marital aggression. Of note here is the general tendency to underreport these behaviors.

Family Measures

The Global Assessment of Relational Functioning

The Global Assessment of Relational Functioning is a simple rating scale on which any relational unit (i.e., family, couple, or other grouping) can be rated for its functionality on a 100-point scale. The goal is to assign a number to the quality of functioning of the particular relationship.

The Beavers-Timberlawn Family Evaluation Scales

The Beavers-Timberlawn Family Evaluation Scales were developed in the 1970s to assess family functioning across a number of continuums of strengths and weaknesses. They have been revised and renamed the Beavers Interactional Competence Scale. The analogous self-report measure, the Beavers Self-Report Instrument, features a global scale, much like that in the clinical rating scale, and four subscales: conflict, leadership, cohesion, and emotional expressiveness.

The Circumplex Measures

The Circumplex model of family functioning developed by David Olson and colleagues (Olson, Russell, & Sprenkle, 1983; Olson, Sprenkle, & Russell, 1979) led to the development of both rater and self-report instruments. The model is based on placing interaction within the context of adaptability and cohesion. Extremes on adaptability and cohesion are viewed as problematic, whereas an array of mid-range responses are viewed as functional. More recently, communication has been added as a third dimension to examine. In contrast to cohesion and adaptability, communication is viewed as a linear measure on which more is better. FACES III and IV measure these dimensions through a series of 5-point Likert scales. The parallel Clinical Rating Scales are structured to assess the same constructs from a rater perspective.

The McMaster Family Assessment Device

The McMaster model of family functioning developed by Epstein and colleagues (Epstein, Baldwin, & Bishop, 1983; Miller, Epstein, Bishop, and Keitner, 1985) postulates six core areas of relational functioning: problem solving, communication, roles, affective responsiveness, affective involvement, and behavior control. The Family Assessment Device is a 60-item self-report inventory covering general functioning plus scoring for each of the six specific dimensions.

Family Environment Scale

The Family Environment Scale (Moos & Moos, 1976, 1981) puts into operation the typology of family social environments through a self-report measure. The scale contains 90 true-false items assessing three domains: relationships, personal growth, and system maintenance.

Systemic Therapy Inventory of Change

This omnibus measure (Pinsof et al., 2005) is targeted to assess therapy progress, and includes scales to assess individual, family, and child functioning and the therapeutic alliance in addition to couple functioning.

CONCLUSION

Clearly, relational diagnosis has advanced monumentally over the past two decades. Progress is clear on two distinct fronts. First, relational diagnosis has moved from the realm of a brilliant global insight of a systemic vision generated by pioneers in the field to a much more fully articulated and readily operationalized vantage point. Research has demonstrated on innumerable occasions the powerful effect of relationships and relational factors on behavior, affects, cognitions, and even physiology. There is now general agreement that it is imperative to track behavior, thoughts, and feelings across multiple system levels, including the levels of individual, the couple, and the family. Relational diagnosis has achieved respect as an essential dimension to track.

Second, the technology and instrumentation for tracking relational variables has advanced remarkably. Whereas two decades ago there were few instruments and many of those poorly validated, today clinicians and researchers can draw from a wealth of instruments designed to assess a wide range of relational factors.

Given the advances in the clarity of the relational view and the growth in the technology to assess relationships, the next decade looks to be a time of far greater utilization of these (now readily available) instruments in clinical work. And we clearly will see the generation of additional research that will help us better understand relational processes.

RESOURCES

Kaslow, F. (1996). *Handbook of relational diagnosis.* New York: Wiley.

REFERENCES

Campbell, D. T., & Fiske, D. W. (1959). Convergent and discriminant validation by the multitrait-multimethod matrix. *Psychological Bulletin, 56:* 81–105.

Epstein, N. B., Baldwin, L. M., & Bishop, D. S. (1983). The McMaster Family Assessment Device. *Journal of Marital & Family Therapy,* 9(2): 171–180.

Fincham, F. D., & K. J. Linfield (1997). A new look at marital quality: Can spouses feel positive and negative about their marriage? *Journal of Family Psychology* 11(4): 489–502.

Gottman, J. M. (1999). *The marriage clinic: A scientifically based marital therapy.* New York: W. W. Norton & Co.

Kaslow, F. (1996). *Handbook of relational diagnosis.* New York: Wiley.

Locke, H., & Wallace, K. (1959). Short marital-adjustment and prediction tests: Their reliability and validity. *Marriage and Family Living, 21:* 251–255.

Miller, I. W., Epstein, N. B., Bishop, D. S., & Keitner, G. I. (1985). The McMaster Family Assessment Device: Reliability and validity. *Journal of Marital and Family Therapy,* 11(4): 345–356.

Moos, R. H., & Moos, B. S. (1976). A typology of family social environments. *Family Process, 15:* 357–372.

Moos, R. H., & Moos, B. S. (1981). *Family Environment Scale manual.* Palo Alto, CA: Consulting Psychologists Press.

Olson, D. H., Russell, C. S., & Sprenkle, D. H. (1983). Circumplex model VI: Theoretical update. *Family Process, 22:* 69–83.

Olson, D. H., Sprenkle, D. H., & Russell, C. S. (1979). Circumplex model of marital and family systems: I. Cohesion and adaptability dimensions, family types, and clinical applications. *Family Process, 18:* 3–28.

Pinsof, W. M., Lebow, J. L., Mann, B., Knobloch-Fedders, L., Freidman, G., Karam, E., et al. (2005). STIC. Evanston, IL: Family Institute at Northwestern.

Snyder, D. K. (1979). Multidimensional assessment of marital satisfaction. *Journal of Marriage & the Family, 41*: 813–823.

Snyder, D. K., & Aikman, G. G. (1999). Marital Satisfaction Inventory–Revised. In M. E. Maruish (Ed.), *The use of psychological testing for treatment planning and outcomes assessment* (2nd ed., pp. 1173–1210). Mahwah, NJ: Lawrence Erlbaum Associates.

Spanier, G. B. (1976). Measuring dyadic adjustment: New scales for assessing the quality of marriage and similar dyads. *Journal of Marriage & the Family, 38*: 15–28.

Straus, M. A. (1979). Measuring intrafamily conflict and violence: The Conflict Tactics (CT) Scales. *Journal of Marriage & the Family 41*(1): 75–88

Weiss, R. L., & Cerreto, M. C. (1980). Development of a measure of dissolution potential. *American Journal of Family Therapy, 8*: 80–85.

Weiss, R. L., Hops, H., & Patterson, G. R. (1973). A framework for conceptualizing marital conflict: A technology for altering it, some data for evaluating it. In L. A. Hamerlynch, I. C. Handy, & E. J. Mash (Eds.), *Behaviour change: The fourth Banff conference on behaviour modification* (pp. 35–52). Champaign, IL: Research Press.

Part IV
Doing Research on Your Practice

23

NEW SCIENCE FOR PSYCHOTHERAPY: CAN WE PREDICT HOW THERAPY WILL PROGRESS?

Progress research looks at how clients change over the course of psychotherapy by assessing how they are doing on a session-by-session basis and whether their gains over time match those that might be expected. In contrast to most psychotherapy research, this form of research focuses on how individual clients change in relation to their own earlier levels of functioning (an example of what is called an ipsative measure) rather than how well kinds of treatment work for groups of clients. This chapter focuses on the research of Kenneth Howard, who was the principal architect of progress research.

Until recently, research examining psychotherapy offered only limited guidance to practicing therapists. The structure of the typical study—from its university setting, to its elaborate controls to assure validity, to its carefully qualified conclusions (e.g., "more research is necessary")—mitigated the opportunity for the direct application of research findings. Over the past few years, however, we have begun to see the emergence of research that is intended to influence practice and is designed for consumption by care providers. A prime example has been the work of Kenneth Howard, a professor at Northwestern University before his untimely death in 2002.

Howard was forever on the cutting edge of practice-relevant psychotherapy research. In the 1960s, well before the interest in understanding the client's perspective and current discourse about the client's voice, Howard and his longtime colleague David Orlinsky asked clients and therapists directly about their experiences in psychotherapy. Their book on the results, *Varieties of Psychotherapeutic Experience*, remains an essential guide to the experience of psychotherapy. Howard then turned to investigate such vital questions as, What progress can be expected in therapy? What does an expected course of treatment for a particular problem look like? and When can we say a therapy has had a fair trial and is not working? This group of studies, which has important implications for clinicians, public-policy makers, and those involved in the funding of mental health care, earned Howard several awards, including the Distinguished Professional Contribution to Knowledge Award from the American Psychological Association.

Howard's work strongly supports the efficacy of psychotherapy. In his sample of 15,000 clients treated in a wide range of settings and modalities, most treatments emerge as highly effective in helping individuals, couples, and families resolve their difficulties and achieve their treatment goals (Howard, Moras, Brill, & Martinovich, 1996; Howard, Lueger, Martinovich, & Lutz, 1999; Sperry, Brill, Howard, & Grissom, 1996). Howard emphasized that a similar level of effectiveness has been found in numerous other samples (Lambert & Bergin, 1994; Smith & Glass, 1977), making psychotherapy among the most tested and empirically validated health interventions.

Howard developed what he terms the "Dosage-Response" Model for charting therapeutic progress (Kopta, Howard, Lowry, & Beutler, 1994). The concept behind the model is fairly simple: psychotherapy, as with other health care interventions, should be evaluated in relation to its effectiveness at various dosages. Just as milligrams are the most appropriate measures for most medications, Howard argued that the most appropriate measure of dose in psychotherapy is the number of sessions. In charting the relation of sessions to outcome, Howard uncovered a number of findings with important clinical implications.

FEELING BETTER WITHOUT TREATMENT

Many clients (5%–10%) feel significantly better even before treatment begins (Kopta et al., 1994; Lyons, Howard, O'Mahoney, & Lish, 1997). Change in these clients occurs between the time they make an appointment and the first session. As clinicians, we should remember to ask clients at the beginning of treatment, "How are you doing now?" rather than "What is the problem?" We should take care not to assume there is a current problem, even though there was one when the first appointment was scheduled. Clients who are no longer distressed may still wish to pursue psychotherapy for self-exploration or to improve their coping skills, but they do not require therapy to feel better. As therapists, we must be cautious about taking credit for these clients' improved feeling states (though scheduling a session may well have been critical in beginning the process of feeling better). Instead, these clients may best be thought of as candidates for interventions that help them to better understand and continue the positive steps they have already taken to improve their lives (e.g., using the "exception" question of solution-focused therapies that asks clients to focus on what is different at those times when they are able to resolve their problems).

For example, Connie had been significantly depressed for two months after the breakup of her relationship with her boyfriend. Setting up an appointment with a therapist meant overcoming her inertia and beginning to take constructive action, which she followed up by engaging more with friends in a variety of activities. By the time she met with a therapist a week later, she felt substantially better. Connie decided there was no need for further therapy, because she had already achieved her goal of feeling better. In their one meeting, Connie and her therapist discussed some of the vulnerabilities that may have made her subject to depression and focused on how she had marshaled her resources to resolve her difficulties. They parted with the agreement that Connie would come back if her depression returned.

Although, as mental health professionals, we know the wide range of benefits that psychotherapy can bring, we must bear in mind that clients are often simply interested in feeling better. Howard's data remind us that, for many, just starting treatment or even making an appointment is enough to ameliorate their distress without any additional interventions.

DIMINISHING RETURN WITH MORE SESSIONS

Although most clients experience significant change early in the treatment process, for those who do not initially respond to treatment, more and more effort is required to produce change (Kopta, Lueger, Saunders, & Howard, 1999; Lyons et al., 1997). Therefore, the minority of clients who respond slowly consume a grossly disproportionate amount of the total number of treatment sessions offered by a typical therapist. According to Howard's research, about 50% of clients are improved after 8 weekly psychotherapy sessions, 75% after 26 weekly psychotherapy sessions, and 85% after 52 weekly sessions. Those who do not respond at this point require many more sessions to improve, if treatment is effective at all.

There are several implications of this finding. The achievement of treatment goals for those who have already received considerable therapy is likely to involve many more sessions. Therapists should plan accordingly, and directly discuss the likely need for longer term treatment, rather than suggesting change is just around the corner.

Howard also suggested that the small number of clients who enter long-term therapy can distort therapists' overall views of their caseloads. Because a small number of clients require most of the therapy sessions, it is likely that, over time, therapists will have cases that are primarily in long-term therapy, even if they do short-term treatment with most clients, leading them to conclude that most actually require long-term therapy.

THE SEQUENCE OF CHANGE

Howard found client change generally proceeds in a clear sequence (Kopta et al., 1994; Kopta, Newman, McGovern, & Sandrock, 1986; Lutz, Lowry, Kopta, Einstein, & Howard, 2001). First, clients feel better, experiencing the relief that comes with seeking help and beginning to face problems directly. This change, termed *remoralization*, usually occurs in the first few sessions. This stage is followed by a change in symptoms, *remediation*, that is the result of developing new coping skills and typically requires about 16 sessions. Finally, the third phase of treatment, *rehabilitation*, focuses on such tasks as unlearning maladaptive behaviors, establishing new ways of approaching one's life, dealing with interpersonal problems, and improving self-esteem, tasks most often conceived of as the essence of psychotherapy. The time needed for these changes depends on the severity of the individual's difficulties and the area of life on which the problem centers. Based on Howard's data, clinicians can expect most clients to feel better fairly quickly, to overcome their symptoms within four months, and to make changes in how they live more slowly—typically between six months and one year.

For example, Bob and Viv, like most couples entering therapy, began treatment feeling hopeless about their relationship. By the third session, their belief that the therapist had something to offer, along with a few glimmers generated in the meetings, left them feeling substantially better, even though none of their problems were resolved. By the eighth session, many of their specific complaints, such as the high level of mutual criticism and low level of support, were substantially ameliorated, and they no longer considered divorce. Nonetheless, they needed 30 sessions to make the kinds of changes that allowed for a close, connected relationship.

BAD BEGINNINGS OFTEN LEAD TO BAD ENDINGS

According to Howard's research (Kopta, Newman, McGovern, & Angle, 1989), if a positive change in the client's feeling state does not occur early in therapy (by the sixth session), change is not likely to occur in that therapy relationship. Feeling worse after beginning therapy is a sign that a change in therapist should strongly be considered. Feeling increasingly worse indicates treatment failure. Far from confirming the old tenet, never supported in research, that the client needs to feel worse to feel better, Howard found that once off on the wrong foot, therapy is unlikely to be productive. Although there are relatively few bad therapists who have consistently poor outcomes, bad matches of client and therapist are quite common.

Howard's work challenges the assumption that trying harder is a solution to a mismatch between client and therapist. If a client is responding poorly to treatment by the eighth session, Howard suggested it would be far better for the therapist to consider referring the client to someone else. Given the vital importance of the client–therapist alliance, it is striking how seldom such mismatches are remedied by this simple response. Howard's data demonstrate that we all need to acknowledge as soon as possible when our therapy is not helping our clients.

Tom initially felt quite uncomfortable with his behavioral therapist's distance and the homework tasks he assigned. In response, the therapist offered many more assignments, which were focused on overcoming anxiety and being more assertive. After one year of unproductive therapy, Tom tried another, more experiential therapist and almost immediately began to feel hopeful. Although the therapy ultimately proved productive, this does not mean that the second therapist was superior to the first, only that a good fit for Tom meant a therapist who was experiential and accepting.

CLIENTS WITH DIFFERENT SYMPTOMS AND PROFILES RESPOND TO TREATMENT AT DIFFERING RATES

Clients differ and can be expected to respond in ways and in amounts of time that are predictable given their characteristics. Those with symptoms of distress, such as anxiety and depression, show the fastest change, whereas those with broad difficulties in personality show the slowest. Using his data pool, Howard and colleagues developed patient profiles that enable therapists to anticipate what an expected course of treatment is likely to be, given such characteristics as the client's symptoms, amount of previous therapy, and overall level of functioning (Lutz et al., 2001). Actual progress is then compared with the expected course.

As an example, Mel began therapy in the average range of overall mental health. He had many depressive signs that were diagnosed as stemming from a dysthymic disorder. His clinical characteristics predicted that therapy would at least be moderately effective. However, even modest progress was not achieved after a year of treatment. Patient profiling showed treatment was much less effective than had been estimated. In contrast, Susan presented with multiple symptoms of anxiety and a diagnosis of panic disorder. After six months of treatment, patient profiling showed that she had profited as expected from psychotherapy.

LOOKING AT OUTCOME AS A PROCESS

Because some early changes predict the course of treatment, Howard emphasized that treatment evaluation should be an ongoing process, not something to be measured at termination. Consider the Smith family, who entered family therapy because of the substance-abuse problem of John, age 15. Assessing the effectiveness of this therapy inevitably includes a comparison of John's drug use before and after treatment, but should also contain interim signs of progress, such as the forming of a therapeutic alliance and the development of a parental coalition that can effectively cope with John's behavior. Knowing early in treatment that John's drug abuse was increasing and that the parents' alliance with the therapist was weak could have considerable value in shaping further intervention strategy. Clearly, just measuring treatment effects after termination has far less impact than using early evaluation data to enhance the treatment process. Evaluation is best conceptualized not as assessing the difference in status before and after treatment, but as the ongoing tracking of change.

AN X-RAY FOR THE CHANGE PROCESS

Howard's research has been extended into the development of a widely used method of outcomes assessment, principally used in managed care, but designed to provide feedback to clinicians in all settings. Howard emphasized the importance of this kind of measurement in managed care because, typically, managed mental health care uses only the number of sessions to measure the effectiveness of clinicians. He suggested that the question is no longer whether managed care will evaluate therapists, but what form the evaluation will take. His efforts moved the question in managed care from the simplistic, "How many sessions?" to the more useful, "What is likely to be accomplished with how many more sessions?" The measures he and his colleagues created intensively track progress along a number of dimensions in each case, and relate that progress to the expected levels of change for other, similar clients. Howard likened these measures to an X-ray that charts the progress of psychotherapeutic healing. The measures include subjective well-being, current symptoms, and current life functioning, summarized into an overall mental health index, along with measures that focus on the process of treatment. The forms are completed by the client and the therapist periodically, providing a profile of how the client is feeling, how symptoms are progressing, how well the client is functioning, and how such core elements of treatment process as the bond between client and therapist are progressing. These forms are sent by the therapist for scoring, leading to regular feedback about progress in the form of written reports, thus providing an additional source of information about treatment progress. Because clients often want to be kind to their therapists, the information from the report sometimes is quite revealing. The reports also compare progress in the individual case with that of other similar clients in the large database. This creates a context for assessing how well the treatment is going.

These reports provide direct feedback to the therapist, who can see how well the client is progressing compared to others like that client. If progress is not at the level expected, the report serves as a launching point for an inquiry about why this has occurred. Have there been special circumstances that would explain the lack of progress (e.g., job loss, death in the family), or is the treatment simply less effective than might have been expected? Grant Grissom, a colleague of Howard's, points out that this kind of feedback provided directly to therapists about their work without an ax to grind is typically found to be very helpful.

Robert Marcovitz, a clinician who has used the Howard measures for several years, has found its major value lies in correcting his own misperceptions. Although 70% of reports from the measures are consistent with his expectations, in the other 30%, the measures identify clients as responding differently to therapy than he expects. For example, some clients who report feeling better in sessions indicate they are feeling no better than before treatment on the measures. He also finds that clients occasionally make disclosures on the forms that they have not shared with the therapist. When clients report better functioning on the measures than in session, Marcovitz uses the findings to discuss dependency and the possibility of termination. In the context of managed care, the use of the measures becomes more complex, serving to help case managers monitor treatment as well as directly helping the therapist learn about treatment. Although the case manager's access to the data creates the possibility that the results will be used to justify limits on service, Howard argues that without measurement of treatment process and outcome, the alternative is simple cost containment (i.e., the manager restricting the number of sessions). Using the patient profiling, client progress can be assessed compared to an expected norm, and in many cases a strong argument for more therapy can be made. Marcovitz finds that in dealing with managed care, the hard data about client progress and need for further treatment are far more convincing than clinician opinion. Of course, at times, the data also call on therapists to understand that therapy is no longer necessary.

Howard's efforts have led to other substantial projects centered on the ongoing assessment of client progress in psychotherapy. Michael Lambert and colleagues have used their measure, the OQ-45, on a client base as large as Howard's (Lambert & Barley, 2002; Lambert & Finch, 1999; Lambert, Hansen, & Finch, 2001). Lambert has also conducted research that has demonstrated the value of feedback to psychotherapists about client progress on the outcomes of psychotherapy (Lambert & Whipple, 2001). Barry Duncan and Scott Miller (2000) use a very simple session-by-session measure of client progress as the central core intervention in their outcome-informed therapy. And Bill Pinsof has extended the Howard paradigm to couple and family therapy in a system of tracking progress that includes feedback to therapists based in the Systemic Therapy Inventory of Change (Pinsof & Wynne, 2000).

In closing, the methods developed by Ken Howard and the evidence marshaled are powerful and convincing. This is good science brought to evaluate clinical practice. In the domain of managed care, measures such as Howard's appear to be enormously useful as an antidote for simplistic decision making. Of course, it remains to be seen whether they will be used in an informed way that includes careful feedback and consultation, as intended by Howard.

Given the strong evidence of psychotherapy's effectiveness, it is a reasonable expectation in most cases that it will yield positive results. It is our responsibility to carefully monitor treatment progress and take special measures if clients do not respond.

RESOURCES

Howard, K. I., Moras, K., Brill, P. L., & Martinovich, Z., (1996). Evaluation of psychotherapy: Efficacy, effectiveness, and patient progress. *American Psychologist, 51*(10): 1059–1064.

Sperry, L., Brill, P. L., Howard, K. I., & Grissom, G. R. (1996). *Treatment outcomes in psychotherapy and psychiatric interventions.* Philadelphia: Brunner/Mazel.

REFERENCES

Duncan, B. L., & Miller, S. D. (2000). *The heroic client: Doing client-directed, outcome-informed therapy.* San Francisco: Jossey-Bass.

Howard, K. I., Lueger, R. J., Martinovich, Z., & Lutz, W. (1999). The cost-effectiveness of psychotherapy: Dose-response and phase models. In N. E. Miller & K. M. Magruder (Eds.), *Cost-effectiveness of psychotherapy: A guide for practitioners, researchers, and policymakers* (pp. 143–152). London: Oxford University Press.

Howard, K. I., Moras, K., Brill, P. L., & Martinovich, Z., (1996). Evaluation of psychotherapy: Efficacy, effectiveness, and patient progress. *American Psychologist, 51*(10): 1059–1064.

Kopta, S. M., Howard, K. I., Lowry, J. L., & Beutler, L. E. (1994). Patterns of symptomatic recovery in psychotherapy. *Journal of Consulting & Clinical Psychology, 62*(5): 1009–1016.

Kopta, S. M., Lueger, R. J., Saunders, S. M., & Howard, K. I. (1999). Individual psychotherapy outcome and process research: Challenges leading to greater turmoil or a positive transition? *Annual Review of Psychology, 50:* 441–469.

Kopta, S. M., Newman, F. L., McGovern, M. P., & Angle, R. S. (1989). Relation between years of psychotherapeutic experience and conceptualizations, interventions, and treatment plan costs. *Professional Psychology: Research & Practice, 20*(1): 59–61.

Kopta, S. M., Newman, F. L., McGovern, M. P., & Sandrock, D. (1986). Psychotherapeutic orientations: A comparison of conceptualizations, interventions, and treatment plan costs. *Journal of Consulting & Clinical Psychology, 54*(3): 369–374.

Lambert, M. J., & Barley, D. E. (2002). Research summary on the therapeutic relationship and psychotherapy outcome. [References]. In J. C. Norcross (Ed.), *Psychotherapy relationships that work: Therapist contributions and responsiveness to patients* (pp. 17–32). London: Oxford University Press.

Lambert, M. J., & Bergin, A. E. (1994). The effectiveness of psychotherapy. In A. E. Bergin & S. L. Garfield (Eds.), *Handbook of psychotherapy and behavior change* (4th ed., pp. 143–189). Oxford, UK: John Wiley & Sons.

Lambert, M. J., & Finch, A. E. (1999). The Outcome Questionnaire. In M. E. Maruish (Ed.), *The use of psychological testing for treatment planning and outcomes assessment* (2nd ed., pp. 831–869). Mahwah, NJ: Lawrence Erlbaum Associates.

Lambert, M. J., Hansen, N. B., & Finch, A. E. (2001). Patient-focused research: Using patient outcome data to enhance treatment effects. *Journal of Consulting & Clinical Psychology, 69*(2): 159–172.

Lambert, M. J., Whipple, J. L., Smart, D. W., Vermeersch, D. A., Nielsen, S. L., & Hawkins, E. J. (2001). The effects of providing therapists with feedback on patient progress during psychotherapy: Are outcomes enhanced? *Psychotherapy Research, 11*(1): 49–68.

Lutz, W., Lowry, J., Kopta, S., Einstein, D. A., & Howard, K. I. (2001). Prediction of dose-response relations based on patient characteristics. *Journal of Clinical Psychology, 57*(7): 889–900.

Lyons, J. S., Howard, K. I., O'Mahoney, M. T., & Lish, J. D. (1997). *The measurement & management of clinical outcomes in mental health.* New York: John Wiley & Sons.

Pinsof, W. M., & Wynne, L. C. (2000). Toward progress research: Closing the gap between family therapy practice and research. *Journal of Marital & Family Therapy, 26*(1): 1–8.

Smith, M. L., & Glass, G. V. (1977). Meta-analysis of psychotherapy outcome studies. *American Psychologist, 32*(9): 752–760.

Sperry, L., Brill, P. L., Howard, K. I., & Grissom, G. R. (1996). *Treatment outcomes in psychotherapy and psychiatric interventions.* Philadelphia: Brunner/Mazel.

24

LEARNING TO LOVE ASSESSMENT: TODAY'S RESEARCH TOOLS TO ASSESS PROGRESS CAN HELP YOU BE A BETTER THERAPIST

Therapists can readily study client progress during psychotherapy through employing measures that track change, client satisfaction, and therapy process. This chapter looks at how therapists can incorporate such sources of information to inform treatment.

Research still intimidates most therapists, who associate it with highly technical methodologies and arcane studies that are indecipherable except to a tiny group of experts. True, rigorous, large-scale research can be daunting to contemplate. A research design may involve hundreds of cases (even small treatment studies are based on 20–30 clients) and tough requirements, including undeviating treatment protocols, homogeneous treatment populations, and randomization of subjects to conditions.

But, research can be far simpler and more user-friendly than most therapists realize. In fact, it's now possible for competent clinicians to make good use of a whole raft of simple and accessible research tools. For a subject base, therapists need only the idiosyncratic, multiply diagnosed clients they are already seeing. The rewards of doing this low-key kind of research are high. Not only does it enable clinicians to demonstrate the objective value of their treatment (managed care tends to be reassured by this), but it helps them discover information they might otherwise miss and become more effective practitioners.

A clinician can carry out with any individual client what method researchers call the "single-case design"—which is simply a more formal and systematic way of documenting what he or she does anyway. By using this design, a therapist uses several questionnaires over the course of therapy to document the changes that occur, both in therapy and in the client's life.

For example, Meg Bartoli, a Midwestern therapist with a master's degree in marriage and family therapy, hated her research courses in graduate school and now works entirely within a humanistic framework. She doesn't remotely think of herself as an academic researcher, but regularly uses a single-case design in treatment, both to help her track the progress of her clients and to enrich her own clinical work. So when Sandy and Tom came in for couples treatment, Meg asked them, as she does with other clients, to complete some self-report measures. Because Sandy had said during the intake call that she and Tom had grown distant from each other and that he seemed depressed, Meg chose to administer the Marital Satisfaction Inventory (MSI) (Snyder & Aikman, 1999) and the Symptom Checklist-90 (SCL-90) (Ogles, Lambert, & Masters, 1996). The MSI is a questionnaire with about 100 items that profile a spouse's marital satisfaction in areas including sexuality, communication, intimacy, and desire to remain in the marriage. The SCL-90, with 90 questions, probes for a range of symptoms, primarily focusing on anxiety and depression. It is probably the field's most widely used questionnaire. For the first session, Meg asked the couple to come in early to complete these instruments, and subsequently asked them to complete the same questionnaires before the first session of every month.

Using the data she obtained from these questionnaires, Meg readily charted not only general improvement in the marriage as therapy moved forward, but also specific patterns of progress within each partner's life. After two months, for example, she could demonstrate that their overall level of marital satisfaction was improving, as were some specific marital areas, such as communication and feelings of intimacy. This result seemed to fit what the couple indicated they were feeling; both reported being more pleased with each other, their marriage, and the therapy. Everything seemed to be going swimmingly. But when Meg administered the monthly questionnaire at the beginning of the third month of therapy, she learned from the instrument that the couple's sexual relationship remained unsatisfactory and Tom's depression hadn't lifted.

Why, one might ask, would a therapist need a questionnaire to find out about these clients' sex life or Tom's depression? Why wouldn't a therapist just ask? At one time, in the palmy days of long-term psychodynamic therapy over the course of several years of therapy, a client's entire personal life would inevitably emerge of its own accord, without need of psychological instruments. In today's world of brief treatment, however, it's far easier for even the most astute and painstaking therapist to miss things. First, there isn't enough time in a few sessions to explore all the areas that might present difficulties in a client's life. Second, if clients are clearly making progress, there's a tendency to maintain a kind of don't-ask/don't-tell attitude in therapy, rather than rock the boat. Clients often shy away from bringing up unpleasant, unresolved subjects, and therapists can remain unaware of issues that don't surface within a few sessions. A questionnaire often allows clients to "talk" about many tough issues—violence, substance abuse problems, sex—that they find almost impossible to mention in therapy. In these days of abbreviated, highly specific, issue-focused therapy, completed questionnaires are like extra therapy sessions; an instrument can expand and deepen clinical work while requiring relatively little time.

After looking at the questionnaires, Meg reviewed the therapy sessions with Tom and Sandy and realized that they'd focused on issues of communication and emotional intimacy, discussing sex and Tom's depression very little. At the next session, Meg shared these findings with Sandy and Tom, which led to a decision to talk more specifically about sexual issues in the couples work and begin individual sessions with Tom focusing on his depression. Tracking a client on an instrument's scales over time conveys the message that change is the goal of therapy, and change is what the therapist is working to achieve.

After four months of therapy, the managed care company representing the couple's insurer questioned the need for further therapy. Meg used Tom's depression scores and the data showing ongoing sexual problems to demonstrate the need for further treatment, and the company approved more sessions without further question. Objective measures make a much better case for approval of more sessions than vague statements based on a clinician's intuitive reading of a client.

In individual sessions with Tom, Meg explored his unresolved grief over the loss of his father at an early age. She began to work with Sandy and Tom on ways to enhance their sexual connection. Ultimately, Tom's depression lifted and the couple's sexual life improved—which were also indicated on the questionnaires. (Meg used these instruments as diagnostic tools and, in sessions, as a form of feedback that provided encouragement to the couple and opened up opportunities for more discussion.) In this case, both the measures and Meg's subjective impression indicated progress, but even measures less positive than the clinician's viewpoint can lead to deeper, richer discussions. A therapist might say, "You do sound less depressed, but the way you answered these items on the questionnaire indicates that you still suffer from bad moods sometime. What do you think that's all about?" When outcomes are not improving as expected, a therapist can bring them up in therapy, and shift strategies.

Doing single-case research allows therapists to reap the rewards of clinical work and scientific investigation. Below are five ideas to bear in mind as you begin to conduct this kind of research in your own practice.

TRACKING YOUR CLIENTS' PROGRESS DOESN'T NEED TO BE DIFFICULT

Progress research requires only that your clients or you complete questionnaires in a few minutes and score the results. For a compendium of such instruments, most of which can be obtained at minimal cost, see *Assessing Outcome in Clinical Practice,* by Benjamin Ogles, Michael Lambert, and Kevin Masters (2000), or the briefer list at the end of this chapter.

YOUR VIEW OF PROGRESS MAY DIFFER FROM YOUR CLIENTS'

Research has repeatedly shown that clients' and therapists' views of change are quite different (Lambert & Bergin, 1994). This is because therapists and clients pay attention to different things: clients notice their own improved feelings, whereas therapists note character, behavior, and symptomatic signs of change. In contrast, clients (particularly depressed clients) sometimes have a harder time than therapists seeing that anything is different. One view isn't necessarily better or more accurate than another, but both complement each other in summarizing what's happening to the client.

DISTINGUISH LIKING YOU FROM CLIENTS' SATISFACTION WITH TREATMENT

A client's view of therapy can be assessed through simple, quickly completed scales that can be given at random times during the course of treatment or mailed to the client after treatment ends; assessing at the conclusion of therapy more accurately taps clients' true feelings (Attkisson & Greenfield, 1994; Lebow, 1983, 1987). About 90% of all clients say they're highly satisfied with treatment. "Satisfaction" can carry many meanings, from simply liking the therapist to genuinely recognizing therapeutic change. A more telling assessment is dissatisfaction with therapy. This does not necessarily mean that the therapist has done something wrong (though it might), but may reflect a client's chronic inability to find satisfaction in anything. Nonetheless, a negative assessment made during treatment indicates that the therapist should talk to the client about possibly making changes in treatment.

ASSESSMENTS CAN MAKE TREATMENT MORE HELPFUL

We can't know what the outcome of therapy will be until after the end of therapy, but examining aspects of the treatment process while it's going on can help a therapist determine whether treatment is more or less likely to be successful. Questionnaires assessing the therapy process include items such as, "I trust my therapist," "My therapist and I share the same goals for therapy," "I think my therapist cares about me," and "I care about my therapist." One of the most replicated findings in psychotherapy research is that the alliance between client and therapist is a robust predictor of treatment success (Norcross, 2002). Psychologist Kenneth Howard even showed that if alliance measures early in therapy pointed to a poor alliance, good treatment outcomes were unlikely (Kopta, Lueger, Saunders, & Howard, 1999). It's better to know how a client feels about a therapist during therapy, when something can be done about it, than after treatment has come to a fizzling dead end.

MEASURE OFTEN

It seems obvious to measure clients at the beginning and end of therapy to learn how successful the treatment has been. But it's actually more informative to assess clients at frequent points during therapy. More frequent assessments give us a better sense of how, and under what circumstances, clients change over time. Research by psychologist Tony Tang of Northwestern University indicates that change in therapy tends to occur more in bursts than in small increments, and with assessment measures, we can track those bursts when they happen (Tang, DeRubeis, Beberman, & Pham, 2005). Additionally, assessing at multiple points protects against the biggest drawback of limiting testing to before and after therapy: we don't know exactly when therapy will end. If we haven't done any tests since a client first entered our offices, a client's decision to terminate therapy may leave us with no "after" measurements to determine what therapy accomplished.

Measures for Your Practice

Client Self-Report of Progress

Outcome Questionnaire-45 (OQ-45), developed by Michael Lambert and Gary Burlingame (Lambert, Gregersen, & Burlingame, 2004). A general measure of symptoms and functioning that assesses clients' personal distress, interpersonal relationships, and satisfaction with social roles.

The SCL-90 and Brief Symptom Inventory (Derogatis, 2000a, 2000b; Derogatis & Fitzpatrick, 2004), developed by Leonard Derogatis. Assesses client symptoms.

The Child Behavior Checklist (Achenbach, 2000), developed by Thomas Achenbach. Assesses the parents' report of child problem behaviors.

The Systemic Inventory of Change (Pinsof & Wynne, 2000), developed by William Pinsof, Jay Lebow, and colleagues. Assesses change in individual, relationship, family, and child functioning.

Specific instruments tailored to particular presenting problems, such as the Beck Depression Inventory (Beck, Steer, & Garbin, 1988), developed by Aaron Beck; the MSI-R (Snyder & Aikman, 1999), developed by Doug Snyder; the Michigan Alcoholism Screening Test (Selzer, 1971), developed by Melvin Selzer; and the Beck Anxiety Inventory (Wilson, de Beurs, Palmer, & Chambless, 1999), created by Aaron Beck and several colleagues.

Therapist's View of Change

Global Assessment Scale, developed by Jean Endicott (Endicott, Spitzer, Fleiss, & Cohen, 1976). A simple rating of the client's functioning on a 0-100 scale at any point in therapy.

Hamilton Rating Scale for Depression. Asks about signs and symptoms of depression (Ogles et al., 1996).

Target Complaints (Ogles et al., 1996), developed by C. C. Battle and colleagues. Focuses on the status of the specific problems being treated in therapy.

Client Satisfaction

Client Satisfaction Questionnaire (CSQ) (Attkisson & Greenfield, 1999; Attkisson & Zwick, 1982), developed by Clifford Attkisson and Daniel Larsen.

Therapy Process

Working Alliance Inventory (Horvath & Greenberg, 1986), developed by Adam Horvath and Leslie Greenberg. For individual therapy.

Couples Therapy Alliance Scales and Family Therapy Alliance Scales (Catherall & Pinsof, 1987), developed by William Pinsof and Donald Catherall. For couples and family therapy.

Therapy Session Report (Orlinsky & Howard, 1967), developed by David Orlinsky and Kenneth Howard. Assesses an array of features of each therapy session.

RESOURCES

Ogles, B. M., Lambert, M. J., & Masters, K. S. (1996). *Assessing outcome in clinical practice*. Needham Heights, MA: Allyn & Bacon.

REFERENCES

Achenbach, T. M. (2000). Child Behavior Checklist. In A. E. Kazdin (Ed.), *Encyclopedia of psychology*. New York: Oxford University Press.

Attkisson, C., & Greenfield, T. K. (1994). Client Satisfaction Questionnaire-8 and Service Satisfaction Scale-30. In M. E. Maruish (Ed.), *The use of psychological testing for treatment planning and outcome assessment* (pp. 402–420). Hillsdale, NJ: Lawrence Erlbaum Associates.

Attkisson, C., & Greenfield, T. K. (1999). The UCSF Client Satisfaction Scales: I. The Client Satisfaction Questionnaire-8. In M. E. Maruish (Ed.), *The use of psychological testing for treatment planning and outcomes assessment* (2nd ed., pp. 1333–1346). Mahwah, NJ: Lawrence Erlbaum Associates.

Attkisson, C., & Zwick, R. (1982). The Client Satisfaction Questionnaire: Psychometric properties and correlations with service utilization and psychotherapy outcome. *Evaluation & Program Planning, 5*(3): 233–237.

Beck, A. T., Steer, R. A., & Garbin, M. G. (1988). Psychometric properties of the Beck Depression Inventory: Twenty-five years of evaluation. *Clinical Psychology Review, 8*(1): 77–100.

Catherall, D. R., & Pinsof, W. M. (1987). The impact of the therapist's personal family life on the ability to establish viable therapeutic alliances in family and marital therapy. *Journal of Psychotherapy & the Family, 3*(2): 135–160.

Derogatis, L. R. (2000a). Hopkins Symptom Checklist. In A. E. Kazdin (Ed.), *Encyclopedia of psychology.* New York: Oxford University Press.

Derogatis, L. R. (2000b). SCl-90-R. In A. E. Kazdin (Ed.), *Encyclopedia of psychology.* New York: Oxford University Press.

Derogatis, L. R., & Fitzpatrick, M. (Eds.). (2004). The SCL-90-R, the Brief Symptom Inventory (BSI), and the BSI-18. In M. E. Maruish (Ed.), *The use of psychological testing for treatment planning and outcomes assessment: Volume 3: Instruments for adults.* (3rd ed.). Malwah, NJ: Lawrence Erlbaum Associates.

Endicott, J., Spitzer, R. L., Fleiss, J. L., & Cohen, J. (1976). The Global Assessment Scale: A procedure for measuring overall severity of psychiatric disturbance. *Archives of General Psychiatry, 33*(6): 766–771.

Horvath, A. O., & Greenberg, L. S. (1986). The development of the Working Alliance Inventory. In L. S. Greenberg & W. M. Pinsof (Eds.), *The psychotherapeutic process: A research handbook* (pp. 529–556). New York, NY: Guilford Press.

Kopta, S. M., Lueger, R. J., Saunders, S. M., & Howard, K. I. (1999). Individual psychotherapy outcome and process research: Challenges leading to greater turmoil or a positive transition? *Annual Review of Psychology 50*: 441–469.

Lambert, M. J., & Bergin, A. E. (1994). The effectiveness of psychotherapy. In A. E. Bergin & S. L. Garfield (Eds.), *Handbook of psychotherapy and behavior change* (4th ed., pp. 143–189). Oxford, England: John Wiley & Sons.

Lambert, M. J., Gregersen, A. T., & Burlingame, G. M. (2004). The Outcome Questionnaire-45. [References]. In M. E. Maruish (Ed.), *The use of psychological testing for treatment planning and outcomes assessment: Volume 3: Instruments for adults* (3rd ed., pp. 191–234). Mahwah, NJ: Lawrence Erlbaum Associates.

Lebow, J. L. (1983). Research assessing consumer satisfaction with mental health treatment: A review of findings. *Evaluation & Program Planning, 6*(3–4): 211–236.

Lebow, J. L. (1987). Acceptability as a simple measure in mental health program evaluation. *Evaluation & Program Planning, 10*(3): 191–195.

Norcross, J. C. (Ed.). (2002). *Psychotherapy relationships that work: Therapist contributions and responsiveness to patients.* London: Oxford University Press.

Ogles, B. M., Lambert, M. J., & Masters, K. S. (1996). *Assessing outcome in clinical practice.* Needham Heights, MA: Allyn & Bacon.

Orlinsky, D. E., & Howard, K. I. (1967). The good therapy hour: Experiential correlates of patients' and therapists' evaluations of therapy sessions. *Archives of General Psychiatry, 16*(5): 621–632.

Pinsof, W. M., & Wynne, L. C. (2000). Toward progress research: Closing the gap between family therapy practice and research. *Journal of Marital & Family Therapy, 26*(1): 1–8.

Selzer, M. L. (1971). The Michigan Alcoholism Screening Test: The quest for a new diagnostic instrument. *American Journal of Psychiatry, 127*(12): 1653–1658.

Snyder, D. K., & Aikman, G. G. (1999). Marital Satisfaction Inventory–Revised. In M. E. Maruish (Ed.), *The use of psychological testing for treatment planning and outcomes assessment* (2nd ed., pp. 1173–1210). Mahwah, NJ: Lawrence Erlbaum Associates, Publishers.

Tang, T. Z., DeRubeis, R. J., Beberman, R., & Pham, T. (2005). Cognitive changes, critical sessions, and sudden gains in cognitive-behavioral therapy for depression. *Journal of Consulting & Clinical Psychology, 73*(1): 168–172.

Wilson, K. A., de Beurs, E., Palmer, C. A., & Chambless, D. L. (1999). Beck Anxiety Inventory. In M. E. Maruish (Ed.), *The use of psychological testing for treatment planning and outcomes assessment* (2nd ed., pp. 971–992). Mahwah, NJ: Lawrence Erlbaum Associates.

25

DO-IT-YOURSELF RESEARCH: THE PRACTICAL ADVANTAGES OF STUDYING YOUR OWN PRACTICE

Research is typically thought of as an activity done by research-ers. Nonetheless, psychotherapists in clinical practice can do "local" research that can help them understand what transpires in individual cases and, more generally, in their practice. Such "local" research can complement what is learned from the larger, better-controlled research. This chapter looks at the kinds of ways psychotherapists can use research tools to examine their practice.

Most clinicians I know tend to think of research as a remote activity, carried out by academics, in large projects that require years to con-duct. In fact, research does not require videotapes, coding systems, computer prowess, or million-dollar budgets, nor does it mean reduc-ing the complexity of human experience to a few summary statistics. Actually, to navigate the subtleties of the therapeutic relationship, cli-nicians must act like researchers every day, forming hypotheses, sifting clinical data, and assessing the impact of treatment. There is no intrinsic reason that clinicians cannot take the additional step of gathering the same kind of quantified information as researchers.

Some might ask, Why quantify? Why not just journal and write down our overall conclusions about our cases? If science and therapy teach us one thing, it is that our subjective biases, our tendency to see what we expect or what we want to see, exert an overwhelming pull on our perceptions. To counterbalance that pull, we need consistent methods of information gathering and consistent measures of that information.

In the era of managed care, data collection has come to have additional value. Having precise information about your clients, the typical duration of treatment, and the level of patient satisfaction is crucial in developing relationships with managed care companies. Having a bank of this kind of information about your practice can be a convincing selling point. In fact, failing to collect these data soon will become a significant liability.

Michael Fox, a family psychiatrist from Baltimore, is one example of a clinician who decided it was finally time to do some research on his own practice (Michael Fox, personal communication, 1996). Having no research background, Fox consulted with a researcher (Michael Rohrbaugh) about ways of collecting and analyzing his data. Using his clinical records and source material, Fox coded a range of clients, treatment processes, and treatment outcome variables from 750 patients he had seen over a 12-year period. He first predicted what the data would show and then looked at the aggregated results.

He was surprised to find that 60% of his patients were seen for fewer than six months, and even though he was aware that much of his work was short-term, he was shocked to find 33% were seen for less than one month. He also found a decline in intake that paralleled the rise of managed care, a decrease in sessions per case over the years, and a changing distribution in client diagnoses over time. These data allowed him to explicitly define what he had previously only vaguely known and helped him to better anticipate the brevity of treatment and to plan accordingly.

Fox's ratings of client outcome on a case-by-case basis were more positive than he had expected. Although his hunch was that 60% of his clients had not improved, the case-by-case ratings he made found only 38% unimproved. In a surprising number of cases that lasted only a few sessions, the presenting problems were significantly reduced. Working with the difficult-to-treat cases Fox frequently encounters, successes can readily be obscured by memories of those not making progress.

Interestingly, Fox also found better outcome in cases having up to 20 sessions, but that beyond 20 sessions, outcomes no longer clearly improved with more sessions. Looking at who improved, he found that families with schizophrenia and substance abuse had the poorest outcomes overall in his caseload, whereas those with eating disorders and marital problems responded most positively to treatment. Fox also found that clients who received medication in addition to family therapy progressed more quickly. From his study, Fox gained a sharpened sense of whom he was seeing and for how long. The study also increased his confidence in the effectiveness of his efforts, pointed to the types of problems on which his treatment had the greatest and smallest effects, and served as a launching point for considering what worked and where he would want to make changes. For instance, he now starts many of his clients on medication much earlier in treatment. He says his research project caused him to trust his global recollections about his practice less and rely more on research data. (Michael Fox, personal communication, 1996)

Here, then, are a few of the ways we as clinicians can use research methods to gather information about our practices.

SIMPLE STATISTICS ABOUT PRACTICE PATTERNS

An easy way to begin is to gather statistics about who you see and for how long. What are the most frequently encountered problems? How many families, couples, and individuals do you see? How old are the clients? What is their gender and ethnicity? How many sessions is typical for each problem area? Which clients account for what percentage of the income to you or your facility? These questions can be answered by keeping a running tally and summarizing on a regular basis (e.g., quarterly) or by simply summarizing from records over a longer period.

It is striking how often we need or are asked for this type of simple information, and how seldom we actually have it. Clients will ask, How long does couples therapy with you usually last? or How often have you worked with my problem? It may be helpful to know what percentage of our clients use managed care. Making a best guess can often prove wrong.

If you decide to gather this kind of information about your practice, start by asking yourself what you really want to know. Pick a few key characteristics and keep them simple. Summarize the data you gather in the form of distributions (e.g., four clients at one session, three at two to five sessions), rather than as means (adding the number of sessions for each client and dividing by the number of clients). Means are too easily affected by those who are at the extreme (the mean of 5 people with 1 session and 1 with 200 is 34 sessions).

SUBJECTIVE MEASURES OF OUTCOME

A method only slightly more complex is to keep a simple record of who improved in treatment and who did not. At termination, globally rate each case you've seen as very improved, improved, unchanged, or worse. Rate each problem encountered as eliminated, much improved, somewhat improved, unchanged, or worse. See how many cases you put in each category. Then examine the cases you have rated at each level of outcome for common threads. Are there patterns that leap out about who improves and who does not? Bear in mind that we are only considering your own rating here. A considerable literature points to the difference among therapists', clients', clients' families', and third-party views of change. Interestingly, therapists are more often *negative* about outcome than are clients. When I rated outcomes in my cases, I uncovered a pattern of which I had not been aware. In cases in which the identified patient was an adolescent, outcomes were better when more than half of the sessions were individual sessions with the adolescent. This led me to move to a higher proportion of individual sessions with adolescents.

CLIENT SATISFACTION DATA

The brave-hearted who are willing to ask their clients about their treatment experience can discover a great deal of interesting information. Surveying client satisfaction involves giving your clients a standardized instrument that asks them to rate their experience in therapy, much like a workshop evaluation form (Lebow, 1983a, 1983b, 1987). My favorite is the Client Satisfaction Questionnaire (CSQ), developed by C. Clifford Attkisson and his colleagues (Attkisson & Zwick, 1982), although there are numerous other good instruments. The CSQ asks several general questions about how clients view their therapy experience and what it did for them. Clients rate the overall quality of service, the extent to which their needs were met, their satisfaction with the amount of help received and how much the service helped. You can add extra questions about specific aspects of treatment in which you are interested (e.g., How helpful did you find the group sessions?).

There are several ways of distributing these questionnaires, ranging from passing them out to all your clients over a short period to giving them to all clients in their last session with you (not a very effective method because many clients don't officially designate their last session) or mailing them to clients a month after the end of treatment (this allows clients to comment about the entire process in privacy, decreasing the likelihood that they will distort their answers; however, such questionnaires only have about a 25% return rate). You need to decide whether you want individuals to identify themselves on the questionnaires (and risk getting less-than-honest responses) or to remain anonymous (limiting your ability to tie that information to a specific case). Bear in mind that most therapists achieve very high levels of satisfaction with most clients. In this kind of survey, 90% satisfaction rates are not uncommon. However, some clients, such as high-conflict couples, can be expected to experience lower levels of satisfaction with treatment than others. A community mental health center where I worked regularly assessed consumer satisfaction. Therapists were surprised to find that many clients, whom they thought had "prematurely" left therapy, were very satisfied with their treatment.

Another approach to assessing client satisfaction is to simply call former clients to follow up about how they are doing, what they think about treatment now that some time has passed, and what they believe helped most. Even the simplest qualitative response provides information about practice that clinicians rarely possess. A colleague wanted to see how her clients in managed care felt about their treatment. Brief phone calls revealed that although the clients did have complaints with some aspects of the care, such as the case management, they remained substantially satisfied with her treatment.

GOAL ATTAINMENT

Also extremely useful is goal-attainment scaling, through which the therapist and client agree on a set of problems and related goals that are to be the focus of treatment (Kiresuk, Smith, & Cardillo, 1994). They then project a range of potential outcomes in the problem area, anchored by what they expect the result to be in a successful treatment (e.g., to be substantially free of depression), also including potential outcomes that are worse than what is expected (e.g., to be still substantially depressed) and better than expected (e.g., for there to be no depression whatsoever). Goal attainment for each problem area is then rated by client and therapist as treatment progresses. New goals can be added over the course of treatment. When I have used goal-attainment scaling with clients, it has helped to sharpen our clinical focus about where the treatment is aimed and to evaluate the success in reaching treatment goals. For example, Tom and Mary's goals included reducing their level of fighting, increasing their level of intimate connection, and improving Tom's self-control during fights. When they assessed their goal attainment after 12 sessions, they agreed that they had achieved a better level of outcome than they expected in reducing fighting and improving Tom's self-control, but rated their intimacy as remaining at the same level. These data helped validate that progress was being made on core goals of treatment, while also helping to redirect further therapy toward the unresolved goal of creating greater intimacy.

MORE COMPLEX PROCESS AND OUTCOME DATA

For those who want to do more research on their practice, more complex information about treatment process and outcome can be gathered. Much of the data in major clinical research studies come from questionnaires and rating scales presented to clients and therapists that are available to therapists, most without cost. Many of these instruments are listed in *Assessing Outcome in Clinical Practice* by Benjamin Ogles, Michael Lambert, and Kevin Masters (1996). These instruments can be used to help describe the types of problems and clients in your practice (how severe is their marital distress or degree of depression?) or can be given to clients at the beginning and end of treatment, tracking the amount of change that has occurred.

NONREACTIVE MEASURES

Among the most informative research measures are those without respondents, eliminating the potential for distortion. These nonreactive measures use information that automatically accrues, but often goes unnoticed. Which clients come back for more treatment? Which refer other clients? Which are regularly late or fail to attend scheduled sessions? How many couples ultimately divorce? Just by observing, following up, and then recording behaviors in which we are interested, a great deal can be learned. In tracking this kind of information, I once found that the referrals from a particular lawyer nearly invariably wanted expert testimony rather than psychotherapy, regardless of what the clients professed at the first session. This information helped me to more quickly focus the work with clients referred by this attorney in a useful way.

POOLING INFORMATION

Efforts to gather data about treatment don't have to stop with the single, interested clinician. Groups of clinicians (whether practicing together or apart) can pool their data. Consider that, at this point, we have virtually no information about the practice patterns and outcomes in many common forms of couple and family therapy. Imagine how much data could be collected if Bowenian therapists, for example, joined together and agreed on how to obtain a standard set of data on their practices. Although this kind of data would not substitute for better-controlled efficacy studies, it would at least begin to provide a database for demonstrating the impact of this therapy. Groups of therapists in Pennsylvania have begun to do something much like this, forming a practice network in which they gather standardized information about their clients and pool the results (Borkovec, Echemendia, Ragusea, & Ruiz, 2001).

TRY IT, YOU MIGHT LIKE IT

A colleague looked at clients who dropped out early in therapy and surveyed client satisfaction. She found that couples were disproportionately represented among early terminators, and that clients in couple therapy frequently mentioned their discomfort with the high levels of conflict in sessions and the therapist's inability to control it. These findings led her to change her approach early in couple therapy, assuming a more active role that set limits on conflict in sessions and focused on building communications skills and collaboration before engaging the high-conflict issues. She soon found less early termination in her couple therapy.

The kind of research described in this chapter is well within the scope of most therapists. Pick a few aspects of your therapy experience you would like to track or form a few questions about your practice you are interested in answering. Formulate some hypotheses about what you will find. Gather the data from records or collect it prospectively over time and see what turns up. A small amount of input from someone with research experience can help a great deal in refining the questions, deciding the relevant variables, and choosing appropriate instruments, but even if you don't have access to that kind of help, give it a try. At the very least, you certainly will learn more about your work and may well be surprised by what you find out.

RESOURCES

Ogles, B. M., Lambert, M. J., & Masters, K. S. (1996). *Assessing outcome in clinical practice*. Needham Heights, MA: Allyn & Bacon.

REFERENCES

Attkisson, C., & Zwick, R. (1982). The Client Satisfaction Questionnaire: Psychometric properties and correlations with service utilization and psychotherapy outcome. *Evaluation & Program Planning, 5*(3): 233–237.

Borkovec, T. D., Echemendia, R. J., Ragusea, S. A., & Ruiz, M. (2001). The Pennsylvania Practice Research Network and future possibilities for clinically meaningful and scientifically rigorous psychotherapy effectiveness research. *Clinical Psychology: Science and Practice, 8*(2): 155–167.

Kiresuk, T. J., Smith, A., & Cardillo, J. E. (1994). *Goal attainment scaling: Applications, theory, and measurement.* Hillsdale, NJ: Lawrence Erlbaum Associates.

Lebow, J. L. (1983a). Client satisfaction with mental health treatment: Methodological considerations in assessment. *Evaluation Review, 7*(6): 729–752.

Lebow, J. L. (1983b). Research assessing consumer satisfaction with mental health treatment: A review of findings. *Evaluation & Program Planning, 6*(3–4): 211–236.

Lebow, J. L. (1987). Acceptability as a simple measure in mental health program evaluation. *Evaluation & Program Planning, 10*(3): 191–195.

Ogles, B. M., Lambert, M. J., & Masters, K. S. (1996). *Assessing outcome in clinical practice.* Needham Heights, MA: Allyn & Bacon.

26

MODELS FOR EVALUATING PSYCHOTHERAPY PRACTICES AND COMMUNITY MENTAL HEALTH PROGRAMS: PUBLIC HEALTH PERSPECTIVES

This chapter explores the evaluation of psychotherapy practice from a public health perspective, examining it through five distinct lenses.

Increasingly, perspectives from the study of public health are being applied to the evaluation of psychotherapy practice and community mental health programs. This makes a great deal of sense because, among other things, psychotherapy is a set of interventions targeted to a set of public health problems. The public health perspective is especially valuable in broadening what, at times, can become a nearsighted vision about what is being done in psychotherapy. There are several overlapping conceptions that are part of the public health perspective (Newman & Ciarlo, 1994; Newman, Howard, Windle, & Hohmann, 1994; Newman, Hunter, & Irving, 1987; Newman & McGovern, 1987).

THE ORGANIZATIONAL MODEL

The organizational model focuses on the management of the treatment facility, be it a hospital, community mental health center, or individual practice. This model is derived from the world of industrial engineering. Management personnel are its most zealous advocates, and its zeitgeist resembles that of most businesses. This model assesses the appropriateness and viability of the organizational structure, the scope of the operation, the efficiency of management, the quantity of services provided, and the relation of services to community need and demand.

The assessment of organizational functioning actually includes several domains. One is the assessment of structure, the "on-paper" ability of the facility to function. Elements of structure that may be assessed include institutional accreditation, type of programs available, number of personnel, number of dollars spent, adequacy of the organizational chart, quality of practitioners' training, quality assurance efforts, and opportunities for professional development.

In addition to structural assessment that focuses on the facility's potential capabilities, the organizational model examines the pragmatics of operation by applying measures of utilization and continuity of service. Utilization measures include the quantity of services offered and the productivity of staff, programs, and facilities. Utilization data also may be combined with community need or demand data to assess availability of service (number of services proportionate to population) and accessibility of service for various groups of community residents. Continuity measures include the movement patterns of clients within the care system. Other relevant management data might include the efficiency of the organization's operation, the cost of services, and the ratio of cost to quantity of services.

Organizational data are used more often in large mental health treatment settings than are data generated by the alternative models. The data most often examined in both internal and external monitoring of agencies are the quantity of services offered; the productivity of staff, program, and facility; the quantity of service in relation to cost; and the extent to which minimal structural criteria are met.

This wide usage points to the importance assigned to these data by individuals who operate facilities and control funding. It also indicates the relative ease and accuracy with which such data can be obtained, as well as the low level of inference required to use these data in decisions. Mental health facilities operate on one level as businesses that require a management perspective; without sufficient attention to management, both clinical service and financial stability are impaired. Organizational data are useful in determining whether appropriate services are available, whether staff time is efficiently used, and whether income is maximized. All of these questions are crucial, especially during times of diminishing resources.

The organizational model does not provide a description of the quality, effectiveness, and acceptability of services. Utilization data can describe only quantity, not quality; structural assessment can describe only whether the facility's structure is conducive to offering good treatment, not how treatment is offered; management data can describe only the organizational functioning, not the care process. Although good service is probably a function of good structure and management, these relationships have yet to be empirically demonstrated in mental health settings. So a complete assessment must encompass more than organizational data.

Organizational data has other shortcomings. Utilization data may show inconsistent patterns across units chosen (hours, sessions, contacts, or clients). Availability and accessibility must be assessed in relation to a standard that almost inevitably will be open to interpretation. Structural assessment must depend on generalized standards that may or may not be relevant in specific instances. Further, structural criteria necessarily accentuate the more easily measured aspects of a facility, and thus may accent insignificant aspects (e.g., the presence of a fire door). Furthermore, systems of assessing management vary; the same information may not be available in all assessments. Thus, while the organizational model is useful in evaluating mental health facilities, it must be augmented to include other forms of evaluation.

THE CARE-PROCESS MODEL

Using the care-process model, the quality of services is compared with some standard of practice. This model focuses on appropriate assignment of clients to services and the effectiveness of service delivery. Its principal strength lies in its assessment of the actual behavior of practitioners. Diagnosis and treatment of clients are the ultimate products of a mental health facility; the facility is reflected in the services offered.

But several problems plague the care-process model. The types of data necessary to evaluate the quality of process are difficult to gather. Clinicians are reluctant to open treatment to examination; constraints of confidentiality and cost are also limiting factors. Tapes of treatment sessions are the best source of process data, but they are rarely available and may be subject to high reactivity (alteration of behavior from the awareness of being evaluated). The principal source of information is therefore limited to records, which may be inaccurate, insufficiently detailed, and incomplete, or may not provide data that directly reflect the quality of services.

The evaluation of process also requires some standard for comparison; setting such standards constitutes a further problem. Even in general medical care the setting of standards for practice is a difficult task; in mental health settings the difficulties are multiplied. There are no widely accepted standards for even the most basic decisions, such as the choice of individual, group, family, or medication therapy, let alone in more specific interventions. The alternative of choosing experts to judge the quality of treatment without explicit criteria similarly remains subject to question, since mental health treatment experts have differing viewpoints. These problems, along with concerns about discouraging innovation through premature establishment of standards for practice, have minimized the use of the process model in evaluation of mental health settings. This method is most applicable where standards for treatment are clear, such as within some very specific forms of treatment (e.g., in multisystemic therapy; Schoenwald, Halliday-Boykins, & Henggeler, 2003; Schoenwald & Henggeler, 2004).

THE CONSUMER-EVALUATION MODEL

The consumer-evaluation model is derived from marketing research and focuses on the consumer's opinions about services offered (Lebow, 1982). From this perspective, mental health services are regarded as products that can be evaluated by the consumer. These consumers may either be clients who assess services they have received, or residents of the community who assess the service system as a whole. Most research has investigated client satisfaction within specific facilities, though some research, such as the *Consumer Reports* study (which found that most people indicated high satisfaction with psychotherapy; Seligman, 1995), has examined satisfaction in a broader population.

The consumer has a unique perspective vital to the evaluation of services. Acceptability of services is an important factor in determining the utilization and funding of services. The satisfaction of clients is also a mediating goal in the pursuit of treatment effectiveness, and an ultimate goal of treatment in its own right. Consumer-evaluation methods are direct and inexpensive, because the data are gathered through simple interviews or questionnaires. These attributes are considerable virtues given the complexity of some of the analyses in the other models for evaluating treatments. Anyone can conduct such a survey, usually with little cost or effort involved. But distortion in reports is a major problem. Consumers' assessment of services may be altered by a desire to respond in a way that they think the provider wants them to respond, by acquiescence to the positive phrasing of questions, by the filtering of specifics through a positive halo response, and by reactivity to fears that their response may have implications for their treatment or their provider. A further problem is that consumer evaluation may not suggest the quality of service even if accurately reported. Clients may be affected by positive or negative transference, poor reality testing, or a lack of knowledge about the elements that constitute appropriate treatment.

There also are other difficulties in getting a valid response from clients, especially problems in obtaining a random sample of respondents. Only those with positive or very negative responses may be likely to respond. The basically positive data obtained through these methods may need to be tempered by other data such as patterns of utilization (especially, for example, data about the number of early terminations). Consumer-evaluation data are valuable, but must be viewed in the proper context; one must consider the source of data and circumstances of the data collection.

THE EFFICACY MODEL

A fourth public health model, the efficacy model, evaluates performance by assessing change in clients. This model has its roots in clinical trials research, in which treatments are assessed by their respective outcomes. Measures of change may assess psychiatric symptomatology as by the Hopkins Symptom Checklist (Derogatis, 2000), or may assess general role functioning, as by the global assessment scales (Endicott, Spitzer, Fleiss, & Cohen, 1976). They may focus on the specific goals of treatment—for example, through using Goal Attainment Scaling (Kiresuk & Sherman, 1968; Kiresuk, Smith, & Cardillo, 1994). Information also may be gathered from various sources: the client, the therapist, significant others, or independent raters. The focus of assessment can be on general functioning or on a much more specific behavior. Each source and type of information has value and suggests a different aspect of outcome.

The efficacy model has the basic strength of testing the stated purpose of most mental health treatment: the facilitation of change in clients. The principal problems of using this model lie in the pragmatic difficulties of measuring outcome and the precarious nature of the relationship between treatment and outcome. Change is difficult to measure; the measures available to assess outcome are necessarily primitive, and the changes are unlikely to coalesce into simple categories. Measures from alternative perspectives also often correlate poorly with one another (Ogles, Lambert, & Masters, 1996), forcing the need for analysis to include complex descriptions of outcome. And, even in a complex descriptive form, outcome assessments may miss the complexity of human experience. Efficacy measures also remain subject to many problems in validation. For example, the influence of reactivity, cognitive dissonance, and desire to maintain socially desirable behavior can distort reports. Data from treatment dropouts become especially important in evaluations of efficacy, but are difficult to obtain. Furthermore, the assessment of outcome easily can become very expensive.

Furthermore, good treatment does not necessarily produce positive outcomes. Many factors that affect outcome may be well beyond the control of the practitioner such as, for example, the chronicity of the client's problem. It is therefore somewhat ironic that assessments of mental health treatment quality have often considered outcome information to be synonymous with evaluation. Outcome data may appropriately serve as the ultimate criteria in comparing treatments in clinical trial research, but certainly cannot take on such a role in the general assessment of practice. Outcome data are valuable, especially when data from groups of providers are involved and when sample characteristics and treatments involved are clearly specified. However, these data do not mitigate the need for other types of analysis.

THE COMMUNITY-IMPACT MODEL

The community-impact model assesses the influence of the provider practice on the community as a whole. Measures of community impact include the community's knowledge of services, as well as the mental health of the community. The latter measure is obviously only salient in considering the impact of large mental health treatment practices, such as that of a community mental health facility.

The principal strength of this model lies in its clear tie to the ultimate goal of many mental health facilities: better mental health functioning in the community served. The model's difficulties are an extension of those encountered in the efficacy model. The mental health of the community is harder to measure than that of particular clients, and the relationship between a center's activity and a community's mental health is unlikely to be strong given the relatively small size of most facilities. Because of these problems, community mental health is seldom employed as a measure of a facility's functioning. The simpler measures of community impact (e.g., knowledge of the facility within the community) offer the best opportunity for the use of this kind of data in most settings.

USING THESE MODELS

Each model has a distinct focus, intent, and place in the evaluation of facilities offering mental health treatment. The organizational model focuses on organization functioning and the ability to offer service, the care-process model concentrates on the care delivered, the consumer-evaluation model assesses the acceptability of care, and the efficacy model stresses the outcome of care, whereas the community-impact model focuses on the effects of the institution on the community. Each model offers unique and valuable data; the optimal evaluation would include data relevant to each of the five models. However, pragmatically, most facilities and providers are unable to draw on each kind of information. Some of these methods involve considerable cost, and some methods, such as impact studies, yield minimal rewards in relation to cost.

Yet, this need not be discouraging. Information nested within any one of these models can be quite valuable, particularly when it addresses a question of interest (e.g., What do our clients think about our treatment?). But it's essential to understand the limitations of each model and consider how additional data generated by other models might affect conclusions. For example, two programs may vary in productivity, but the one with the lower patient count may be more effective. In this instance, failing to consider efficacy might lead to oversimplified and counterproductive decisions. Each model also has a natural constituency; managers prefer organizational data, while consumers prefer consumer-evaluation data. Thus various stakeholders are likely to assign different importance to the assorted models. The collection and presentation of data are only one step in assessment and decision making. The full process must include establishing priorities among goals and models of evaluation.

Each of us, within our various organizations, can find ways to examine our work through the lens of each of these public health perspectives. And we can benefit from gathering and examining data that assesses our practice from a variety of these perspectives.

RESOURCES

Newman, F. L., Hunter, R. H., & Irving, D. (1987). Simple measures of progress and outcome in the evaluation of mental health services. *Evaluation & Program Planning, 10*(3): 209–218.

Newman, F. L., & McGovern, M. P. (1987). Simple measures of case mix in mental health services. *Evaluation & Program Planning, 10*(3): 197–200.

Ogles, B. M., Lambert, M. J., & Masters, K. S. (1996). *Assessing outcome in clinical practice.* Needham Heights, MA: Allyn & Bacon.

REFERENCES

Derogatis, L. R. (2000). SCl-90-R. In A. E. Kazdin (Ed.), *Encyclopedia of psychology.* New York: Oxford University Press.

Endicott, J., Spitzer, R. L., Fleiss, J. L., & Cohen, J. (1976). The Global Assessment Scale: A procedure for measuring overall severity of psychiatric disturbance. *Archives of General Psychiatry, 33*(6): 766–771.

Kiresuk, T. J., & Sherman, R. E. (1968). Goal attainment scaling: A general method for evaluating comprehensive community mental health programs. *Community Mental Health Journal, 4*(6): 443–453.

Kiresuk, T. J., Smith, A., & Cardillo, J. E. (1994). *Goal attainment scaling: Applications, theory, and measurement*: Hillsdale, NJ: Lawrence Erlbaum Associates.

Lebow, J. (1982). Consumer satisfaction with mental health treatment. *Psychological Bulletin, 91*(2): 244–259.

Newman, F. L., & Ciarlo, J. A. (1994). Criteria for selecting psychological instruments for treatment outcome assessment. In M. E. Maruish (Ed.), *The use of psychological testing for treatment planning and outcome assessment* (pp. 98–110). Hillsdale, NJ: Lawrence Erlbaum Associates.

Newman, F. L., Howard, K. I., Windle, C. D., & Hohmann, A. A. (1994). Introduction to the special section on seeking new methods in mental health services research. *Journal of Consulting & Clinical Psychology, 62*(4): 667–669.

Newman, F. L., Hunter, R. H., & Irving, D. (1987). Simple measures of progress and outcome in the evaluation of mental health services. *Evaluation & Program Planning, 10*(3): 209–218.

Newman, F. L., & McGovern, M. P. (1987). Simple measures of case mix in mental health services. *Evaluation & Program Planning, 10*(3): 197–200.

Ogles, B. M., Lambert, M. J., & Masters, K. S. (1996). *Assessing outcome in clinical practice.* Needham Heights, MA: Allyn & Bacon.

Schoenwald, S. K., Halliday-Boykins, C. A., & Henggeler, S. W. (2003). Client-level predictors of adherence to MST in community service settings. *Family Process, 42*(3): 345–359.

Schoenwald, S. K., & Henggeler, S. W. (2004). A public health perspective on the transport of evidence-based practices. *Clinical Psychology: Science & Practice, 11*(4): 360–363.

Seligman, M. E. P. (1995). The effectiveness of psychotherapy: The *Consumer Reports* study. *American Psychologist, 50*(12): 965–974.

Part V

Research in Psychology That Informs
the Practice of Psychotherapy

27

DEFENDING THE FAMILY: BEWARE OF THE BIOGENETIC BANDWAGON

The practice of psychotherapy is very much affected by findings having to do with the debate over nature vs. nurture. If biology is ultimately the key, then therapy becomes largely about working within the limits of biology, whereas if nurture is more important, such considerations do not apply. In the last two decades, having an understanding of the role of biology has emerged as increasingly important to the practice of psychotherapy. This chapter describes the debate over the influence of nature vs. nurture, here organized around one of what now are many radical views that suggest that genetics is what ultimately matters in human development.

Although therapists tend to argue among themselves about differences in clinical theories and about practical issues in treatment, they have agreed about one thing: The family matters. The cornerstone of the field has been the fundamental idea that family structure and family-of-origin experiences are the central determinants of who we are and how we behave. But as the interest in the genetic influences on behavior grows, one increasingly hears highly respected researchers and practitioners question the role of the family in human development.

Perhaps the best summary of the research challenging the psychological importance of the family is the provocatively titled, *The Limits of Family Influence,* and is by psychologist David Rowe (1994), professor of family studies at the University of Arizona (Rowe, 2001a, 2001b, 2003; Rowe & Jacobson, 1999). Rowe strongly argues that much of who we are is shaped by our biology, and that the family environment has little impact on children's development of personality and other traits, except as a negative factor and then only in extreme circumstances, such as abuse and neglect.

Rowe presents data from numerous studies that consistently show genetic inheritance mattering far more than family life across such widely varying characteristics as intelligence, gender differences, personality, risk for divorce, criminality, schizophrenia, manic depression, and other affective disorders. Further, he views the family as relatively unimportant even among environmental influences. As a corollary, he argues that changes in parenting styles will make only a small dent in social problems.

He asserts that when all the possible contributing factors in people's lives are ranked in order of their relative importance, the qualities of a family's life emerge as significantly less important than other factors, such as biology, present life circumstances, and even chance events. "Socialization science," concludes Rowe, "has placed too heavy an emphasis on the family as the bearer of culture" (Rowe, 1994).

What are we to make of these findings that seem to dispute so directly the central tenet of the clinical work many of us do? Do family experiences really make no difference, or only make a difference in the worst deprivation? Are therapists merely deluding themselves and their clients when they focus on childhood experience or family-of-origin factors?

First, let us acknowledge that studies such as those Rowe discusses do, in fact, address limitations in traditional clinical thinking. For all the important contributions of the early therapists, their theories were largely blind to the importance of biological factors. By now there is a substantial body of research that has used variation in degrees of relatedness to examine the relative importance of biology, the family, and other environmental factors and found that biology plays a pivotal role for a range of individual aptitudes, temperamental styles, and psychological disorders.

Nonetheless, admitting the importance of biology in some areas of human functioning and development is a far cry from dismissing entirely the psychosocial impact of family experience. As informed consumers of research, we must always ask of any theory or finding: Does it make sense based on everyday experience? If the answer is no, we should be careful to examine the methodology of the studies in question.

It is important to understand how the research cited by those suggesting that family life has little impact is conducted. The logic of this research is clear and simple: examine how various individual characteristics are influenced by varying degrees of shared heredity and environment, then create an equation that tells us how much variability each source, such as family life and heredity, is responsible for. For example, when studying a personality trait like extroversion, individuals in a group of families may be given the Minnesota Multiphasic Personality Inventory (MMPI), and then the relative contributions of heredity and environmental factors are calculated by comparing the scores of individuals with various degrees of genetic relatedness and similarities in their environment. Specific methods for deciding what should be in the equation include looking at identical twins (who have the same genetics) raised apart, looking at adoptive children (who lack genetic commonalties with each other and parents) raised together, looking at the differences in similarities between siblings and identical twins, and looking at intergenerational patterns within families. In these studies, family members are individually evaluated, based on self-report or historical information about them, to assess their characteristics. Statistical techniques are then used to infer the relative contributions of genetics, family, and other environmental factors to the development of various traits. But significantly, the impact of family processes is never directly studied. No one looks at actual families interacting together to determine whether these interactions matter. No one even tracks the individual development of children exposed to special circumstances, such as depression or abuse, in the family. Instead, this research basically focuses on whether people from the same family are similar or dissimilar as a way of determining the psychosocial impact of the family. The assumption seems to be that if the family is such a potent influence, it should affect all members in more or less the same way. All of the research evidence supporting the idea that the family barely matters, or only matters in the most extreme conditions, relies on a methodology measuring the contribution of family entirely through these kinds of statistical methods without ever actually looking at the process of influence.

In addition, minimizing the impact of the family requires virtually ignoring the entire body of research in family science and developmental psychology, which has repeatedly demonstrated strong relationships between family processes and child and adult development. Let us consider a few studies that actually look at how family experience impacts on individuals.

PARENTAL CONFLICT

High levels of parental conflict have repeatedly been shown to have deleterious effects on all family members, most particularly on children. This is a prominent finding of the longitudinal studies of nuclear families by Philip and Carolyn Cowan of the University of California, Berkeley (Cowan, Cowan, Heming, & Miller, 1991; Cowan, 1991), and of postdivorce family systems and remarried families by Mavis Hetherington and her colleagues at the University of Virginia (Henderson, Hetherington, Mekos, & Reiss, 1996). The effects on children are numerous and powerful, among them anxiety, depression, and various forms of acting out.

PARENTAL DISCIPLINE

For more than 30 years, psychologist Gerald Patterson of the Oregon Social Learning Institute, among others, has studied the effects of consistent and inconsistent parental discipline (Patterson, 1996, 2002). Patterson's work makes it clear that when rewards and punishments are not consistently dispensed in families, conduct disorders and oppositional defiant disorders in children are far more likely than in families with consistent discipline. Patterson's research goes on to show that cycles of cause and effect emerge, in which inconsistent parenting and child opposition beget one another.

ATTACHMENT

Studies over four decades by researcher John Bowlby (1978) and many others have consistently shown, in what is perhaps the most replicated finding in the social sciences, the powerful effect on children of being raised in families that provide warmth, empathy, and connection. Such children are better able to form positive attachments, have higher levels of self-esteem, are happier, are better able to empathize and form bonds, and are less likely to show psychopathology than children from families that are less able to create such attachments.

CONCLUSION

These are a few of many well-documented relationships between family experience and individual functioning. Those who minimize the importance of family impact discount this family research, suggesting that these powerful effects can be explained by underlying genetics. For example, they claim that oppositional children and their parents begin with a genetic makeup that then causes the behavioral patterns observed. Although genetic similarity between parents and children may play some role in creating these effects, the critics of family influence go well beyond what the data tell us in suggesting a strong impact of biology in traits for which such an impact has yet to be demonstrated, such as the tendency to engage in conflict and the ability to form attachments. Further, this rationale offers no explanation for why interventions that change how parents behave can make such a difference in their child's behavior.

The behavior-genetic research seems to miss an obvious point: all family members will not react in the same way to the same family environment, or even experience exactly the same environment. It is not how your family functions in general, but how the family treats you as an individual, and how that affects you and vice versa. That one person might remain free of a family's negative impact whereas another becomes depressed speaks to the power of the interaction of family, the individual, and the outside environment, not to the lack of importance of the family.

The evidence that biology is wired into behavior also varies enormously, depending on which aspect of human functioning is being studied. When we lump together such disparate attributes as intelligence, gender, alcoholism, homosexuality, shyness, criminality, and personality into one discussion, as does David Rowe, it becomes easy to create an exaggerated impression of the strength of the evidence for biology in our behavior. Some characteristics, such as early tendencies toward basic temperaments, general intelligence, and the risk for becoming schizophrenic or hyperactive, clearly have been demonstrated to have a strong genetic basis. For other traits, such as sexual orientation, criminality, getting divorced, and personality, there is only limited evidence for a powerful genetic influence.

The more important point that behavior-genetic research illuminates is how nature and nurture work together, not the argument that the family does not matter. It is clear that the relationships between nature and nurture in families are complex; parents transmit genes that promote traits and then construct the rearing environment that will support a child's genetic propensities. Therefore, depressed children are likely to have depressed parents who provided them both with the genes and the environment that promote the development of depression, while artistically inclined children are likely to have artistically inclined parents who provide them with the genes and the environment that promote being artistically inclined.

Further, genetically distinct people evoke different reactions from parents, peers, and others. Teachers may pay special attention to those who are depressed or artistically inclined. Children may also select experiences that fit their genetically influenced preferences, as when a depressed child seeks out depressed friends or artistic children find others like them.

The result of all these influences is momentum in certain directions, but the specific sources of the momentum (genes/environment) become very difficult to separate from one another (Plomin, 2004). David Lykken (2004), one of the principal espousers of the new behavioral genetics, says,

> The traditional argument over nature versus nature is plainly fatuous, like asking whether the area of a rectangle is more dependent on its length or its width. . . . Without environmental inputs, your genome would have created nothing more than a damp spot on the carpet. Nature works through nurture, even in the fabrication of bone and neurons.

If we are to further develop the art and science of biopsychosocial intervention, we need to remember that biology is but one in a complex system of interdependent factors that includes the family, peers, the rest of the environment, and the never-to-be underestimated effect of chance occurrences. Biology creates risk factors and potential, but so does our life in our families of origin and in the families we create. It certainly is a distortion of scientific evidence to conduct a case conference about an autistic or schizophrenic child today and only focus on family causation. Let's hope that in future years, this skewed clinical thinking won't be reversed so that biology reigns and the role of the family is once again forgotten.

RESOURCES

Plomin, R. (1994). *Genetics and experience: The interplay between nature and nurture*. Thousand Oaks, CA: Sage Publications.

Plomin, R., & McClearn, G. E. (Eds.). (1993). *Nature and Nurture, & Psychology*. Washington, DC: American Psychological Association.

Rowe, D. C. (1994). *The limits of family influence: Genes, experience, and behavior*. New York: Guilford.

REFERENCES

Bowlby, J. (1978). Attachment theory and its therapeutic implications. *Adolescent Psychiatry, 6*: 5–33.

Cowan, C. P., Cowan, P. A., Heming, G., & Miller, N. B. (1991). Becoming a family: Marriage, parenting, and child development. In P. A. Cowan & E. M. Hetherington (Eds.), *Family transitions* (pp. 79–109). Hillsdale, NJ: Lawrence Erlbaum Associates.

Cowan, P. A. (1991). Individual and family life transitions: A proposal for a new definition. In P. A. Cowan & E. M. Hetherington (Eds.), *Family transitions* (pp. 3–30). Hillsdale, NJ: Lawrence Erlbaum Associates.

Henderson, S. H., Hetherington, E., Mekos, D., & Reiss, D. (1996). Stress, parenting, and adolescent psychopathology in nondivorced and stepfamilies: A within-family perspective. In E. Hetherington & F. A. Blechman (Eds.), *Stress, coping, and resiliency in children and families*. (pp. 39–66). Hillsdale, NJ: Lawrence Erlbaum Associates.

Lykken, D. (2004). The new eugenics. *Contemporary Psychology, 94*: 677–679.

Patterson, G. R. (1996). Some characteristics of a developmental theory for early-onset delinquency. In M. F. Lenzenweger & J. J. Haugaard (Eds.), *Frontiers of developmental psychopathology* (pp. 81–124). London: Oxford University Press.

Patterson, G. R. (2002). The early development of coercive family process. In J. B. Reid & G. R. Patterson (Eds.), *Antisocial behavior in children and adolescents: A developmental analysis and model for intervention* (pp. 25–44). Washington, DC: American Psychological Association.

Plomin, R. (2004). Genetics and developmental psychology. *Merrill-Palmer Quarterly, 50*(3): 341–352.

Rowe, D. C. (1994). *The limits of family influence: Genes, experience, and behavior*. New York: Guilford.

Rowe, D. C. (2001a). The nurture assumption persists. *American Psychologist, 56*(2): 168–169.

Rowe, D. C. (2001b). Do people make environments or do environments make people? In A. R. Damasio, A. Harrington, J. Kagan, B. S. McEwen, & H. Moss (Eds.), *Unity of knowledge: The convergence of natural and human science*. New York: Annals of the New York Academy of Sciences.

Rowe, D. C. (2003). Assessing genotype-environment interactions and correlations in the postgenomic era. In R. Plomin, J. C. DeFries, I. W. Craig, & P. McGuffin (Eds.), *Behavioral genetics in the postgenomic era* (pp. 71–86). Washington, DC: American Psychological Association.

Rowe, D. C., & Jacobson, K. C. (1999). In the mainstream: Research in behavioral genetics. In R. A. Carson & M. A. Rothstein (Eds.), *Behavioral gentics: The clash of culture and biology* (pp. 12–34). Baltimore: John Hopkins University Press.

28

AGING: FACT AND FICTION

Psychotherapists need to understand the research that is perti-
nent to the kinds of clients they treat. To fail to understand what
the research tells us about various populations is to remain sus-
ceptible to the kinds of distortions that can come with stereotypes.
One group that often is subject to such stereotyping in society is
the elderly. This chapter centers on what can be learned from a
recent study of the elderly, which challenges many commonly held
beliefs.

Albert Einstein, Eubie Blake, Georgia O'Keeffe, Brooke Astor, Bob
Hope. It is common to hear that people such as these, who live vital
lives into their 80s and 90s, somehow have beat overwhelming odds
to achieve a fulfilling old age. The bleak assumption about old age is
that it dooms us to being lonely, sick, and unproductive. In an effort
to develop an empirically based "new gerontology" that moves from
such outdated myths about aging to reflect the realities of successful
aging today, the MacArthur Foundation Study of Aging in America
conducted a wide range of research projects led by an array of scholars

over the past decade. The results of the study, presented in *Successful Aging* by physician John Rowe of Mount Sinai Hospital in New York and psychologist Robert Kahn of the University of Michigan, show that far from being doomed to inevitable decline, the vast majority of older people maintain their health, enjoy good quality of life, and contribute substantially to society well into old age (Rowe & Kahn, 1998).

By examining how older members of our society actually live and looking at what we can learn from people who age successfully, the research study shifted the focus away from the deficits experienced in aging to the factors that permit individuals to function effectively, both physically and mentally, well into old age. The findings debunk many common myths about aging.

MYTH: ILLNESS, DECLINING MENTAL CAPACITY, AND DISENGAGEMENT FROM LIFE ARE INEVITABLE

The research found that a high percentage of aging respondents were mentally and physically healthy and actively engaged in life. Only 21% had any significant disability, only 10% showed significant signs of dementia, and only 5% lived in institutional settings. Indeed, 39% viewed their health as very good or excellent.

MYTH: GENES DETERMINE OUR EXPERIENCE OF AGING

The MacArthur Study reveals that lifestyle choices, not genetics, most powerfully determine how people age. Diet, exercise, mental stimulation, a sense of self-efficacy, and connection to others emerged as key factors in maintaining high function and being content in life. In a study of twins designed to identify the specific effects of heredity and environment, only 30% of the quality of life was determined by genes; lifestyle and environment were the major determinants of how the elderly aged physically. The research shows that even the likelihood of developing genetic-related diseases, such as cancer and heart disease, is powerfully affected by lifestyle and environment. In addition, lifestyle far outweighs genetics in determining whether the elderly maintain high physical and mental function and active engagement in life, two key characteristics of successful aging.

The study also looked at the impact of specific lifestyle choices on the experience of aging. Inactivity, for example, emerged as more harmful than the combination of smoking and exercising regularly. Beginning regimens of good diet, exercise, and health-related behaviors, such as stopping smoking and losing weight, *at any age* appears to improve the quality of life and experience of aging.

Social supports and connections to family and friends not only have positive effects on health, but also buffer the effects of aging when illness does strike. Instrumental support (having meals prepared or the house cleaned) was not as important as emotional support in maintaining physical functioning, however.

Interesting trends also emerged in looking at the relative quality of life among the elderly. Those with incomes of more than $10,000, those who were more physically fit (as measured by lung capacity), and those who participated in moderate or strenuous physical activity generally reported better quality of life than others. Those with high mental functioning were more likely to retain physical functioning as well. A sense of self-efficacy also proved vital to successful aging.

MYTH: THE ELDERLY ARE NOT PRODUCTIVE

The MacArthur Study shows that this myth derives in part from where we look. Our studies of productivity typically only consider employment, ignoring the variety of other contributions made by the elderly. As Rowe and Kahn point out, a service carried out by an employee in a hospital is not typically considered productive activity when done in one's home for other family members (1998). The MacArthur research redefines productive behavior as any activity, paid or unpaid, that generates goods or services of economic value. Using this broader notion, the study found that most older people continue to do substantial productive work throughout their lives. More than 40% of the elderly report at least 1,500 hours of productive activity a year. Only 2% report not engaging in any productive activity. Providing informal help to friends and relatives reaches its peak among individuals ages 55–64, and even individuals age 75 and older often still provide the same level of help to others as people half their age.

The MacArthur Study challenges the myths and assumptions about aging. As therapists, we need to recognize the contributions made by our elderly clients and pay attention to the kinds of productive activity in which older people engage. We can educate our clients young and old about the realities of the "new gerontology" and successful aging. Without glossing over the difficulties older people face, therapists can help elderly clients identify their strengths, realize the extent of their contributions (which often go unrecognized), and develop ways to maximize their chances of aging successfully (Zarit & Knight, 1996). Therapy approaches aimed at improving self-efficacy and social connection appear to fit particularly well with promoting successful aging. Finally, we should remember that psychotherapy offers a potentially life-enhancing contact for older adults.

The MacArthur Study shows us that being old does not necessarily mean fading away. Far from demonstrating that older people can only benefit from medication to ameliorate their symptoms, the study underscores the fact that most of society's elders are not drains on their communities, but active contributors to the well-being of others.

RESOURCES

Gatz, M. (Ed.). (1995). *Emerging issues in mental health and aging.* Washington, DC: American Psychological Association.

Rowe, J. W., & Kahn, R. (1998). *Successful aging.* New York: Pantheon Books.

Zarit, S. H., & Knight, B. (Eds.). (1996). *A Guide to psychotherapy and aging.* Washington, DC: American Psychological Association.

REFERENCES

Rowe, J. W., & Kahn, R. (1998). *Successful Aging.* New York: Pantheon Books.

Zarit, S. H., & Knight, B. (Eds.). (1996). *A guide to psychotherapy and aging.* Washington, DC: American Psychological Association.

29

KEYS TO ENHANCING PERFORMANCE

Psychotherapists are often in the role of helping clients enhance their performance, either in helping reduce deficit, augment competencies that are already present, or build new competencies. This chapter describes a ground-breaking study that isolated the key factors in successful performance.

We are a culture endlessly searching for how to do things better. We want to work faster, play harder, and live longer. Such desires have spurred what is virtually a growth industry in ways to enhance performance. Hundreds of books on the market describe methods for learning and achieving—from altering our minds with chemicals to acquiring skills subliminally while asleep. So how is it possible to evaluate the learning approaches out there in light of the grand claims of success so many of them make?

Fortunately, the Committee on Techniques for the Enhancement of Human Performance, organized by the National Research Council of the National Academy of Sciences and comprising a group of America's foremost experts on learning under the direction of Daniel Druckman and Robert Bjork (Druckman & Bjork, 1991, 1994; Druckman & Swets, 1988), have tracked the vast research literature on enhancing performance for over a decade. Expanding from an original mandate to review all the relevant research to help the military decide what methods to best employ in the training of personnel, this group has published a kind of consumer report of what we know about improving learning and performance.

What do they and other experts about human ability tell us? First, they found the claims to furthering learning and performance by such unusual and intensely marketed methods, such as Neurolinguistic Programming (NLP), Suggestive Accelerative Learning and Teaching Techniques, integrating brain hemispheres, sleep learning, and subliminal learning remained unproven. In reviewing the empirical literature examining NLP, for example, the committee found no support for the widely circulated assumptions NLP makes about how individuals use their visual, auditory, and kinesthetic systems. They also found negligible evidence in support of the effectiveness of the specific NLP learning methods beyond that which any system would achieve. Further, they suggest that when individuals attribute their learning to NLP, the effects are more likely the product of the generic attention and organization that inevitably go with any effort to learn rather than the complex methods used by NLP.

The committee endorsed the following methods to enhance learning and performance flow directly from general long documented principles of learning.

PRACTICE

Practice skills until they become second nature. The level of original learning for a task is the best single predictor of long-term retention. Continued practice after the point of being able to be skillful, called overlearning, improves performance further (although there is a point of diminishing return). Practice over time results in longer-term retention than massed practice at a single time. Mental practice and visualization are helpful in a wide range of activities, from sports to surgery.

For example, consider Sandy, who wants to develop her ability to recall and explain information about real estate development in her community as part of her presentation to potential clients of her firm. Sandy should review the facts to be remembered many times and practice explaining what needs to be communicated numerous times. She should not try to fully learn want she needs to know in one sitting, but across a number of occasions, and should also visualize presenting the information many times. She should continue to review and practice even after the facts are readily recalled and spoken about. The same principles apply across such diverse goals as developing social skills, public speaking ability, a tennis stroke, or the ability to work with numbers.

To gain the most from practice, it is useful to create simulations of the situation in which the skill ultimately is to be invoked. Thus, a swimmer does best to practice in pools that are similar in size and feel to the one in which the meet will occur. However, performance does not appear to be enhanced by learning in the specific setting for the performance: practicing in the very pool of the meet will not help more than practicing in similar venues.

MODELING

Watching individuals who are skillful and copying their methods significantly improves performance. However, modeling is not very effective without experience to try out skills. For example, a young man who wants to learn how to be effective socially with women should carefully observe how his more socially adept roommates meet women and how they relate. However, these models will not be of much help unless that man creates opportunities to try out the ways of relating that he sees. Unfortunately, much of our system of education consists of didactic presentations without either modeling or hands-on practice, methods of pedagogy that are most likely to be effective.

RECEIVE INTERMITTENT FEEDBACK

Constant feedback about the quality of performance is not as effective for developing a skill as delayed and intermittent feedback, which allows learners to detect and correct errors on their own. For example, a dancer does better to receive feedback at intervals during practice, not as each error is detected by his or her instructor, so that the dancer can develop his or her own sense of when errors are occurring and how to avoid or correct them. This principle has great relevance for us as therapists, given the pull in therapy from clients to help them avoid pain by providing continual guidance. Opportunities to try skills out without feedback are a necessary part of learning.

BEWARE OF TRAINING THAT DOES NOT CHALLENGE

Without sufficient challenges, it is easy for teachers, trainers, and students to reach the judgment that they are more proficient than they are.

For example, a couples therapist may feel quite confident in treating the simulated couples that respond well to their interventions in their training group, only to emerge feeling totally inadequate when they encounter real clients who do not respond readily. Learning through experience with the range of real-life situations that will be encountered ultimately leads to better performance.

EVALUATE PERFORMANCE ACCURATELY

A common problem in building skills is that assessment often occurs primarily in training situations, which may not entirely be like the situations in which the skills ultimately need to be invoked. For example, a police cadet may do well on a shooting range, but this may not generalize to how he or she shoots at escaping bank robbers. The reliable evaluations occur in actual situations well after training is completed.

BUILD ON SUCCESS

The creation of a sense of hope and self-confidence is a crucial ingredient in the process of change. Programs of learning work best when they build on successful experiences. For example, Tom, a young actor, considerably improved his performance after receiving his instuctor's feedback, which accentuated what he was doing right. Positive critical reviews in the school newspaper further added to his sense of confidence. It also is helpful to have opportunities to observe others succeeding; this provides both models for the ingredients for success (observing what to do) and opportunities to vicariously participate in the other's success ("If she can do it, so can I"). However, self-confidence also depends on a realistic appraisal of one's ability: developing an unrealistic sense of how one will do is not helpful, leaving the individual very vulnerable to deterioration in performance when encountering failure. If Tom has limited skill in comic acting, he will not be helped by his acting coach providing him with an inflated sense of his ability. Given an unrealistic positive self-appraisal, he is likely to be shocked and deflated when he receives negative critical reviews. Mistakes are a necessary part of learning, and therefore important to accept as part of the process of developing a skill. There is a fragile balance in optimal learning experiences between encountering and accentuating success and having opportunities to learn from mistakes and gain a realistic appraisal of one's abilities.

MAKE REWARDS CONTINGENT ON PERFORMANCE

Whether they are offered from the outside or by the person to himself or herself, providing rewards for attaining goals increases effectiveness. Buying yourself that new dress when you achieve your goal can help you run farther.

REDUCE ANXIETY

Anxiety interferes with performance because it competes for attention with the skill to be invoked. Relaxation and meditation techniques that diminish anxiety, such as progressive relaxation or transcendental meditation, improve performance. Former all-star baseball pitcher Rick Ankiel is said to still be able to throw straight and hard in practice. However, in front of the thousands who attend games, he mostly bounced the ball to home plate at the end of his career. Anxiety has a range of similar effects on performance across such disparate skills as running, sex, and solving math problems.

LEARN HOW TO MAKE IT MORE LIKELY TO FIND A STATE OF FLOW

Psychologist Mihaly Csikzentmihalyi (1991) of the University of Chicago has termed *flow* a state we all occasionally know: that feeling of being positively absorbed in a challenging activity. Moments of flow offer our best opportunities of optimal performance. Flow offers not only pleasure and productivity, but also an antidote for many difficulties, such as depression and demoralization. Although we cannot live our lives fully in a state of flow, we can improve performance by doing those things that help make this state present more frequently, such as taking on challenging tasks, preparing well for them, and working to reduce anxiety.

CONCLUSION

As psychiatrist Henry Grunebaum has suggested, therapy is ultimately a form of learning. The report of the Committee on Techniques for the Enhancement of Human Performance suggests the basic principles of learning transcend the specific focus of what is to be learned. Experts across activities typically acquire skills in similar ways and show many commonalties in how they function. As therapists, our work should remain rooted in these principles. Always, we should remember we are the principal teachers of another kind of higher education.

RESOURCES

Csikzentmihalyi, M. (1991). *Flow*. New York: Harper Perennial.

Druckman, D., & Bjork, R. (Eds.). (1991). *In the mind's eye: Enhancing human performance*. Washington, DC: National Academy Press.

Druckman, D., & Bjork, R. (Eds.). (1994). *Learning, remembering, believing: Enhancing human performance*. Washington, DC: National Academy Press.

Druckman, D., & Swets, J. (Eds.). (1988). *Enhancing human performance: Issues, theories, and techniques*. Washington, DC: National Academy Press.

REFERENCES

Csikzentmihalyi, M. (1991). *Flow*. New York: Harper Perennial.

Druckman, D., & Bjork, R. (Eds.). (1991). *In the mind's eye: Enhancing human performance*. Washington, DC: National Academy Press.

Druckman, D., & Bjork, R. (Eds.). (1994). *Learning, remembering, believing: Enhancing human performance*. Washington, DC: National Academy Press.

Druckman, D., & Swets, J. (Eds.). (1988). *Enhancing human performance: Issues, theories, and techniques*. Washington, DC: National Academy Press.

30

BEYOND THE SUGAR PILL: CLARIFYING THE PLACEBO EFFECT

Psychotherapy draws on common factors such as the generation of hope and positive feeling as part of its process. Because of this, it remains vitally important to sort out whether a treatment is effective because of something special about the treatment or simply because it invokes such common factors. This chapter looks at what research can tell us about placebo effects.

Franz Anton Mesmer, the 18th-century German physician, put forth a theory of "animal magnetism," in which he viewed health as being affected by the gravitational pull of the various planets. Mesmer traveled far and wide throughout Europe "curing" a wide range of illnesses through the practice of "mesmerism," which featured his passing magnets and his hands over people. Mesmer's work was even in his time quite controversial. In 1784, Louis XVI (the king later beheaded in the French Revolution) assembled a commission of scientists that included Benjamin Franklin to assess Mesmer's techniques. The commission concluded that Mesmer's claims could not be backed up by evidence.

Although some people felt better, these changes could in no way be related to Mesmer's specific techniques. The changes Mesmer described were not as marked as the testimony of his patients suggested they were and the changes that did occur were in no way attributable to the techniques he employed or the theory he espoused. The changes that occurred could better be explained by the impact of engendering hope and positive expectation in his patients, that is, what we now term a placebo effect.

Today, such placebo effects are widely recognized, yet there remain debates just as acrimonious as that between Mesmer and the French scientists about whether methods are efficacious or merely impact to the extent they generate such effects. What constitutes a placebo? Placebos (be they medical, psychological, or physical) are treatment-like interventions that invoke a sense that they are likely to be effective without containing active ingredients that specifically impact on that disorder. Thus a placebo pill looks and feels like medicine, but contains nothing that should directly affect, say, a headache.

Placebos are usually defined as treatment-like interventions that evoke patients' expectations of improvement despite lacking any active ingredient specifically intended to affect a particular disorder. Just as a placebo pill may look and feel like medicine but contain only sugar, placebo therapy looks like therapy—it may involve two people talking—but it entails no intervention designed to have an effect on the problem at hand.

A RECENT CONTROVERSY

In medicine, placebos have been assumed to have a marked impact on health since 1955, when Henry Beecher, in a milestone review of 15 studies, documented their effect. Yet, a recent meta-analysis of research published in the *New England Journal of Medicine* stirred up some well-publicized controversy by casting doubt on the long-held assumption that the placebo effect is a potent source of change in health care. Asbjorn Hrobjartsson and Peter Gotzsche (Hrobjartsson, 1996; Hrobjartsson & Gotzsche, 2004a, 2004b), physicians at the University of Copenhagen, found that placebos—by which they meant the simple belief that one is receiving an effective treatment—had little affect on patients. Hrobjartsson and Gotzsche's analysis included 114 subsequent studies, covering such diverse problems as pain, asthma, colds, seasickness, high blood pressure, myocardial infarction, alcoholism, and schizophrenia. Many had been more carefully constructed than those reviewed by Beecher. Their report challenged a tenet held by researchers and practitioners alike since the 1950s—the premise that as long as people *think* they're receiving useful treatment, improvement will occur, even when the treatment is only a sugar pill.

Hrobjartsson and Gotzsche concluded that where outcomes could be divided clearly between success and failure, placebos didn't have a sufficient impact to have a useful influence. When outcomes ranged along a continuum (as in producing, for example, a certain degree of pain relief), the authors found that placebos had small positive effects, but because many studies that reported such effects were based on small samples, Hrobjartsson and Gotzsche suggested the results were erroneous. They concluded that the effects of placebos are too meager to have much effect on clinical practice.

ASPECTS INCLUDED IN THE PLACEBO EFFECT

A side effect of their study was to highlight the variety of the processes subsumed under the umbrella of the placebo effect and how sloppy the common usage of the term has become. Following up on similar concerns, Richard Bootzin (Bootzin, 2003; Bootzin & Bailey, 2005), professor of psychology at the University of Arizona, has led a movement aimed at achieving a better understanding of what we mean by a placebo. In research on treating insomnia, he has seen some methods appear to produce significant results only to learn that these results derived from factors other than his intervention, such as the way bedroom lighting can affect sleep cycles (Bootzin, Herman, & Nicassio, 1976). To establish a more rigorous methodology for studying how interventions work, Bootzin has focused on separating the effects of treatment from effects that have other causes.

Bootzin points out that a patient may improve for many reasons that have little to do with the treatment. These include

- Spontaneous remission unrelated to treatment, as when people get better just because of the natural recovery cycle of a disorder.
- The tendency of people presenting extreme behavior to develop less extreme behavior later, so a client initially assessed as extremely depressed may become less depressed without any intervention.
- Clients who report nonexistent improvement to please their treatment provider.
- Clients who improve after presenting their illness as more acute than it is.

Bootzin's point is that patients can improve in many ways that have little to do with the treatment. Bootzin argues that even if thinking one is receiving a treatment has as little impact as the Danish researchers suggest, expectation, relationship, and other factors can significantly influence the process of change. Further, he suggests that the potency of what's loosely described as the placebo effect depends on the interactive mix of patient, provider, and treatment. In general, he reports, placebo effects are likelier in the presence of an experienced, competent, optimistic provider and where the outcome is less inevitable from physical causes.

The therapeutic weight given to the placebo effect varies among clinicians. Some view the generation of hope and positive expectancy as nonspecific, not very potent, treatment factors; others view it as a key to successful treatment. Four decades ago, psychiatrist Jerome Frank (1963) said that the "active ingredient" in psychotherapy lies in the generation of hope and positive expectancy, rather than in the impact of any specific therapeutic techniques. More recently, psychologists Mark Hubble, Barry Duncan, and Scott Miller (1999) have cited evidence that much of the change that occurs in therapy can be traced to such powerful general factors, whereas the specific impact of therapeutic technique accounts for only a small part of the outcome.

So what are we to make of this controversy raised by Hrobjartsson and Gotzsche? It appears that, for patients, the impact of receiving something that resembles a treatment is not, in and of itself, likely to be great. It looks especially small when the outcomes in focus are clearly defined and dichotomous, such as, to take the most extreme example, whether the patient dies from the disorder. However, it also appears that when treatments focus on broader and "softer" outcomes, such as the extent to which a patient feels better, factors such as the patient's expectations and the quality of the provider–patient relationship have considerable impact. Such factors may outweigh the power of specific treatment techniques, particularly in situations in which feeling more positively represents a core aspect of the preferred outcome. The impact of these factors can be expected to be less in extreme and incapacitating conditions, such as schizophrenia and manic depression, where treatment success is difficult, requiring changes that go well beyond feeling better and becoming remoralized.

USING AN UNDERSTANDING OF PLACEBO EFFECT

All this leads to specific suggestions about how therapists can use an understanding of nonspecific treatment factors to assess their personal impact and the potencies and limitations of their technical methods.

"Placebo effects" can contribute to positive outcome. Positive effects based on hope and positive expectancy aren't bad; in fact, they're valuable, as long as we don't confuse the placebo effect with the specific impact of our clinical procedures. The late researcher Kenneth Howard often pointed out that 10% of clients get better in therapy before the first appointment, just by making the decision to enter treatment (Kopta, Howard, Lowry, & Beutler, 1994). Helping clients generate hope and realistic positive expectations about the changes they're likely to experience can be important in helping them accomplish their goals. Tell them you've seen their problem before and have helped others with it. Cite evidence that the methods you follow can help them deal with it. Highlight your qualifications and competence in a way that gives them confidence in your work.

Consider rival hypotheses about what has occurred. However wedded we may be to a clinical theory, we should bring a questioning attitude to our work. For any client, change may come from many factors, including the mere passage of time. To enhance our effectiveness, we should try to distinguish between effects produced by specific interventions and effects produced by the more global impact of meeting with someone who cares and focuses attention on a problem. As we become more disciplined and effective in what we offer clients, we should ask ourselves what we're doing that's specifically useful for the client.

Don't assume that a promising clinical technique works in and of itself. The history of the field of psychotherapy is filled with charismatic leaders who have strongly believed in the power of their discoveries (McNally, 1999). Their charisma and their faith in the power of what they're doing have profoundly affected their clients. However, these individuals' clinical effectiveness has contrasted sharply with the effectiveness of their methods as practiced by others. Clinicians lacking these gurus' charisma and armed only with their techniques have often been ineffective. Always look for evidence that methods work when practiced by a range of practitioners. Most of us have learned exciting new methods at workshops, only to see them prove ineffective as we practice them. The history of therapy includes many methods that time has shown to have little or no universal value. This fact sends a two-pronged message: use your enthusiasm for new methods as potentially important ingredients in helping clients change, but pay attention to what works over the long haul.

Don't overestimate the clinical efficacy of positive expectations. Research has consistently demonstrated that when clients are led to expect positive changes that don't occur, the result is a particularly disheartening experience, likely to lead to further medical deterioration (Caspi & Bootzin, 2002). Telling chronic schizophrenic clients they will fully recover sets up the majority for failure. Be realistic in what you forecast: don't promise what you can't deliver.

When claims of efficacy are made for a treatment, be sure these claims have been tested in relation to a placebo-control group. One essential function of research lies in establishing the effects of methods beyond those of placebo effects. Look to summaries of findings about methods, such as in sources such as Nathan and Gorman's *Guide to Treatments that Work* for the state of evidence about a particular treatment (2003).

Ultimately, the controversy about the role of the placebo effect should humble us all. As clinicians, we must be careful to view our practices as long-term research projects, in which we help clients achieve the best possible outcomes while questioning our explanations of the means by which we do so.

RESOURCES

Caspi, O., & Bootzin, R. R. (2002). Evaluating how placebos produce change: Logical and causal traps and understanding cognitive explanatory mechanisms. *Evaluation & the Health Professions, 25*(4): 436–464.

Frank, J. D. (1963). *Persuasion and healing.* Oxford, UK: Schocken.

Hrobjartsson, A., & Gotzsche, P. C. (2004a). Is the placebo powerless? Update of a systematic review with 52 new randomized trials comparing placebo with no treatment. *Journal of Internal Medicine, 256*(2): 91–100.

REFERENCES

Bootzin, R. R. (2003). Studying the context in which treatments are delivered: Observations on "open versus hidden medical treatments." *Prevention & Treatment, 6*: 1–6.

Bootzin, R. R., & Bailey, E. T. (2005). Understanding placebo, nocebo, and iatrogenic treatment effects. *Journal of Clinical Psychology, 61*(7): 871–880.

Bootzin, R. R., Herman, C., & Nicassio, P. (1976). The power of suggestion: Another examination of misattribution and insomnia. *Journal of Personality & Social Psychology, 34*(4): 673–679.

Caspi, O., & Bootzin, R. R. (2002). Evaluating how placebos produce change: Logical and causal traps and understanding cognitive explanatory mechanisms. *Evaluation & the Health Professions, 25*(4): 436–464.

Frank, J. D. (1963). *Persuasion and healing.* Oxford, UK: Schocken.

Hrobjartsson, A. (1996). The uncontrollable placebo effect. *European Journal of Clinical Pharmacology, 50*(5): 345–348.

Hrobjartsson, A., & Gotzsche, P. C. (2004a). Is the placebo powerless? Update of a systematic review with 52 new randomized trials comparing placebo with no treatment. *Journal of Internal Medicine, 256*(2): 91–100.

Hrobjartsson, A., & Gotzsche, P. C. (2004b). Placebo interventions for all clinical conditions [update of Cochrane Database System Review 2003;(1):CD003974; PMID: 12535498]. *Cochrane Database of Systematic Reviews, 3.*

Hubble, M. A., Duncan, B. L., & Miller, S. D. (Eds.). (1999). *The heart and soul of change: What works in therapy.* Washington, DC: American Psychological Association.

Kopta, S. M., Howard, K. I., Lowry, J. L., & Beutler, L. E. (1994). Patterns of symptomatic recovery in psychotherapy. *Journal of Consulting & Clinical Psychology, 62*(5): 1009–1016.

McNally, R. J. (1999). EMDR and mesmerism: A comparative historical analysis. *Journal of Anxiety Disorders, 13*(1–2): 225–236.

Nathan, P. E., & Gorman, J. M. (2003). A guide to treatments that work. *Psychotherapy Research, 13*(1): 128–130.

INDEX

A

Acceptance, 80
Accountability, 31, 111
Achenbach, T. M., 157, 216
Ackerman, S. J., 132
Action stage, 57
Active listening, 164, 166
Addictions treatment, 97–102
    change process, 98–99
    confrontation, 100–101
    intense treatments, 100
    motivation, 99–100
    social support, 101–102
    therapeutic alliances and, 100
Addis, M. E., 72
Adolescents, *see* Children and adolescents
African-American families, 90–93
Aging, 249–252
    contributions/productivity of elderly,
        251–252
    lifestyle choices and, 250
    myths of, 250–252
    new gerontology research, 249
    stereotyping of elderly, 249
Agoraphobia, 70
Ahrons, C. R., 171, 173
Alcoholics Anonymous (AA), 98,
        102
Alcoholism, 53, 98–99, 101, 143,
        148
Alexander, J. F., 8, 65, 144
Alternative treatments, 127
Amato, P. R., 173

American Association of Marriage and
        Family Therapy (AAMFT), 14,
        141–142
American College of
        Neuropsychopharmacology,
        118
American Psychiatric Association, 118,
        189
American Psychological Association
        (APA), 14, 22, 24, 29, 31–32,
        35, 42, 48, 108, 202
Anderson, C. M., 5, 144
Anderson, E. R., 182
Anderson, P., 73
Andolfi, M., 5
Antidepressants, 115–121
Anxiety disorders, 23, 40, 42, 127
    evidence-based treatments for,
        69–75
    generalized anxiety disorder, 74
    obsessive-compulsive disorder,
        72–73
    panic disorders, 70–72
    simple phobia, 73–74
Archives of General Psychiatry, 14
Areas of Change Questionnaire, 195
Assessing Outcome in Clinical Practice
        (Ogles, Lambert, and Masters),
        214, 226
Assessment, 127, 189, 207, 211–217; *see*
        also Relational assessment
        methods
At-risk children, 93–94
Attachment, 244
Attention deficit disorder, 42, 143

D